OXFORD WORLD'S CLASSICS

FOUR MAJOR PLAYS

FEDERICO GARCÍA LORCA was born into a landowning family in the Vale of Granada in 1898. Nine years later, his family moved to Granada itself, the scene of his formative artistic and intellectual contacts. After abandoning early plans for a musical career, Federico turned to literature; *Impressions and Landscapes* appeared in 1918. A year later began his long association with the *Residencia de Estudiantes* in Madrid. His many friends there included the poets Guillén and Alberti, the future film director Buñuel, and most importantly for Lorca, Salvador Dalí. Lorca's early plays and poems draw on aspects of Andalusian tradition, but always as part of a sophisticated language of highly personal expression. Dalí too encouraged him to make the exploration of his own unconscious a spur to more radical literary experiment. Thus when in 1928 his *Book of Gypsy Ballads* achieved its outstanding popular success, Lorca had in a sense already moved beyond it. Partly in reaction to an unhappy homosexual love-affair he left Spain in 1929 to study at Columbia University. In the event his New York experiences sharpened his sense of crisis, confirming his sexual orientation and introducing new extremes of experiment into his writing: *Poet in New York* and the 'unperformable' drama, *The Public*. In 1931, the year following his return to Spain, the Second Republic was established. It brought Lorca a new commitment as director of the student theatre company *La Barraca*, touring classic Spanish plays about the country. His literary projects of the early 1930s included new poetic ventures—*The Diwan of Tamarit*; the *Lament* for his bullfighter friend, Ignacio Sánchez Mejías—and, in *Blood Wedding*, *Yerma*, and *Doña Rosita the Spinster* a new kind of theatre: poetic, radical, questioning, but also accessible and popular. His success in this, his broad identification with progressive public causes, and his seemingly inexhaustible creativity made the Republican years a rewarding time for him. That was cut short when, in August 1936, a few weeks into the Civil War, and soon after finishing *The House of Bernarda Alba*, he was arrested and murdered by the Nationalist authorities in Granada.

JOHN EDMUNDS founded the Department of Theatre, Film, and Television Studies at the University College of Wales, Aberystwyth, and was Director from 1973 to 1985. Four of his translations of plays by Racine and Molière have been broadcast on BBC Radio Three.

NICHOLAS ROUND began his career as a Hispanist in Belfast in 1962, later becoming Professor of Hispanic Studies in the universities of Glasgow (1972–94) and Sheffield. His published and performed translations of Spanish and Portuguese theatre range from the seventeenth-century *comedia* to the 1950s.

OXFORD WORLD'S CLASSICS

*For over 100 years Oxford World's Classics have brought
readers closer to the world's great literature. Now with over 700
titles—from the 4,000-year-old myths of Mesopotamia to the
twentieth century's greatest novels—the series makes available
lesser-known as well as celebrated writing.*

*The pocket-sized hardbacks of the early years contained
introductions by Virginia Woolf, T. S. Eliot, Graham Greene,
and other literary figures which enriched the experience of reading.
Today the series is recognized for its fine scholarship and
reliability in texts that span world literature, drama and poetry,
religion, philosophy and politics. Each edition includes perceptive
commentary and essential background information to meet the
changing needs of readers.*

£7·99

OXFORD WORLD'S CLASSICS

═══

FEDERICO GARCÍA LORCA

Four Major Plays

═══

Translated by
JOHN EDMUNDS

Introduction by
NICHOLAS ROUND

Notes by
ANN MacLAREN

OXFORD
UNIVERSITY PRESS

OXFORD
UNIVERSITY PRESS

Great Clarendon Street, Oxford OX2 6DP

Oxford University Press is a department of the University of Oxford.
It furthers the University's objective of excellence in research, scholarship,
and education by publishing worldwide in

Oxford New York

Athens Auckland Bangkok Bogotá Buenos Aires Calcutta
Cape Town Chennai Dar es Salaam Delhi Florence Hong Kong Istanbul
Karachi Kuala Lumpur Madrid Melbourne Mexico City Mumbai
Nairobi Paris São Paulo Singapore Taipei Tokyo Toronto Warsaw

with associated companies in Berlin Ibadan

Oxford is a registered trade mark of Oxford University Press
in the UK and in certain other countries

Published in the United States
by Oxford University Press Inc., New York

First published as a World's Classics paperback 1997
Reissued as an Oxford World's Classics paperback 1999

British Library Cataloguing in Publication Data

Data available

Library of Congress Cataloging in Publication Data

García Lorca, Federico, 1898–1936.
[Plays. English. Selections]
Four major plays / Federico García Lorca ; translated by John
Edmunds ; introduction by Nicholas Round ; notes by Ann MacLaren.
(Oxford world's classics)
Includes bibliographical references (p.   ).
Partial Contents: Blood wedding—Yerma—The house of Bernarda
Alba—Doña Rosita the spinster.
1. García Lorca, Federico, 1898–1936—Translations into English.
I. Edmunds, John. II. Title. III. Series.
PQ6613.A763A2265 1997 862'.62—dc20 96–20870

ISBN–13: 978–0–19–283938–1
ISBN–10: 0–19–283938–1

8

Printed in Great Britain by
Clays Ltd, St Ives plc

CONTENTS

TRANSLATOR'S NOTE

THE translator of García Lorca is a tilter at windmills, but I have had the good fortune to be prodded and cajoled by Professor Nick Round, whose meticulous and sensitive comments have occasionally retrieved me from error and frequently urged me to seek ever more supple (and subtle) refinements. Many of his proffered alternative renderings I have been happy to incorporate, and I record my gratitude for his constructive encouragement.

As an actor and director I have been particularly conscious of the need to produce actable scripts for the theatre as well as trustworthy texts for the drama student and general reader. If translations of plays differ, it is in part because dramatic dialogue is, by its nature, elliptic. A translator, just like an actor, has to work out the subtext, that is, the unspoken thoughts and feelings which give rise to what is spoken—either to reveal or to conceal. Translators, like actors, will make differing judgements in this area, and their conclusions will colour their interpretations. The best one can do is to endeavour to capture in the new language the tone, the degree of emotional intensity, and the shade of meaning as they strike one's own sensibility—and pray that the dramatist is somewhere smiling approval.

J.E.

INTRODUCTION

I

ALMOST uniquely among Spanish writers—the other exception is Cervantes—Federico García Lorca (1898–1936) can be said to need no introduction for an English-speaking public. His figure is memorably defined between two widely known and sharply opposite realities: the vibrant, troubling verbal energy of what he wrote, and the brute absurdity of his murder by Nationalist firing-squad in the first weeks of the Spanish Civil War. Yet neither the writings nor the death can readily be made to yield an unambiguous set of meanings. Any image of Lorca formed on that basis alone is likely, then, to prove unreliable. Perhaps he does need some introduction after all.

It seems a truism that Lorca's work belongs decisively to our own century. But its relevant context in Spanish culture begins rather earlier. The Liberal revolution of 1868 against the Bourbon monarchy achieved less in socio-political terms than its hopeful epithet of *la Gloriosa* implied. Yet it did inaugurate a period of some three generations in which Spain produced a succession of writers, artists, and intellectuals of authentically European stature. It is still none too clear how this robust cultural flowering relates to the tardy, defensive, patchily efficacious, and broadly corrupt public hegemony of Spain's upper bourgeoisie in these same years. But the quality of the cultural achievement stands in no doubt. Writers, especially, sustained an urgent and creative double dialogue: with the specific and Spanish experiences available to them, and with modes of understanding—still more, of questioning—which were recent and European in their origins. Coming late into this process, Lorca and his contemporaries enjoyed a familiar access to movements and developments beyond Spain which had been altogether less assured in the case of their elders. Yet these too had been important makers and remakers of literature and thought. Lorca's various debts to them shaped his own work and thinking in ways which are too easily overlooked.

It makes a difference, for example, to familiar views of him as a 'surrealist' or anti-realist writer to be reminded how much he admired the massy representational force and intractable Liberal tolerance of the great novelist Pérez Galdós (1843–1920). The image—again conventional—of a Lorca attuned by birthright and instinct to all things Andalusian is modified a little by his own account of seeking out conversations with 'shepherds and woodcutters'.[1] It seems all too like those self-conscious strategies for getting to know authentic peasant life which found favour among writers of the '1898 Generation'. His decisively (not to say aggressively) modern and cosmopolitan cultural stance was formed in his early twenties at the Residencia de Estudiantes in Madrid. But the Residencia owed its existence and its ethos to Francisco Giner de los Ríos (1839–1915), the great secular teacher of late nineteenth-century Spanish dissent. The whole protracted shift in Spanish culture between *la Gloriosa* and the Second Republic was, overwhelmingly, a shift towards pluralism. Lorca and his immediate contemporaries were there to catch the tide.

More specific literary debts are often traceable. Lorca's evocation of a Granadine provincial past in *Doña Rosita the Spinster* is not far removed in sensibility from the Sevillan childhood memories which flood the early poetry of Antonio Machado (1875–1939). That harsh, implicit degradation of dialogue which marks such work of his as *The House of Bernarda Alba* could hardly have been carried through without the examples furnished by the idiosyncratic theatre of Ramón María del Valle-Inclán (1869–1936). The structuring of relationships in Lorca's plays —those clashes of self with other where love and its opposites emerge as paradigms of competing will—express a sense of selfhood closely akin to that explored in the philosophy and fiction of Miguel de Unamuno (1864–1936). Unamuno's drama *The Other*, produced in Madrid in December 1932, may well have influenced the starkly schematic speech-strategies employed between Yerma and Juan, or among members of the Alba household.

---

[1] Interview in *La Voz*, 18 Feb. 1935; text in *Obras completas*, ed. Arturo del Hoyo, 3 vols. (Madrid: Aguilar, 1986), iii. 623. This edition hereafter cited as OC.

Unamuno, it is worth recalling, attended the dress rehearsal of *Yerma*, and spoke warmly of the play.[2]

In theatre, even so, the generation preceding Lorca's own offered fewer growing-points than it did in poetry or fiction. Commercially popular genres—costume drama, or stereotyped Andalusian regional comedy—held much of the stage. There was still a public for the portentous, melodramatic problem-play such as José Echegaray had made famous in the previous century. The *género chico* of unpretentiously popular farce was cultivated within its limits with much technical skill. But the attempts of more serious writers to break into the repertoire had met with little success.

From the 1890s onward, Galdós had tried to apply a basic realism of character and language to the treatment on stage of substantial issues and ideas. These aspirations, shared by such younger writers as Unamuno and Jacinto Benavente (1866–1954), were never entirely fulfilled. Galdós, in the event, deferred too readily to the demands of well-made theatre, urged upon him by actors and managers. Benavente, albeit with a bolder sense of theatrical possibilities, came to play an increasingly canny ideological hand. His carefully modulated ironies troubled his bourgeois audiences little more than would encourage them to find the price of a ticket. Unamuno's theatre, its language by turns austerely plain and austerely knotty, tended to remain unperformed.

Other playwrights sought room for a non-realistic imagination (stylized or lyrical or merely eccentric) to develop a theatre beyond the norms laid down by commerce or convention. The most striking achievement in this vein was the clutch of harsh satirical caricatures which Valle-Inclán created for the stage during Primo de Rivera's dictatorship of the late 1920s.[3] These, however, suffered from the double disability of being both a political

---

[2] See *Federico García Lorca: El escritor y la crítica*, ed. Ildefonso-Manuel Gil (Madrid: Taurus, 1973), 473–5. This is one of very few details to escape the massively inclusive Ian Gibson, *Federico García Lorca: A Life* (London: Faber and Faber, 1989).

[3] Valle-Inclán's personal sub-genre of the *esperpento*, with its systematic distortions of human speech and behaviour, constituted an important exception to Lorca's general dislike of his work (see *OC* iii. 530–1).

and a box-office risk. Lorca himself admired them, but his own quest for a non-naturalistic, 'poetic' theatre was more strongly influenced by non-Spanish models—Wedekind, for example, or Pirandello. His earliest plays are rather tentative and unfocused forays into this domain. The much-acclaimed historical drama *Mariana Pineda* (1927) illustrates their limitations. Lorca took evident pains to make it poetic, through its heroic and romantic story-line and its lyrical expression. But it is not yet a theatrical experience totally framed as poetry. The power of poetic organization is not being applied at that level.

Lorca's first substantial attempt to do so came in the two plays which arose most directly from the time which he spent in New York and Havana in 1929–30. Both *The Public* and *Once Five Years Pass* are strikingly experimental: Lorca, indeed, regarded the former as 'unperformable' for many years to come. Doubtless he was thinking chiefly of the play's homosexual content. But the theatrical idiom of both pieces was disconcerting. Lorca seemed driven to communicate what now concerned him most by fusing together the most disparate cultural and expressive resources at his command. Yet this same grasping at an absolute originality of form actually put that communicative aim at risk. In our own time, as Lorca foresaw, these plays have come to be better appreciated. But the appreciation still requires much explanatory glossing.

The four plays in this volume represent a second strategy, arguably less radical, because of Lorca's use of pre-existing dramatic models. He drew on classical tragedy, on seventeenth-century Spanish *comedia*, on Synge and Chekhov—a list whose sheer eclecticism makes clear his continuing concern to remake, rather than merely follow tradition. Even so, audiences had more to hold on to here than in the more uncompromisingly experimental works. *Blood Wedding*, *Yerma*, and *Doña Rosita*—all produced in Lorca's lifetime—brought him public acclaim and a close creative relationship with professionals in the theatre. But the experience scarcely altered his view of Spanish theatre at large, which he described in 1933 (*OC* iii. 531) as being written 'by swine for swine'. Rescuing it from wholly commercial interests and from 'that horrible thing called *killing time*' (*OC* iii. 459) remained as work in progress to the end of his life.

II

One reason why Lorca is often deemed to need no introduction is that he tends, in any event, to get one. We are variously and unhelpfully offered Lorca in a whole series of roles. There is, for example, the Gypsy balladeer—an identification which particularly annoyed him. Others, in varying degrees, have greater warrant: the local laureate of Andalusia; the surrealist sworn-brother of Dalí and Buñuel; the poet of the people, a fallen soldier in the wars of the proletariat; the martyred homosexual, fully understandable only within the parameters of the gay imagination; the *poeta maldito*, living out through all these his version of the old Romantic Agony. None of these accounts is without its value as a point of reference; none approaches the whole truth.

His *Book of Gypsy Ballads*, of course, made him more famous than anything else he wrote. But its poetic voice—neither a Gypsy voice, nor even particularly traditional—was adopted for that collection, as others were for other collections or poems. So was the Gypsy imagery. Lorca knew the Gypsies of Andalusia from childhood, and from his adult interest in the *cante jondo*, the 'deep song' that was—far more than the ballad—their particular music. His work displays an evident imaginative sympathy for them. Yet that sympathy is scarcely the main subject-matter even of the *Gypsy Ballads*. In Lorca's Andalusia generally, the Gypsies are only one element: they are virtually absent from the plays. These are about people (mostly women) who live in villages, own or rent land which they or others labour to make productive, observe peasant—but not Gypsy—customs. They are often contrasted with people who are not bound into the nexus of land-tenure, property, and settled abode. But these are not Gypsies either. Leonardo is a poorer landholder; Victor a shepherd; the itinerant reapers in *The House of Bernarda Alba* are unemployed day-labourers. This is not the Andalusia of the actual 1930s, or even of earlier times. The political agitation, the violence and counterviolence are absent; the sense of oppression always oblique (Juan's dogged attachment to his labour; Bernarda's savage contempt for her farmhands). The picture is selective. But the Gypsy part is not the part selected.

On Lorca's attachment to Andalusia at large, we can take him at his word. His childhood, spent on the family estate at Fuentevaqueros in the vale of Granada, had been richly privileged: his father, a major local landowner, had made a fortune from up-to-date sugar-beet production—but there were other reasons too. Federico García Rodríguez was no village tyrant like Bernarda Alba or her husband: an easygoing man and humane landlord, from a family of talented musicians, he chose as his second wife (his first had died childless and young) a penniless but earnest and gifted schoolmistress, Vicenta Lorca.

Wealth, comfort, and family affection, were augmented by the attentions of servants and tenants, from the wet-nurse Dolores Cuesta—supposed model for the salt-tongued, earthy country-women of Lorca's plays—to the village herbalist. To such early contacts the poet owed his immersion in Andalusian oral culture: lullabies, songs, ceremonies, superstitions, seasonal customs, and sharp tropes of popular speech. This lore informs his adult writing on several levels. Sometimes he sought more of it, and brought aspects, especially of *cante jondo*, directly into his work. More pervasively, it formed a repertoire of images, enriching his range of metaphor and allusion. And it allowed him to construct settings—the wedding feast; the river where the women wash clothes; the funeral formalities of the Alba household—which are convincingly characterized because culturally coherent.

Yet the Andalusia of these plays is itself, in a sense, only a representation of something wider. Bernarda Alba's house has aspects, material and human, recalling a house in Asquerosa, the village where Lorca's family lived for a while after Fuentevaqueros. One fairly attentive reader, not knowing this, found nothing in the play's atmosphere to shake his belief that it was set in Castile.[4] The orgiastic fertility-pilgrimage in *Yerma* is based on annual excesses at the shrine of Moclín, which Lorca had heard of, and perhaps visited. But the male and female figures at the centre of the ritual are not Andalusian at all. Lorca had apparently lifted them from Asturian folklore; his description—'They are in no way grotesque, but singularly beautiful and redolent of pure

[4] Alfredo de la Guardia, *García Lorca, persona y creación* (Buenos Aires: Schapire, 4th edn., 1961), 383.

earthiness'—implies a strong claim to universality. One might claim that too for the Old Woman Death of *Blood Wedding*, while the young Moon Man there clearly belongs to Lorca's private iconography, not to any specific local tradition.

Another Andalusian influence was the city of Granada—always, as Antonio Machado put it, 'his' Granada. If Lorca had learned to see and hear and develop his imagination in the villages of the vale, Granada itself was the place of his adolescence, and supplied the first of those supportive circles of friendship which he built up wherever he went. Its contrasts fed his increasingly complex cultural responses. The matchless Alhambra, relic of lost Islamic splendour, confronted the Gypsy town of Albaicín on its opposite hill; between lay a seemingly commonplace Spanish provincial city. Yet modern, middle-class Granada had never been wholly commonplace. A minority of its citizens had long upheld traditions of artistic creativity and political dissent despite their neighbours' derision and occasional persecution. The martyred Liberal heroine Mariana Pineda was part of that history. Another part went into *Doña Rosita the Spinster*. The *cursilería*, the faded gentility of Rosita's decline into old-maidhood has its own dimension of art and ideas—albeit belittled by its deep provinciality. Lorca, even so, saw the play as reflecting Spanish, not Granadine, *cursilería* and marginality. Commenting on the period of the final act (1911), and hinting at larger issues off-stage, he remarked 'one step further on lies war'.[5] But in the war of 1914 no one from Granada or from Spain was called upon to fight.

The surrealist association, again, is a biographical fact. Surrealist and avant-garde movements greatly interested Lorca's contemporaries at the Residencia de Estudiantes—notably his two close friends, Luis Buñuel and Salvador Dalí. In the mid-1920s the latter had a powerful influence over him. Dalí urged Lorca to make the unconscious the organizing principle of his imagination, thereby developing a more radically irrational, personally authentic aesthetic. Whether either man was ever formally a 'surrealist' is doubtful, and not especially important. The real

---

[5] Interview in *Crónica*, 15 Dec. 1935 (*OC* iii. 667). Interviewed for *El Sol* on 1 Jan. 1935, Lorca had spoken of the final act of *Doña Rosita* as taking place in 1910 (*OC* iii. 619).

objection to applying that term to Lorca is that it is too handy
for the lazy reader. It enables us, conveniently, to discount any
imagery which fails to make immediate sense. 'That', we can
always argue, 'is surrealism, random association. We should not
even try to rationalize it.' But this ignores that great part of
Lorca's imagery which does, once analysed, yield itself as following out some specific associative code. These may be private
codes, or even a private language; critics write perceptively about
Lorca's 'grammar of images'. But they are neither arbitrary nor
automatic. In those other, apparently irreducible cases, we may
simply lack a full enough knowledge of Lorca's extraordinarily
eclectic range of cultural reference. Martínez Nadal's wholly
credible claim that, of all the poets of his generation, he bore the
most substantial *cultural* load hints at enormous interpretative
challenges.[6]

The notion of Lorca as a martyr of the Left has fewer devotees
now than it once had, though it retains a certain credibility. He
belonged to the radical minority among Granada's middle-class
élite. His father, the enlightened landowner, ensured that young
Federico's education was decisively secular. The Socialist academic Fernando de los Ríos was a family friend; young left-wing
intellectuals formed part of Lorca's own circle. When the Second
Republic brought Socialists and advanced Liberals into government (and los Ríos to a Ministry), Lorca shared in the hopes
of social betterment inspired by the change. He expressed this
allegiance actively in 1932–4 by directing *La Barraca*, the company of Madrid University student actors who toured towns and
villages, bringing the Spanish classics to popular audiences. This
was by no means the specific self-definition in party terms of
poets like Rafael Alberti or Miguel Hernández. But the commitment was unmistakable.

His broader adherence to the cause of the less privileged is
repeatedly affirmed in statements of his own. The precise bearing of these assertions on the plays is less clear-cut. His explicit
acknowledgement that people of his class and cultural formation
have to 'make sacrifices' came in an interview given just before

[6] See Rafael Martínez Nadal, *Lorca's 'The Public'* (London: Calder & Boyars,
1974), 219.

the première of *Yerma*—his most politically controversial play.[7] That controversy may owe much to external factors: the supposed links between the leading actress Margarita Xirgu, the director Rivas Cherif, and Manuel Azaña, leader of the Republican Left. But it was Lorca himself who wrote into the text the Old Pagan Woman's emphatic dismissal of God, and who would later build the arrogance of ownership into the opinions of Bernarda Alba and the conduct of her husband. Such issues arise in all these plays, precisely because Lorca put them there.

Their primary content, though, is not overtly political. Typically, it concerns a woman protagonist's passage from one state to another: from bride-as-chattel to outlawed lover; from barren wife to mother. What does resonate politically is the pattern marking each transition: at first desired as a liberation; then pursued, frustrated, inexorably denied. It is surely relevant to find here a note of protest, even rebellion. Admittedly the rebellion addresses things inherent in the condition of these human lives, rather than specific social abuses. But the immediate images of constraint evoke a traditional social framework, simultaneously upholding the claims of propriety and property. That, in the febrile ideological climate of the 1930s, ensured that Lorca's theatre was seen as political. Even the universally admired *Blood Wedding* was rumoured—no doubt falsely—to have been staged in a militant version as *Bodas de dinamita*.

If these plays have a political dimension, it is clearly not of that kind. Lorca's political orientation doubtless helped to turn his theatre in the 1930s towards more publicly accessible forms. And the subject-matter of the plays obviously coheres with the dramatist's sense of a wider social reality. But that does not make them the direct expressions of a socio-political outlook. The real case is more complex, and will bear further examination. But at the time it was all too readily over-simplified. In that sense, all enquiries into the causes of Lorca's death tend to issue in a 'discovery of the Mediterranean'. He was killed (like many people, in many wars) for being in the wrong place at the wrong time, and because the Nationalists who controlled Granada identified him as being on the wrong side. *Ex illis est*—the perceived fact

[7] Interview in *El Sol*, 24 Dec. 1934 (OC iii. 614).

of being 'one of the others'—was, as so often, warrant enough for condemnation.

It had, as we now understand more clearly, another application to Lorca. His homosexuality is an important fact about both the man and his writing. There remain questions concerning how it is important, and the difference which it makes to ways of reading him or reading about him. With regard to his death, it seems to have brought him additional and predictable abuse, but not to have been the specific occasion for his murder. As to his work, it is evident that it requires to be understood with the facts about his sexuality in mind; it by no means follows that it can only be understood from within such a sexuality. This would be like arguing that homosexual readers could never understand Robert Burns as a love poet. Clearly it would be an impertinence to mark down such understanding as inauthentic. Lorca, like any poet, speaks from within his own nature both to those who share it and to those who do not.

This does not mean, though, that everything which he writes has to be referred to the sexual dimension of that nature. It would be naïve to see Lorca's sexuality and the situations into which it brought him either as what his work was 'all about' or as what it was 'really about'. Through most of what he wrote (including his later plays) there runs a theme of 'desire denied', which could scarcely have mattered to him so universally but for his own sexual history. Here, however, that theme is specifically embodied—that, rather than 'envisaged', seems the right word —in the lives of women: the Bride of *Blood Wedding*, Yerma, Rosita, the Alba daughters. Nor can we plausibly take these female representations as mere allegory or disguise, for Lorca, consciously or unconsciously, has crafted them in ways which that, of itself, would not have required. If he took that trouble, this fact in turn requires its explanation.

Again, to raise a point which certainly relates to Lorca's sexuality, three of his female protagonists—the Mother in *Blood Wedding*, Yerma, and Bernarda Alba—are responsible in some way for the deaths of their own children. One recalls cryptic remarks by Lorca regarding his single state, his insecure identity, and the relevance of his mother to such concerns. The mother–son relationship as a source of danger appears elsewhere in his work:

' "Mother, stitch me to your pillow!" | "Yes, I will!" '[8] But there are also parallels in classical tragedy: behind the Mother, Hecuba; behind Yerma, the Agave of Euripides' *Bacchae*; behind Bernarda, most clearly of all, Seneca's Medea. The interesting question regarding this particular terror, might not be its role in Lorca's psychological formation, but his coming to view it here as part of a *female* tragedy: the tragedy certainly of the first two women, and possibly even of the appalling Bernarda. What Lorca is able to imagine is not necessarily co-terminous with his psychosexual make-up.

All these images of Lorca are at best partially valid. Even their summation in the figure of the *poeta maldito* furnishes only a conventionalized view, and one which assimilates into late Romanticism a writer very much of the 1920s and 1930s. 'Late Romantic', admittedly, is an elastic term: in music one might attach it to Walton or Britten—composers not far removed, chronologically or aesthetically, from Lorca. Yet, applied to them as to him, it obscures specific links with their own times. Often associated with the *poeta maldito* motif are epithets like 'dionysiac', 'demonic', or 'telluric'. These displace the inapt image of Lorca the happy folklorist, only to supplant it with folklore of another kind, playing down that consciously modern input of craft and culture which so largely shaped his creative process. Here it is not the nineteenth-century reference which misleads, but the easy assertion of a timeless spontaneity. As with other encapsulations of Lorca, a natural desire for simplicity is flattered; understanding of the more complex reality risks being lost.

III

These familiar a-priori notions of Lorca have other things in common. Revolutionaries aspire to change society; surrealists and rebel poets subvert meanings and values; homosexuality questions categories once seen as fixed and safe; Gypsies are popularly credited with both magic and shiftiness; Andalusians

---

[8] 'Mamá. | Bórdame en tu almohada. | ¡Eso sí! | ¡Ahora mismo!' ('Canciones para niños: Canción tonta', in *Canciones* (1927); *OC* i. 304.)

with fluent and plausible speech. All conjure a sense of something protean, hard to pin down or rely on.

In this they evoke the sheer virtuosity of Lorca's artistic and social self-expression—the gift for music and drawing as well as poetry; the captivating personality; the restless dazzle of his creativity. 'One could scarcely think of him', Luis Cernuda wrote 'as being still, even in death.' He could exasperate as well as captivate: Borges' barbed dismissal—'a professional Andalusian'—has substance enough to be hurtful.[9] But what others saw as bravura self-assurance, could be a source of profound self-doubt. 'I have just made a terrible discovery ... *I have not yet been born* ... I live off borrowed substance; what I have within me is not mine.'[10] That was written when he was 22; it might have been at almost any period of his life. Some of our shrewdest witnesses—Vicente Aleixandre, Helen Grant—sensed, behind the seeming completeness of his social self, an inward loss and lack.[11] The contradiction is matched in the plays and poems: rich, imagistic affirmation, forever threatened with death and denial; forever colluding with that threat.

This pattern powerfully serves the breadth of Lorca's appeal. Abundant possibility, successively affirmed and negated, represents a universal trajectory: people first live, then die. More specific histories of defeat through repression or fatality are anything but rare. The sense that such defeats are facilitated, perhaps justified, by flaws within the self is integral to the notion of tragedy. Yet this alone cannot guarantee the quality of Lorca's work. A fully tragic vision must do more than insist—however memorably—that these defeats happen; it must offer insight into what they are. That too Lorca supplies, though how he supplies it is too easily misrepresented.

All those familiar stereotypes of Lorca signal some form of marginality or outsider status. Under their sign, he becomes particularly the poet of those marked by some acknowledged

[9] Gibson, 372 (the source is a conversation recorded in the 1970s); see also Luis Cernuda, 'Federico García Lorca (Recuerdo)', in *Prosa completa*, ed. D. Harris and L. Maristany (Barcelona: Barral, 1975), 1338.

[10] Letter [sc. 1921] to Regino Sanz de la Maza (OC iii. 782–3).

[11] See OC ii, pp. ix–xi (Aleixandre) and Gibson, 240–1 (Helen Grant).

'difference'—and indeed of many not so marked, who very much wish that they were. But if all such readings of him are granted some validity, then a much more powerful notion emerges. Difference itself becomes a human universal: in the perspective thus offered, to be human at all is to be left out of some much-desired form of belonging. That, indeed, is a conclusion towards which his writing tends, and a major source of its poignancy.

But it seems disconcertingly predictable—almost a stock response among writers since Romanticism—and strangely at odds with the subtle effects which illustrate it. Rosita, pining away against a backdrop of Granadine *cursilería*, is culturally placed with Chekhovian ironic exactitude. But the ground of her despair —her lover's failure to return from Argentina—has an operatic arbitrariness about it. We are made disturbingly intimate with Yerma's particular humiliations. Yet her childlessness is simply a 'given': attempts to make rational sense of it seem doomed. Such contrasts can foster an account of Lorca's appeal which again favours the self-indulgence of spectators or readers. This complex dramatic poet is seen as confirming certain grand, tragic, essentially simple propositions—visceral truths, unattainable by pedantic intellect. This very comfortable finding flatters our competence in handling the difficult and modern, whilst offering a licensed holiday from the obligation to think. A Lorca who did only this could hardly be the major dramatist which it is claimed he was.

Attempts to make good that claim need to begin by admitting something not often stated in terms: virtually no major twentieth-century Spanish writer offers less by way of conceptual content. Quality of mind is not the issue: Lorca's intelligence is unmistakable. But his writing very seldom generates any sense of a process of thought impressively accomplished. This is true even of his discursive prose. His lecture on Góngora begins to sketch a substantive poetic theory.[12] But the famous piece on children's lullabies is charmingly anecdotal and little more, while the equally well-known talk on the inspirational *duende* of Andalusian song

---

[12] 'La imagen poética de Don Luis de Góngora' (OC iii. 223–47); see Nadine Ly, 'Lorca y la teoría de la escritura', in *Valoración actual de la obra de García Lorca* (Madrid: Casa de Velázquez; Universidad Complutense, 1988), 163–79.

remains shamelessly—perhaps fittingly—pure performance-art.[13]
So too with the plays translated here. As theatrical experience,
they are searchingly profound; what they *say* is another matter.
This has nothing to do with Lorca's modernity. The line of intellectual process is present and important in poets like Jorge Guillén
and (even in his pre-Marxist phase) Neruda; others, like Alberti,
sought such conceptual shaping through their Marxist attachment.
Nor is it a consequence of visceral, passionate, or delinquent
aspects of Lorca's sensibility. All that can be just as emphatically
asserted of Luis Cernuda, and no poet gives more richly of
argument. The frugality of thought in Lorca's writing is simply,
inexplicably, there.

Shorn of such conceptual support, all Lorca's work risks itself
on the hope that as a master of images, a shifter and changer of
shapes, he can achieve mastery too over inchoate experience.
This is a bold venture, bringing a real sense of danger—of *duende*,
one might say. Yet text after text—*Don Perlimplín*, *The Public*,
Blood Wedding, *The House of Bernarda Alba*—dramatizes the
fact that mastery of images is not enough. Whether exercised
to avert a personal doom, to achieve a work of artistic creation,
to give a social transition like marriage its ritual potency, or to
control the rebellious lives of others, the manipulation of linguis-
tic and social signs will not serve. It will not hold up the sky
from falling.

Lorca's theatre, then, does not merely display the fated struggle to resist isolation and meaninglessness; it embodies the struggle and it risks the loss. In that, rather than in any conceptual
process, its full seriousness resides. Should we, then, speak of a
tragic seriousness—as 'fated struggle' surely implies? Lorca himself would probably have found that appropriate. The subtitles
of *Blood Wedding* and *Yerma* define both plays as tragedies. So
do several of his statements about them, though these refer prin-
cipally to formal features which they share with the classical
genre. There is less certainty over *Doña Rosita the Spinster*, to
which he once referred in a single interview (OC iii. 667–8) as
comedia, *drama*, and *tragedia*. Manuel Altolaguirre remembered

---

[13] 'Canciones de cuna españolas' (*OC* iii. 282–300); 'Juego y teoría del duende'
(*OC* iii. 306–18). For Lorca the inspirational power of *duende* is closely bound up
with a sense of risk and of impending death.

him calling *The House of Bernarda Alba* 'this tragedy',[14] but it is hard to evaluate that as evidence. Certainly the subtitles of these later plays say nothing about tragedy, and their tonality is more mixed. Both draw on modes of ironic presentation which lie closer to comedy. Yet all four plays at least aspire towards the tragic. Their power to move audiences seems proof of some success.

But how is it that those audiences are being moved? Tragedy is more than the mere spectacle of terror and distress. It may end in 'the place | where lies, trembling, enmeshed, | the dark root of the scream' (*Blood Wedding*, Act 3, below, p. 65), but this does not define the tragic way of getting there. That assumes a story of both worth and waste, and an awareness of the gulf between them—that is to say, of the 'tragic fall'. To assess that fall requires an agreement about value, acknowledging some things as better and others as worse. That can prove problematic for modern writers, among whom belief in any transcendent value-system is rare. Lorca's shape-shifting facility with images, indeed, impugns the stability even of wholly secular languages of valuing. Things appear captivatingly, vertiginously as they are: yet we are denied reliable knowledge of *what* they are. The more powerfully that facility is exercised, the less authoritatively the fullness of tragedy can be conveyed.

Audiences needed to know what mattered in the plays, and how it mattered. Lorca needed to find agreement with them about the language used and the values invoked. There was no going back to transcendence: though he uses the cultural motifs of Andalusian popular religion, there is no trace of natural theology in his plays. The search for new mythologies, mediating private imagery through Freudian or other psychologically based schemes, interested him, as it interested many artists of his time. But even at his most hermetic, he never identified the problem of language solely as one of self-expression. It was always a problem of communication. His most 'unperformable' play, in which self-expression and self-generated mythic imagery are most prominent, was not entitled *The Theatre Director*, but *The Public*.

---

[14] Manuel Altolaguirre, 'Nuestro tiempo', *Hora de España*, 9 (Sept. 1937), 36.

Throughout his development as a playwright Lorca was searching for a 'society of the play'—for that audience whose existence
might give him the capacity to speak. In these last plays he came
closest to success, though not all limitations were overcome. The
virtuosity of his image-based expression is still a debatable asset.
He renders with haunting specificity the objects, the circum-
stances, and the force of his protagonists' desires: Yerma's passionate, pained vision of motherhood; Adela's fantasy of Pepe el
Romano; the soaring, amorous arias of Rosita and her cousin.
But there is no equivalent clarity as to how far these are, authentically, goods whose forfeiture is tragic—or if so, what leads to
their denial. Is it an oppressive social and cultural order, affronting
nature? Or is it nature, indifferent to all human desires? Or a
disabling contradiction, ingrained in desire itself? If this last, is
the disablement perhaps the thing *really* desired? The answers
might leave either more or less room for tragedy. We might, for
example, be faced instead with a cold poetry of defeat—an endlessly elaborated variation on the Moon's soliloquy in *Blood
Wedding*.

It matters to know such things, and Lorca does not altogether
help us to know them. Possibly he did not know them himself.
But his theatre of the 1930s still stands as the kind of achievement he wanted it to be. The poet-dramatist who had for some
years, and in some desperation, been asking 'Is there anyone out
there?' was emboldened in those years to think that there might
be, if he went to meet them. They were there, and their number
is still growing.

IV

The chronology of Lorca's writings is complex. He liked to keep
several projects in being, sometimes for years, before completing them in a final burst of energy. His earliest notes for *Doña
Rosita* go back to 1922, two years before José Moreno Villa
showed him the botanical description of *rosa mutabilis* which
supplies that play's central image. A chance meeting in Argentina, nine years later, revived his interest. Three times in 1935 he
promised friends a reading of the play, finally delivering it in
September, three months before the première. *Blood Wedding*

too had a long gestation: inspired by press reports of an incident in Níjar (Almería) in 1928, and completed four years later, it was first played in March 1933. *Yerma* already existed in part when Lorca visited Cuba early in 1930, but the last act was delayed until August 1934; by December the play was in performance. *The House of Bernarda Alba*, by contrast, was written entirely in the summer of 1936; the autograph is dated 19 June. Thus the completion-dates of all four plays fall within a four-year span (September 1932 to June 1936).

These were the years of the Second Republic, and of Lorca's identification with it. Neither his direction of *La Barraca* nor his statements and gestures of solidarity with the Republican project meant that his plays of this period were either propaganda or political advocacy. The issues which they address were not those debated in *Cortes* or fought out on the Republic's turbulent streets. Yet their images of rural poverty, the restricted lives of women, the abuses of petty and domestic power, and the dysfunctions of moral and social convention could hardly escape a political meaning. Their panorama of 'liberation denied' offers no warrant for believing in any particular political response to that denial. But it does make such responses appear relevant. Lorca's emphatically expressed belief in the 'social action' of theatre suggests that this was not accidental.

Even so, he remained clear-sighted about the implications of that belief. It did not mean that every possible political allusion must always bear an ideological meaning. That most directly political of images, the revolutionary crowd invading the theatre, featured already in *The Public*, without making that play political any more than its use of the crucifixion motif made it a religious drama. The incident emerges again in the draft of Lorca's *Untitled Play*. This unfinished piece from early 1936 does manifest a directly political intention, though Lorca displays no very secure grasp of what to do about it. The manuscript reflects many continuing uncertainties, and he never did give it a title. It seems, on balance, unlikely that he would have come readily to terms with this mode of political drama. But he did quite clearly recognize it as a distinctive mode from his other plays of the time. He defined the *Untitled Play* unambiguously as 'social drama', echoing a statement of February 1935 that he planned several 'dramas of a human and social type', differing in subject-matter (*materia*) and technique from *Yerma* or *Blood Wedding*.[15]

The distinctive scope which Lorca claimed for the 'social action' of plays like *Yerma* is made clearer in his address to an audience of Madrid actors, gathered for a special performance in March 1935. The occasion lent itself all too well to sweeping rhetorical claims on behalf of the theatre; Lorca's chosen rhetoric echoed the language of many Republican pronouncements on cultural policy. Didactic, humanistic, ethical, it dwelt on the power of culture to transform the horizons and sensibilities of audiences, and the entitlement of the people at large to a place in that process of change. Yet such commonplaces of public debate were not necessarily insincere. Lorca often talked like this as spokesman for *La Barraca*, and we have good evidence that his commitment to *La Barraca* was authentic: he had actually made its work a priority over finishing *Yerma*. We may take it that in describing how theatre might be socially effectual, he meant what he said. Yet he referred to no specifically political ends, merging these, rather, into a broadly drawn but challenging ethical programme: theatre as 'a forum of debate, where old and wrong moralities can be brought to the bar of criticism' (*OC* iii. 459). For Lorca, the socio-political contribution of theatre remains at this level of generality. It does so even when he links his writing with protest against 'a world of injustice and wretchedness of every kind' (*OC* iii. 623), or inveighs against inequalities of wealth (674), or declares himself 'on the side of the poor' (614). He nowhere links the ethical authority of his theatre to programmes—much less party programmes—of concrete political action. If anything, he tends to broaden—politically, to dilute—the theatrical agenda. Theatre, his 1935 speech continued, should instruct audiences in 'the eternal norms of the human heart and feelings' (*OC* iii. 459).

Overwhelmingly, the experience of later audiences confirms this, finding in his plays not ideology or indoctrination, but

---

[15] *OC* iii. 624; see also the reference to 'a social drama, still untitled, with the public intervening . . . from the streets', in an undated interview of 1936 (*OC* iii. 679).

these larger human resonances. Yet his strong didactic assurance raises its own problems. Triumphantly affirming the theatre's mission to instruct, Lorca presupposes that someone—playwrights, poets, himself—has a secure entitlement to instruct. That seems to contradict the moral economy of his plays—so absolute for the individual self against any moral authority whatsoever. The sufferings of Yerma, of Adela, of Rosita deny anyone such authority. One could argue that this denial witnessed to a more inclusive truth: the 'eternal norms of the human heart'. But that only introduces a fresh contradiction—this time with the implied philosophical thrust of Lorca's theatre.

For as each play unfolds, the possibility of any uncontradictory truth about humanity is ruthlessly discounted. The elopement in *Blood Wedding*, experienced first as a movement towards spontaneous life, reveals itself as a flight into death. All that play's crucial images—the stallion, vital and violent; the knife that cuts victuals and kills men; blood itself—stand poised on that edge of ambivalence. Rosita's fidelity, which seemed so absolutely a value, proves to have been a grotesque burden to her. The talkers in Bernarda's household, endlessly contending, shape, reshape, and deform every reality. Everything dissolves in the relentless flux of desire, and desire consumes itself. Yerma has killed her husband, or (as she says) her son, or the lover she might have had, or the figure at the heart of patriarchy—who can tell which? And does it matter? Identities, images, values, language, appear endlessly, pointlessly commutable. How can Lorca draw a sufficiently robust view of human nature—'eternal norms', no less—out of such radical instability?

These contradictions are not pedantic matters, of no application to a major writer. They are part of what made Lorca a major writer in and for his time. The unresolved tension over his mission to instruct embodies a central problem of the whole republican project. The Republic sought, by applying a body of public wisdom, to create a better, freer society. Yet a powerful section of its natural supporters held that such wisdom could define itself only in the active recovery by the dispossessed of their alienated freedoms. The debate took many forms: reformers against revolutionaries; socialists against anarchists; the communist security apparatus against the doomed idealists of the POUM.[16] Its arguments shaped the Republic's political life; they played a major part in its death. Lorca's insistent, shakily founded didacticism neither resolves nor even directly addresses that debate. Yet it bears a special witness to how and why the debate mattered.

Much the same applies to his aspiration to deal in human universals. He was one of many writers and artists whose modernity in the 1920s led them away from humanism, but who in the newly politicized 1930s felt challenged to give their work a more humanistic sense. A truculent minority—Lorca's old friend Dalí among them—resisted the demand. Others, like Alberti and Neruda, were willing to alter both the premises and the manner of their writing in order to meet it. Lorca, eager to offer a humanistic content, yet pursuing a practice which constantly jeopardized it, faithfully reflected the dilemma of his whole artistic generation.

But his chosen stance as a would-be propagator of timeless human truths was ill-adapted to his ever resolving that dilemma. The anomalies to which it could lead are exemplified in an interview of April 1936:

My first plays are unperformable . . . my real intention is here, in these impossible plays. But in order to establish a personality and make good my right to be respected, I have turned out other things.[17]

The problem is not that the 'impossible' plays—*Once Five Years Pass* and *The Public*—are being overvalued. Rather, it is that the 'other things'—*Yerma* and the eminently performable *Blood Wedding*—are being downgraded. Seen as a retreat from full integrity, a second-best, created for purposes of public reputation, how can they express the 'eternal norms' of human inner life? If we turn to *The Public*, as the authentic expression of Lorca's 'real intention', the contrast becomes plainer yet. Two kinds of theatre were distinguished there—one unperformable but speaking unspeakable truths; the other publicly accepted but inauthentic (OC ii. 599–610). Lorca naturally identified *The*

[16] *Partido Obrero de Unificación Marxista* ('United Marxist Workers' Party'), forcibly suppressed by the more authoritarian Communists in May–June 1937.
[17] Interview in *La Voz*, 2 Apr. 1936 (OC iii. 674).

Public itself and *Once Five Years Pass* as instances of the former: the 'theatre beneath the sand'. But if his two Andalusian tragedies belong to the other theatre—the 'theatre in the open air'—they must surely be cut off from those levels of truth-telling to which he elsewhere presents them as committed.

Much of the difficulty stems from Lorca's philosophical idealism. For him the truths which theatre can tell are guaranteed as true because they derive from the dramatist's privileged access either to the inner world of his own authentic intention or to a world of overarching human universals. Since Lorca attributes an absolute, ideal reality to both these domains, he has no way of mediating between them. Yet we need not follow him into that impasse; we can find what his plays communicate on either score, credible or important without investing it with that absolute authority. Between his relatively hermetic plays and the more public and accessible dramas which followed them, there is both contrast and continuity. The anxieties of *The Public* over effective communication—whether it is achieved; whether, if achieved, it must falsify the thing communicated—apply to both kinds of theatre. Lorca's later plays revisit these issues, from premises which, like those of his 'unperformable' theatre, are not absolutely but provisionally, experimentally valid.

The cultural politics of the Republic were decisive in underwriting the provisional validity of Lorca's communicative intent. The commitment to redistribute wealth and advantage implied a wider diffusion of Spain's cultural and artistic patrimony. Hence the work of *La Barraca*. Lorca's experience in that work, bringing classic Spanish drama to popular audiences, convinced him that uneducated audiences could be brought to understand emotionally things which they could never comprehend intellectually. His own attempt to locate and address a very different audience primarily through image and feeling was demonstrably rooted in this lesson of his *La Barraca* days. In turn, the widely shared perception of cultural issues as issues of social moment meant that his efforts were reinforced by enthusiastic audiences, admiring critics, and loyal helpers. The identification with his plays of a major actress like Margarita Xirgu, for example, brought them into the very centre of contemporary theatre.

Yet he had by no means found a secure formula for ready and

replicable communication. The very diversity of these plays under-
lines their continuing experimental character. Their present status
as 'classics' tends to mask a certain rough-edged, risk-taking quality, present in them all. Lorca's own dubiously sustainable insist-
ence that they bear witness to timeless human attributes only
obscures the more important extent to which they remain prod-
ucts of their particular time and circumstance.

V

Blood Wedding, the earliest of these plays, was relatively predictable in terms of Lorca's previous work. Though not itself
about Gypsies, it recalls the *Gypsy Ballads* in its rich remaking
of traditional poetry, its ritualistic passage from custom to fatality, and the deceptive ease with which it offers itself as melo-
drama in a 'primitive' setting. But it also reflects Lorca's recent
La Barraca experience, especially that company's staging of Lope
de Vega's *The Knight of Olmedo*. In this, the last three scenes
were cut, making the murder of the Knight, like the killings in
Lorca's play, the climax of the drama. The mood and pace of both
plays exhibit a thickening of atmospheres, a fatalistic undertow
from joyous ceremonial to death in the dark. The only two personal names in *Blood Wedding*—Leonardo and Félix—are themselves Lopean in background.[18]

Practical experience in the theatre had also reinforced Lorca's
growing mastery of dialogue. Phases of functional plainness here
alternate with others of suppressed stress and antagonism, marked
by sharp images out of Andalusian popular speech. This alter-
nating rhythm is played off in complex polyphony against others:
verse and prose; fraught domesticity and exuberant public ritual;
human struggle and destructive fatality. At each level, the design
embraces both climax and pause: the stillness about the cradle,
the lull in the wedding preparations, the silences of the wood, all
build towards the wilder clashes which follow. Much of this was
a necessary affirmation of plenitude in a piece whose final scenes
fathom an absolute negation. Yet the threat of that negation is

[18] He was, of course, Lope Félix de Vega Carpio; the literary alias of the young
woman to whom he dedicated a late volume of short stories was 'Marcia Leonarda'.
For Lorca's curtailment of *El caballero de Olmedo* see OC iii. 654.

ever-present—sustained by the imagery, and centrally by the images implicit in the play's title.

In the society depicted here all weddings are 'blood weddings': in the defloration of the wedding night, and the mingling of bloodlines. But another social form—the blood-feud—is also structured by blood. The plot of *Blood Wedding* reflects the clash between these two. Its imaginative power goes far deeper. Blood can seal or sunder the union of lovers. It is passed on in lineages; it spills from murdered bodies when lineages are cut off. For men and women it is the stuff of both life and death. Their predicament is marked as inescapable here through further imagery of the four elements: earth, water, fire, air. Through this culturally powerful complex of references, the vital and vulnerable human heritage of blood emerges as an irresistibly self-destructive natural force.

All this establishes a potent claim to universality, underlined by the general and generic naming of all the characters save Leonardo. The illusion of archetypal truth is shaken neither by the feeble Bridegroom's implausible transformation into a self-sufficient mythic avenger, nor by minor discrepancies of timescale or topography. The abrupt shift to the dreamlike symbolic mode of Act 3 actually intensifies the play's effect. It also reinforces a certain reassuring linearity, a succession, rather than a fusion of contrasting styles. Lorca, with some justification, regarded it as a favourite moment (*OC* iii. 524). Unsurprisingly, *Blood Wedding* brought him all the popular success he could have wished, but it also suggests a Lorca who was capable of more. Indeed, he had already identified the dramatic model which would underwrite his next advance. The chorus passages, the off-stage violence, and most obviously of all, the subtitle of *Blood Wedding* all point towards classical tragedy.

Yerma, subtitled *poema trágico*, he later described as 'a tragedy pure and simple'[19]—and indeed it adheres very closely to the design of Greek (especially Euripidean) tragedy. It has a chorus, relating the heroine's plight to more conventional and communal perspectives. Its tightly defined group of main characters are all named. Its protagonist is powerfully foregrounded. Its story—

---

[19] Interview in *El Día Gráfico*, 17 Sept. 1935 (*OC* iii. 651).

Lorca called it 'plotless' (OC iii. 650)—is simply Yerma's struggle against her fate. It is essentially an inner struggle: unknown
to Yerma, its decisive event has already happened. Its concern
with what that does to her is reflected in scenes wholly classical
in their framing: chorus; conflictive *agon*, confronting one protagonist with another; self-revelatory soliloquy. Unity of place is
not observed—successive locations—indoors or out of doors; the
village environs or the distant pilgrim-shrine—are importantly
contrasted. Unity of time is strangely handled. Various overt
references establish the corrosion of Yerma's marriage and spirit
as taking place over years. Yet the vague treatment of the intervening periods suggests something more instant and more ca-
lamitous. It is a duality familiar from examples such as *Othello*
or *Celestina*—both, like *Yerma*, tragedies of passion. But in the
most important of the unities—that of theme and action—*Yerma*
is classically single-minded. The question 'Why am I barren?'
and its corollary, 'What can I do?' haunt Yerma throughout.
And there are no answers to either.

It is repeatedly hinted that Juan—canny and grudging in deal-
ing with her as with his little parcel of land—might be impotent.
Yet Yerma's demands on herself similarly highlight a potential
defect in her. Her view of motherhood is disquietingly absolute:
an exalted state, transcending pain, neutralizing desire, valid
only within the marriage to which she is bound. She will not
leave niggardly Juan for free-spirited Victor; she scornfully re-
jects the orgiastic liberation of the pagan pilgrimage. Is she the
author of her own dilemma? Or a victim of social norms, tyran-
nous for women and their hopes, which she has somehow inter-
nalized as a life-negating 'second nature'? Possibly, but her
constraining sense of honour is hard to separate from her selfhood. If hers is a social tragedy, it cannot be put right by facile
social adjustment. Society aspires to be a 'second nature'—as
comprehensive as nature itself. It offers roles and norms; it pro-
vides releases as well as rigidities: the licensed sexual piquancy
of gossip; the nature-magic of the village 'wise woman'; the
promiscuous pilgrimage. Yet neither here nor in the primary
world of fertile nature can Yerma find herself. The play's central
nexus of images defines nature's domain as one of flow—flow of
water, flow of maternal milk, flow of blood. But Yerma is *seca—*

'barren', but more literally, 'dry'. Perhaps (the thought torments her) she is outside nature altogether, made monstrous against her will.

That fear broods over the play, unspoken, like so much else here. Its climaxes are forced admissions: truths about the marriage which the partners do not want to speak or hear. The tension as the dialogue builds towards these self-revelations is impressively controlled. The verse-passages weave the key images into lyrical highlights of great beauty. But there is a disciplining of picturesque elements: echoes of popular lyric are now only pretexts for Lorca's more radical imagery. He is fully—even chillingly—the master of his medium. The bodily flaw of Yerma's barrenness contrasts hauntingly with the willed perfection of an expression through whose artful transparency the realities of her suffering—and of whatever griefs of Lorca's own it represents—escape unnamed.

Doña Rosita the Spinster suggests at first a tactical retreat from these extremes. The setting, neither abstract nor elemental, is a solidly furnished provincial bourgeois interior. There is abundant cultural and historical reference to the Granada of Lorca's childhood and earlier. The characters are gently caricatured eccentrics. The heroine's story, increasingly tinged with melancholy, is also punctuated with moments of life-affirming absurdity. *Doña Rosita* is easily dismissed as a holiday from seriousness, 'a delightful miniature'.[20] Even its poetic passages tend towards pastiche. Indeed, the whole play can be taken as pastiche—an attempt to do knowingly what was once done naïvely in the artistic modes of a past generation. Yet pastiche as skilled and self-aware as this is itself inherently theatrical. The pleasure offered by *Doña Rosita* stems as much from its transparent contrivances as from what it contrives to represent. This rather sets the play apart from the example of Chekhov—often cited as a fruitful influence. That example is certainly present in the inconsequential, self-absorbed household dialogue, and still more in the low-key ending—the empty room and the curtain flapping in the wind. Yet Chekhov's 'precise emotional balance', as Virginia

[20] Francisco Umbral, prologue to *La casa de Bernarda Alba; Doña Rosita la soltera* (Barcelona: Ediciones B, 1987), 5.

Higginbotham rightly observes, is very different from Lorca's willed 'dissonance'.[21] The latter gathers within its dramatic idiom techniques of pastiche, Chekhovian shifts of mood, poetic models drawn from Romanticism and seventeenth-century Baroque, and the cultural codes of turn-of-the-century bourgeois Granada.

In Lorca's 'unperformable' theatre, dissonance had multiplied confusion; in *Blood Wedding* it issued in sharp, discrete contrasts. Here it is made fully communicative. The raw inwardness of tragedy, glimpsed when Rosita breaks out in bitter remembrance of what her life has really been, remains mysterious and troubling. But the insertion of Rosita's story into an actual cultural history opens the way to other meanings. Act 2 especially evokes in richly allusive detail the mental world of a particular class in a particular time and place. Its virtuoso parody, affectionate without sentimentality, is something unique in Lorca's theatre—a theatre whose human substance often seems to vanish in abstraction just when we are being invited to lament its loss as something real. Here, instead, there is an engagement with the historical conditions of that loss. It remains oblique, but it was clearly both authentic and new.

The House of Bernarda Alba is startlingly different again. Margarita Xirgu had asked Lorca to create a 'hard' character for her after the gentle Rosita.[22] But the contrast goes much further. There is a conscious rejection of the poetic, a purging of images not rooted in natural speech. The speech-styles are plainer, coarser than in the earlier pieces. There are still abstract elements: the geographically vague setting; the allegorical-sounding names; the enclosed space of the house, simultaneously location and symbol. But Lorca's express desire is for a 'documentary' effect. Above all, *The House of Bernarda Alba* is incontestably 'social' drama in that it explores the working out of a pattern of social relations. In *Doña Rosita* Lorca had dealt with cultural textures; here his attention goes to structure—the structures of authority.

Bernarda Alba is doubly a tyrant: rigid in her assertion of social hierarchy and of control over her family. Her absolute will

[21] Virginia Higginbotham, *The Comic Spirit of Federico García Lorca* (Austin: University of Texas Press, 1976), 110.

[22] Antonina Rodrigo, *Margarita Xirgu y su teatro* (Barcelona: Planeta, 1974), 268.

to dominate distorts any possibility of truth-telling. Inferiors conform in transparently perfunctory ways; tests of obedience turn on absurdly arbitrary prohibitions; formulaic civility-rituals, once gone through, are flouted in contempt; fears of sexual contamination coexist with scabrous gossip. This regime corrupts the response of all Bernarda's daughters, their dealings shot through with evasion, jealousy, and spite. The small resentments and readjustments, the larger rivalries—centrally that of Angustias and Adela over Pepe el Romano—are represented in a peculiar language: in one aspect, commonplace and even restricted; in another, iridescent with bad faith and ambiguity. The truth of any situation, then, has to emerge consistently against the grain of the language used.

Lorca, moreover, allows himself only minimal elements of variation: the handful of incursions from outside, or events glimpsed in the street; a few shifts of lighting; quarrels and challenges among the daughters; the mad grandmother, María Josefa. In all these plays, the life-affirming elements tend to be suspect: neither the romantic fugitives of *Blood Wedding*, nor Yerma's vibrant call to motherhood, nor even the demurely lost Rosita are quite what they seem. But the worn-down self-assertion of Bernarda's dependants against the norms which she so crushingly imposes seems little enough in the first place. Hope cannot even be represented as possible. Here, no less than in the phantasmagoria of *The Public*, Lorca looks into a personal heart of darkness. That play had named it with a more naked truth; in *The House of Bernarda Alba* the thing is seen with the more level eye.

What audiences are made to see goes beyond the events on stage. Somewhere beyond, other lives go on; yet these too seem marked as the life of the Albas is marked. Prudencia's family feuding and the grotesque tale of Adelaida are manifestly of a piece with that life.[23] Bernarda's double standards are matched by the villagers' blend of puritan savagery and orgiastic prurience. In this half-glimpsed, absent world—largely the world of men—some, like Enrique Humanes or La Poncia's put-upon spouse, are as powerless as the Alba daughters; others—the dead

---

[23] See, for example, Robin W. Fiddian, 'Adelaida's Story and the Cyclical Design of *La casa de Bernarda Alba*', *Romance Notes*, 21 (1980), 1–5.

patriarch Benavides; the predatory Pepe el Romano—are distinc-
tively figures of power. And here, as in Bernarda's enclosed world,
power means power to dominate and betray.

The House of Bernarda Alba, with its wilful distortions and
troubling linkages of imagery, is no work of social realism. Yet
it remains distanced from any conventional rhetoric of tragedy.
Much of it could be played successfully as broad domestic farce,
with the ending as a powerful dissonance. Its mood, even so,
remains corrosively negative, its tragic potential actually height-
ened by the affinities between Bernarda and her wider social
setting. For if she too is what that setting has made her, she is,
to that degree, a victim: the waste of spirit over which she pre-
sides becomes the extension of a wasted self. Here was matter
for pity and terror—and if that process of deformation did have
social causes, matter too for protest and redress. Did Lorca see
it in those terms, completing this, his last play, in that turbulent
summer of 1936?

This is not to ask whether *The House of Bernarda Alba* is
about social and political oppression, or about sexual roles, or
about some more broadly universal 'human condition'. Rather,
it is to ask whether Lorca's engagement with any of these—all
of which mattered to him—had become an engagement with
history. Ultimately, we cannot know, and none of his plays can
tell us unambiguously whether Lorca himself knew. Here, as in
Doña Rosita, his dramatic language seems more historically
rooted. He cut several lyrical interludes in pursuit of 'severity
and simplicity'.[24] The elements which identify Bernarda with her
social milieu are not folkloric and archetypal, as in the earlier
rural plays, but anecdotal and illustrative. As Lorca's subtitle
insists, this play is about 'the women who live in the villages of
Spain'. Yet it issues in a terminal acknowledgement of emptiness
which verges perilously on celebration of that nullity. Bernarda's
demand that her daughter's death be met with silence may be set
before us as the last act of her tyranny—or as the only possible
response.

Such tensions are never resolved in Lorca's theatre—though
the struggle to resolve them gives these last plays much of their

[24] Quoted by Altolaguirre (above, n. 14).

power. His large number of uncompleted dramatic projects might be evidence either that he was content to go on trying, or that he would eventually have moved on to another genre.[25] But the shift towards a more directly historical focus does suggest that his next move could have taken him towards the novel. What a Lorca in his forties and fifties might have become as a novelist one can scarcely begin to imagine. Notions of a Spanish Proust, or of a 'magical realism' developed importantly in the Peninsula are certainly not far-fetched. None of it happened, of course. All we know is that elements in his theatre of 1935–6 hint at a more creative involvement with history than had marked his previous work. It might have taken him in many directions. Unluckily, history met him on the road.

[25] The texts are presented, with an introduction by Marie Laffranque, in Federico García Lorca, *Teatro inconcluso* (Granada: Universidad, 1987).

SELECT BIBLIOGRAPHY

Biography

García Lorca, Francisco, *In the Green Morning: Memories of Federico* (London: Peter Owen, 1989). Less than definitive (first published in Spanish in 1965), but interesting and evocative.

Gibson, Ian, *Federico García Lorca: A Life* (London: Faber & Faber, 1989). As full as one could wish.

General studies of Lorca and his theatre

Adams, Mildred, *García Lorca: Playwright and Poet* (New York: George Braziller, 1977).

Allen, R. C., *Psyche and Symbol in the Theater of Federico García Lorca* (Austin: University of Texas Press, 1974).

Anderson, Reed, *Federico García Lorca* (London: Macmillan, 1984).

Binding, Paul, *Lorca: The Gay Imagination* (London: GMP, 1985).

Cobb, Carl, *Federico García Lorca* (New York: Twayne, 1967).

Edwards, Gwynne, *Lorca: The Theatre Beneath the Sand* (London: Marion Boyars, 1980).

Higginbotham, Virginia, *The Comic Spirit of Federico García Lorca* (Austin: University of Texas Press, 1976).

Honig, Edwin, *Federico García Lorca* (London: Jonathan Cape, 1968).

Klein, Dennis A., *'Blood Wedding', 'Yerma', and 'The House of Bernarda Alba': García Lorca's Tragic Trilogy* (Boston: Twayne, 1991). A treatment angled towards non-Hispanist readers.

Lima, Robert, *The Theatre of García Lorca* (New York: Las Américas, 1963).

Martínez Nadal, Rafael, *Lorca's 'The Public': A Study of the Unfinished Play ('El público') and of Love and Death in the Work of Federico García Lorca* (London: Calder & Boyars, 1974).

Collected essays on Lorca's writing

Among many volumes of this kind, the following are recent, of interest to readers of the plays, and at least partially in English.

Durán, M., and Colecchia, F. (eds.), *Lorca's Legacy* (New York: Lang, 1991).

Havard, Robert (ed.), *Lorca: Poet and Playwright. Essays in Honour of J. M. Aguirre* (Cardiff: University of Wales Press, 1992).

Morris, C. B. (ed.), *'Cuando yo me muera': Essays in Memory of Federico García Lorca* (Lanham, Md.: University Press of America, 1988).

Rees, Margaret A. (ed.), *Leeds Papers on Lorca and Civil War Verse* (Leeds: Trinity and All Saints College, 1988).

Zdenek, Joseph W. (ed.), *The World of Nature in the Works of Federico García Lorca* (Rock Hill, SC: Winthrop College, 1980).

Individual plays

Two of the plays here translated are covered in the Critical Guides to Spanish Texts series, published by Grant & Cutler:

Morris, C. B., *García Lorca: 'Bodas de sangre'* (London: Grant & Cutler, 1980).

Morris, C. B., *García Lorca: 'La casa de Bernarda Alba'* (London: Grant & Cutler, 1990).

Three of the four have been edited, with extensive introductions in English, for the Manchester Hispanic Texts series:

Bodas de sangre, ed. Herbert Ramsden (Manchester: University Press, 1980).

La casa de Bernarda Alba, ed. Herbert Ramsden (Manchester: University Press, 1983).

Yerma, ed. Robin Warner (Manchester: University Press, 1994).

Though intended for readers of Spanish, the critical material in all of these is useful to anyone with an interest in the plays. The bibliographies provided will guide that interest yet further. Regrettably, there is no similar treatment of *Doña Rosita la soltera*; indeed, English-based treatments, beyond those works listed above, are relatively few. Even in Spanish, the play has had less attention than it deserves.

A CHRONOLOGY OF
FEDERICO GARCÍA LORCA

1898   Born in Fuentevaqueros in the vale of Granada.

1907   Family move to Asquerosa (setting for *Bernarda Alba*).

1909–19 Granada. Early musical studies, but enters University Faculty of Letters (1915). Among family friends are Socialist professor Fernando de los Ríos and composer Manuel de Falla.

1918   First book, *Impressions and Landscapes* published.

1919–28 Based in Residencia de Estudiantes, Madrid. Friends there include Luis Buñuel, poets Jorge Guillén, Rafael Alberti (1924), and Salvador Dalí (1923).

1920   First play, *The Butterfly's Evil Spell*, performed.

1921   Publishes *Book of Poems*. Begins *Songs*, and the *cante jondo* poems.

1922   With Falla, organizes *cante jondo* festival in Granada.

1923   Begins *Mariana Pineda*, *Book of Gypsy Ballads*, *The Prodigious Shoemaker's Wife*.

1924   José Moreno Villa shows him a description of *rosa mutabilis*.

1925–8 Close friendship and collaboration with Dalí. Growing interest in literary experiment: *Ode to Salvador Dalí*, *Buster Keaton's Walk*, *Love of Don Perlimplín and Belisa in her Garden*.

1927   Participates in Góngora tercentenary. Publishes *Songs*. *Mariana Pineda* performed (June). Exhibition of his drawings in Barcelona (July).

1928   *Book of Gypsy Ballads* published. Rupture with Dalí. Reads press reports of Níjar murder case (kernel of *Blood Wedding*).

1929   Personal and artistic anxieties multiply. Goes to study at Columbia University (June). Experiences of New York, Wall Street crash, Black life of Harlem, evoke more radical forms of expression: *Poet in New York*, *The Public*.

1930   Travels to Cuba (March). *Yerma* in progress. In Madrid from June: reads the explicitly homosexual *The Public* to friends. *The Prodigious Shoemaker's Wife* performed (December).

1931   Writes *Once Five Years Pass*. Publishes *Cante jondo Poem*. Second Republic proclaimed in April.

1932–4   Director of travelling student theatre, *La Barraca* (part of Republican government's cultural outreach).

1932   Reads the complete *Blood Wedding* to friends (September).

1933   *Blood Wedding* performed (8 March). Theatre-club performance of *Don Perlimplín*. Centre-right government takes office in autumn. Lorca visits Argentina (September 1933–March 1934). Partial reading of *Yerma*. Meets cousin's former fiancé (story featured in *Doña Rosita*).

1934   Completes *Yerma* and *The Diwan of Tamarit* (poems). Composes *Lament* for bullfighter Ignacio Sánchez Mejías, killed in August.
Abortive October Revolution followed by repression. Lorca supports appeals for clemency. *Yerma* performed (29 December).

1935   *Lament for Ignacio Sánchez Mejías* published (May). Final drafting of *Poet in New York* (August). Signs anti-fascist manifesto (November). *Doña Rosita the Spinster* performed (12 December).

1936   Popular Front wins elections (16 February). Lorca signs appeal for peaceful co-operation. Joins in homage to Alberti (February), Luis Cernuda (April), and French Popular Front delegates (May). Writing *Sonnets of Dark Love*, and projects for theatre. *The House of Bernarda Alba* completed (19 June); read to friends (24 June).
Political tension increases. Lorca travels to Granada on 13 July.
Military uprising (17 July) seizes power in Granada (20–3 July). Mass arrests and killings.
19 August: Lorca murdered by firing-squad at Víznar.

1945   *The House of Bernarda Alba* performed in Buenos Aires (8 March).

BLOOD WEDDING

[*BODAS DE SANGRE*]

A Tragedy in Three Acts
and Seven Scenes

(1932)

CHARACTERS

The Bridegroom
The Bridegroom's Mother
The Neighbour
Leonardo
Leonardo's Wife
Leonardo's Mother-in-law
The Bride
The Bride's Father
The Servant
Three Woodcutters
The Moon* (a young woodcutter)
Death* (an old beggar woman)
Three Girls
Two Youths
A Little Girl
Wedding Guests
Women Neighbours

ACT 1

SCENE 1

A room painted yellow.

BRIDEGROOM [*entering*]. Mother.

MOTHER. What?

BRIDEGROOM. I'm going.

MOTHER. Where to?

BRIDEGROOM. The vineyard.   [*He turns to go*

MOTHER. Wait.

BRIDEGROOM. Is there something you want?

MOTHER. Your food, son.

BRIDEGROOM. No, leave it. I'll eat some grapes. Give me the knife.

MOTHER. What for?

BRIDEGROOM [*laughing*]. To cut them with.

MOTHER [*muttering, looking for the knife*]. Knives, knives. . .
Curse them all, and the villain who invented them.

BRIDEGROOM. Let's keep off that.

MOTHER. And shotguns and pistols, and the smallest little knife,
even mattocks and pitchforks.

BRIDEGROOM. All right.

MOTHER. Everything that can cut a man's body. A fine-looking
man, in the flower of his life, who goes out to the vineyards
or his very own olives, because they belong to him, they're his
inheritance. . .

BRIDEGROOM [*looking down*]. Be quiet.

MOTHER. . . . and that man doesn't come back. Or if he does
come back it's to be laid out with a palm-leaf put on his
chest,* or a plate of rock salt to keep his body from swelling.
I don't know how you can bring yourself to carry a knife on
you, or how I can let the little snake lie in the drawer.

BRIDEGROOM. Have you done now?

MOTHER. If I lived a hundred years, I'd talk of nothing else. First your father, like a carnation he smelt to me, and three short years he was mine. Then your brother. Is it right, is it possible that a little thing like a pistol or a knife can do away with a man, a man built like a bull? No, I'd never be quiet. The months pass, and I still feel the rage pricking at my eyes and reaching out to the very tips of my hair.

BRIDEGROOM [*vehemently*]. Will you have done?

MOTHER. No. I'll never have done. Can anyone bring your father back to me? Or your brother? Then there's prison. What's prison? They eat there, they smoke, they make music. My dead ones smothered with grass, unable to speak, turned into dust; two men who were like two geraniums. . . And their murderers in prison, fit and healthy, looking out at the mountains.

BRIDEGROOM. Should I kill them, then; is that what you want?

MOTHER. No. . . If I speak like this it's because. . . How can I not speak when I see you go out through that door? It's because I don't like to see you carrying a knife. It's because. . . I'd like you not to go out to the fields.

BRIDEGROOM [*laughing*]. Come on!

MOTHER. Because I'd like you to be a woman. Then you wouldn't be going to the stream now, we'd be embroidering hems and little poodles together.

BRIDEGROOM [*putting his arm round his mother and laughing*]. Well, mother, what if I took you with me to the vineyards?

MOTHER. What would an old woman do there? Did you think of laying me down under the vine-shoots?

BRIDEGROOM [*lifting her up in his arms*]. Old woman, you old, old woman, you ancient old woman.

MOTHER. Your father used to take me with him all right. That's how it is with good stock. Red blood. Your grandfather left sons all over the place. That's what I like. For men to be men; for wheat to be wheat.

BRIDEGROOM. And what about me, mother?

MOTHER. What about you?

BRIDEGROOM. Do I have to tell you again?

MOTHER [*serious*]. Ah!

BRIDEGROOM. Are you against it?

MOTHER. No.

BRIDEGROOM. Well, then. . .?

MOTHER. I don't know, really. All of a sudden like this, it's a shock. I know she's a good girl. Isn't she? Quiet. Hard-working. She bakes her bread and sews her skirts, and yet when I speak her name it's like being hit in the face with a stone.

BRIDEGROOM. That's just silly.

MOTHER. It's not silly. I'm being left alone. I have only you now and I'm sorry to see you go.

BRIDEGROOM. But you'll come with us.

MOTHER. No. I can't leave your father and your brother here alone. I have to go and be with them every morning, and, if I went away, one of the Félixes could easily die, one of the murderers' family, and be buried alongside them. And that I won't have! Oh no! That I won't have! I'd dig them up with my nails, and all on my own I'd smash them to pieces against the wall of the cemetery.

BRIDEGROOM [*sternly*]. There you go again.

MOTHER. I'm sorry. [*Pause*] How long have you known her?

BRIDEGROOM. Three years. And now I've managed to buy the vineyard.

MOTHER. Three years. She had a young man once, didn't she?

BRIDEGROOM. I don't know. I don't think so. Girls have to take a hard look at who they marry.

MOTHER. Yes. I didn't look at anybody. Only your father; and when they killed him I looked at the wall in front of me. One woman with one man, and that's it.

BRIDEGROOM. You know my girl is all right.

MOTHER. I'm sure she is. I just wish I knew what her mother was like.

BRIDEGROOM. What does that matter?

MOTHER [*looking at him*]. Son.

BRIDEGROOM. What is it?

MOTHER. Only that you're right. It doesn't matter. When do you want me to ask for her?

BRIDEGROOM [*happy now*]. Does Sunday seem all right to you?

MOTHER [*gravely*]. I'll take her the bronze earrings, they're really old, and you can buy her. . .

BRIDEGROOM. You know best. . .

MOTHER. You can buy her some fancy stockings, and for yourself two suits—No, three! You're the only one I've got!

BRIDEGROOM. I'm going. Tomorrow I'll go and see her.

MOTHER. Yes, yes, and we'll see if you can make me happy with six grandchildren, or as many as you feel like having, since your father didn't have the chance to give any more to me.

BRIDEGROOM. The first-born will be your boy.

MOTHER. Yes, but I hope there are girls. I want to be able to sit with my embroidery and lace-making and be at peace.

BRIDEGROOM. I'm sure you'll love my wife.

MOTHER. I'll love her. [*She makes to kiss him but draws back*] Get away with you. You're too big now for kisses. Give them to your wife. [*Pause. To herself*] When she is your wife.

BRIDEGROOM. I'm going.

MOTHER. Be sure and give the ground a good digging over, all round the little mill; you've been letting it go.

BRIDEGROOM. Right you are!

MOTHER. God bless!

    [*The* BRIDEGROOM *leaves. The* MOTHER *remains seated with her back to the door*

    A NEIGHBOUR *appears in the doorway dressed in dark colours with her head tied in a kerchief.*

MOTHER. Come in.

NEIGHBOUR. How are you?

MOTHER. As you see.

NEIGHBOUR. I came down to the shop, so I thought I'd call in. We live so far apart!

MOTHER. It's twenty years since I went up to the top of the street.

NEIGHBOUR. You're looking well.

MOTHER. Do you think so?

NEIGHBOUR. Things happen. The other day they brought back my neighbour's son with both arms cut off by the machine.*

[She sits

MOTHER. Rafael?

NEIGHBOUR. Yes. So he's done for. Many's the time I've thought your son and mine are better off where they are, asleep, at rest, in no danger of being made useless.

MOTHER. Be quiet. That's just a lot of rigamarole, it's no consolation.

NEIGHBOUR. Ah!

MOTHER. Ah!   [Pause

NEIGHBOUR [sadly]. So what about your son?

MOTHER. He's gone out.

NEIGHBOUR. He's bought the vineyard, then!

MOTHER. He was lucky.

NEIGHBOUR. Now he'll get married.

MOTHER [as if pulling herself together, drawing her chair closer to the NEIGHBOUR's]. Listen.

NEIGHBOUR [adopting a confidential manner]. Yes. What?

MOTHER. You know my son's sweetheart?

NEIGHBOUR. A fine girl!

MOTHER. Yes, but. . .

NEIGHBOUR. But there's no one knows what she's like deep down. She lives out there alone with her father, all that way off, it's ten leagues to the nearest house. But she's a good girl. She's used to her own company.

MOTHER. What was her mother like?

NEIGHBOUR. Her mother I did know. Beautiful she was. She had a face that shone like a saint's; but I'd no time for her. She didn't love her husband.

MOTHER [*forcefully*]. Well, there's not much people don't know!

NEIGHBOUR. Sorry. I meant no offence; but it's the truth. Now whether she was a respectable woman or not, nobody's ever said. That wasn't talked about. She was proud all right.

MOTHER. There you go again!

NEIGHBOUR. You did ask me.

MOTHER. I just wish no one knew either of them, the living one or the dead one. I wish they were like two thistles that no one talks about but they scratch you if you get too close.

NEIGHBOUR. You're right. Your son's a good catch.

MOTHER. He is. That's why I take care of him. They tell me the girl had a sweetheart some time ago.

NEIGHBOUR. She'd have been fifteen. He got married two years ago, to a cousin of hers as it turned out. Nobody remembers she was engaged to him.

MOTHER. So what makes you remember?

NEIGHBOUR. The questions you ask me!

MOTHER. We all like to know about things that hurt us. Who was the boy?

NEIGHBOUR. Leonardo.

MOTHER. What Leonardo?

NEIGHBOUR. The Leonardo of the Félix family.

MOTHER [*rising*]. The Félixes!

NEIGHBOUR. But, woman, how can Leonardo be blamed for anything? He was eight years old when all that happened.

MOTHER. That's right. But I hear that name Félix, and for me that word Félix [*with gritted teeth*] is like a mouthful of slime [*spitting*] and I have to spit because I can't kill.

NEIGHBOUR. Control yourself. What good does it do you?

MOTHER. None. But you can understand.

NEIGHBOUR. Don't get in the way of your son's happiness. Say nothing to him. You are old. And so am I. What you and I have to do is keep quiet.

MOTHER. I'll say nothing to him.

NEIGHBOUR [*kissing her*]. Nothing.

MOTHER [*calm now*]. The things that happen. . .!

NEIGHBOUR. I'm going. My people will soon be back from the fields.

MOTHER. Have you ever seen it so hot?

NEIGHBOUR. It's hard on the children, the ones that take water to the reapers. Goodbye now.

MOTHER. Goodbye.

> [*The* MOTHER *moves towards the door on the left. Half-way across the stage she stops and slowly crosses herself*

CURTAIN

SCENE 2

A room painted pink, hung with copperware and sprigs of common flowers. In the middle a table covered with a cloth. It is morning.

Leonardo's MOTHER-IN-LAW *is rocking a child in her arms. His* WIFE, *in the other corner, is knitting.*

MOTHER-IN-LAW.
> Hushaby, my baby,
> Oh, the great proud stallion
> that would not drink the water.
> The water was all black there
> down among the branches.
> When it nears the bridge, see,
> there it stops and murmurs.
> Who can tell, my baby,
> tell what ails the water,

winding its long tail there,
through its dark green parlour?

WIFE [*softly*].

Little carnation, sleep,
the stallion does not want to drink.

MOTHER-IN-LAW.

My little rose tree, sleep,
the stallion is starting to cry.
His hooves are all wounded,
his mane is all frozen,
in his eyes a-shining
there's a silver dagger.
Oh, down to the river,
ay, down they were riding!
And blood there was gushing,
thicker far than the water.

WIFE.

Little carnation, sleep,
the stallion does not want to drink.

MOTHER-IN-LAW.

My little rose tree, sleep,
the stallion is starting to cry.

WIFE.

His muzzle all steaming
with fly-flecks of silver
would not touch the soaking
dark bank of the river,
but neighed to the mountains,
the far-off, hard mountains,
while the dead river's water
was at his throat lapping.
Oh, the great proud stallion
that would not drink the water!
Ay, cold as snow his sorrow,
great stallion of the dawn!

MOTHER-IN-LAW.

Don't come near us! Stay there!
Oh, seal up the window
with branches of dreams
and dreams made of branches.

WIFE.   My baby is sleeping.

MOTHER-IN-LAW.
              My baby is quiet.

WIFE.   Great stallion, my baby
               has a pillow for his head.

MOTHER-IN-LAW.
              And a cradle made of steel.

WIFE.   And a linen coverlet.

MOTHER-IN-LAW.
              Hushaby, my baby.

WIFE.   Oh, the great proud stallion
               that would not drink the water!

MOTHER-IN-LAW.
              Don't come in! Keep away!
              Be off to the mountain,
              Through the grey valleys
              where your mare is waiting.

WIFE [*looking*].
              My baby is sleeping.

MOTHER-IN-LAW.
              My baby is resting.

WIFE [*softly*].
              Little carnation, sleep,
              the stallion does not want to drink.

MOTHER-IN-LAW [*getting up, very softly*].
              My little rose tree, sleep,
              the stallion is starting to cry.*

              [*The* MOTHER-IN-LAW *goes off with the child*

              LEONARDO *enters.*

LEONARDO. Where's the boy?

WIFE. He's gone to sleep.

LEONARDO. He wasn't well yesterday. He cried in the night.

WIFE [*full of joy*]. He's bright as a dahlia today. What about
  you? Did you go to the smithy?

LEONARDO. I've just come from there. Would you believe it? For more than two months I've been putting new shoes on that stallion, and he keeps losing them. It looks as if he works them off against the stones.

WIFE. Couldn't it be because you ride him a lot?

LEONARDO. No. I hardly ever ride him.

WIFE. The neighbours told me yesterday they'd seen you over on the far side of the plains.

LEONARDO. Who said that?

WIFE. The women who go picking capers. I couldn't believe it. Was it you?

LEONARDO. No. What would I be doing over there, in that desert?

WIFE. That's what I said. But the horse had sweated fit to drop dead.

LEONARDO. Did you see him?

WIFE. No. My mother did.

LEONARDO. Is she with the boy?

WIFE. Yes. Do you want some lemonade?

LEONARDO. With the water really cold.

WIFE. Not coming back for your meal!

LEONARDO. I was with the wheat buyers. They always take so long.

WIFE [*making up the drink, very tenderly*]. Are they paying well?

LEONARDO. A fair price.

WIFE. I need a new dress, and the boy needs a cap with ribbons.

LEONARDO [*getting up*]. I'll just go and see him.

WIFE. Careful, he's asleep.

MOTHER-IN-LAW [*entering*]. So who's been driving the horse so hard? He's stretched out down there with his eyes popping out of his head as if he'd come from the other end of the earth.

LEONARDO [*sharply*]. I have.

MOTHER-IN-LAW. Sorry, I'm sure; it's your horse.

WIFE [*timidly*]. He was with the wheat buyers.

MOTHER-IN-LAW. The creature can drop dead for all I care.

[*She sits. Pause*

WIFE. Is your drink all right? Is it cold enough?

LEONARDO. Yes.

WIFE. Have you heard they're going to ask for my cousin?

LEONARDO. When?

WIFE. Tomorrow. The wedding will be in less than a month. I expect we shall be invited.

LEONARDO [*gravely*]. I don't know.

MOTHER-IN-LAW. I don't think his mother was very happy about the marriage.

LEONARDO. She may be right. That girl needs watching.

WIFE. I don't see why you should think badly of her. She's a good girl.

MOTHER-IN-LAW [*meaningfully*]. If he says that, it's because he knows what she's like. Don't forget he courted her for three years.

LEONARDO. I left her, though. [*To his* WIFE] Are you going to cry now? Stop that! [*He roughly pulls her hands away from her face*] Let's go and see the little chap.

[*They exit with their arms round each other*

A GIRL *comes running in, looking radiant.*

GIRL. Señora!

MOTHER-IN-LAW. What is it?

GIRL. The bridegroom came into the shop and bought the best of everything.

MOTHER-IN-LAW. Was he by himself?

GIRL. No, with his mother. Very serious, tall. [*She imitates her*] And so extravagant!

MOTHER-IN-LAW. They're not short of money.

GIRL. The fancy stockings they bought! Oh! Those stockings! Stockings every woman dreams about! Just think: here a swallow [*pointing to her ankle*]; here a boat [*pointing to her calf*]; and here a rose [*pointing to her thigh*].

MOTHER-IN-LAW [*reprovingly*]. Really!

GIRL. A rose with its seeds and the stem and everything! Ooh! And all in silk!

MOTHER-IN-LAW. Money marrying money, that's what you've got there.

LEONARDO *and his* WIFE *appear.*

GIRL. I came to tell you what they're buying.

LEONARDO [*harshly*]. We're not interested.

WIFE. Let her be.

MOTHER-IN-LAW. Leonardo, there's no call for that.

GIRL. I'm sorry.   [*She goes out in tears*

MOTHER-IN-LAW. Why do you have to be so unpleasant to people?

LEONARDO. I didn't ask for your opinion.   [*He sits*

MOTHER-IN-LAW. I'll say no more, then.   [*Pause*

WIFE [*to* LEONARDO]. What's the matter with you? There's something eating away at you inside your head: what is it? Don't leave me like this, not knowing what's wrong...

LEONARDO. Stop it!

WIFE. No. I want you to look at me and tell me what it is.

LEONARDO. Leave me alone.   [*He gets up*

WIFE. Where are you going, dear?

LEONARDO [*sharply*]. Be quiet, can't you?

MOTHER-IN-LAW [*vehemently, to her daughter*]. Be quiet!
            [LEONARDO *exits*

MOTHER-IN-LAW. The child!
            [*She goes off and returns with the child in her arms. The* WIFE *has remained standing, motionless*

MOTHER-IN-LAW.
>His hooves are all wounded,
>his mane is all frozen,
>in his eyes a-shining
>there's a silver dagger.
>Oh, down to the river,
>ay, down they were riding!
>And blood there was gushing,
>thicker far than the water.

WIFE [*turning slowly, as if in a dream*].
>Little carnation, sleep,
>the stallion is starting to drink.

MOTHER-IN-LAW.
>My little rose tree, sleep,
>the stallion is starting to cry.

WIFE.   Hushaby, my baby.

MOTHER-IN-LAW.
>Oh, the great proud stallion
>that would not drink the water!

WIFE [*dramatically*].
>Don't come in! Keep away!
>Be off to the mountain!
>Ay, cold as snow his sorrow,
>great stallion of the dawn!

MOTHER-IN-LAW [*weeping*].
>My baby is sleeping. . .

WIFE [*weeping and slowly drawing closer*].
>My baby is resting. . .

MOTHER-IN-LAW.
>Little carnation, sleep,
>the stallion does not want to drink.

WIFE [*weeping and supporting herself on the table*].
>My little rose tree, sleep,
>the stallion is starting to cry.

CURTAIN

SCENE 3

Interior of the cave where the BRIDE *lives. At the rear,
a cross of large pink flowers. The doors are rounded,
with lace curtains and pink ties. On the walls,
made of a hard, white substance, are hung circular fans,
blue jugs, and small mirrors.*

SERVANT. Come in.   [*She is ingratiating, full of false humility*

Enter the BRIDEGROOM *and his* MOTHER. *The* MOTHER *is
dressed in black satin with a lace mantilla. The* BRIDEGROOM
is in black corduroy with a great gold chain.

SERVANT. Would you like to sit down? They'll be here in a
moment.

> [*She exits. The* MOTHER *and* SON *are left seated, as
> still as statues. Long pause*

MOTHER. Are you wearing your watch?

BRIDEGROOM. Yes.   [*He takes it out and looks at it*

MOTHER. We must allow time to get back. How far away these
people live!

BRIDEGROOM. It's good land here, though.

MOTHER. It's good, but it's too lonely. Four hours' journey and
not a single house or tree.

BRIDEGROOM. These are the dry lands.

MOTHER. Your father would have filled them with trees.

BRIDEGROOM. With no water?

MOTHER. He'd have soon found some. In the three years he was
married to me he planted ten cherry trees. [*Thinking back*]
And the three walnut trees by the mill, a whole vineyard, and
a plant called Jupiter with crimson flowers, but it dried up.
> [*Pause*

BRIDEGROOM [*referring to the* BRIDE]. She must be getting
dressed.

The BRIDE'S FATHER *enters. He is very old, with shining
white hair. His head is bowed. The* MOTHER *and*
BRIDEGROOM *get up, and they shake hands in silence.*

FATHER. Long journey?

MOTHER. Four hours.   [*They sit*

FATHER. You must have come the long way round.

MOTHER. I'm too old now to be jolted up and down the river road.

BRIDEGROOM. She gets giddy.   [*Pause*

FATHER. Good crop of esparto.

BRIDEGROOM. It *is* good.

FATHER. In my day this land wouldn't even grow esparto. We've had to punish it, we've had to break our hearts over it before it would give us anything useful.

MOTHER. But now it does. There's no need to complain. I haven't come to ask you for anything.

FATHER [*smiling*]. You're richer than I am. Your vineyards are worth a fortune. Every shoot a silver coin. What I'm sorry about is that our lands—you follow me?—are separated. I like everything to be together. One thing makes my heart sore, and it's that little orchard stuck in the middle of my land, that they won't sell me for all the gold in the world.

BRIDEGROOM. It's always the same.

FATHER. If we could just get twenty pair of oxen to pull your vineyards over here and set them up on the hillside, how happy I'd be!

MOTHER. Why?

FATHER. What's mine is hers and what's yours is his. That's why. To see everything together. When things are together, that's beautiful!

BRIDEGROOM. And it would be less work.

MOTHER. When I die, you can sell that over there and buy more land close to this.

FATHER. Sell, sell! Bah! Buy, my dear, buy all you can. If I'd had sons, I'd have bought up all of this hill as far as the stream. It may not be good land, but strong arms can make it good, and, as nobody passes by, they don't steal your fruit, and you can sleep in peace.   [*Pause*

MOTHER. You know why I've come.

FATHER. Yes.

MOTHER. So?

FATHER. It seems good to me. They've talked it over.

MOTHER. My son is willing and able.

FATHER. So is my daughter.

MOTHER. My son is a gem. He's never known a woman. His name is cleaner than a sheet spread in the sun.

FATHER. What shall I say of my girl? She's up at three, before first light, frying the men's breakfast. She keeps a still tongue in her head, she's soft as wool, she does all kinds of embroidery, and she can cut through a rope with her teeth.

MOTHER. God bless their house.

FATHER. God bless it.

The SERVANT *appears with two trays, one with glasses on and the other with sweetmeats.*

MOTHER [*to her son*]. Have you agreed when you want the wedding?

BRIDEGROOM. Next Thursday.

FATHER. Her twenty-second birthday.

MOTHER. Twenty-two! That's how old my first-born would be if he were alive. Warm-hearted he was, a real man, and he'd still be with us if men hadn't invented knives.

FATHER. It doesn't do to think about that.

MOTHER. I do, every moment. Think how you'd feel.

FATHER. Thursday, then. Is that right?

BRIDEGROOM. That's right.

FATHER. The bride and groom and the two of us, we'll go in a carriage to the church, it's a long way, and the rest can go in the carts and on their own horses.

MOTHER. Agreed.

The SERVANT *enters.*

FATHER. Tell her she can come in now. [*To the* MOTHER] It will gladden my heart if you like her.

> *The* BRIDE *appears. She holds her hands in a demure attitude and her head bowed.*

MOTHER. Come closer. Are you happy?

BRIDE. Yes, señora.

FATHER. You needn't be so stiff. After all, she's going to be your mother.

BRIDE. I'm happy. When I said Yes, it's because that's what I want.

MOTHER. Of course. [*She takes her by the chin*] Look at me.

FATHER. She's exactly like my wife in every way.

MOTHER. Is she? What lovely eyes she has! Do you know what getting married means, my dear?

BRIDE [*solemnly*]. Yes, I know.

MOTHER. A man, children, and a wall two yards thick to keep out everything else.

BRIDEGROOM. What more could she want?

MOTHER. Nothing. Just let them all stay alive, that's all! Just let them stay alive!

BRIDE. I shall know my duty.

MOTHER. Here are some presents for you.

BRIDE. Thank you.

FATHER. Aren't we going to take something?

MOTHER. I won't. [*To the* BRIDEGROOM] Will you?

BRIDEGROOM. I'll have something.

> [*Takes a sweetmeat. The* BRIDE *takes one too*

FATHER [*to the* BRIDEGROOM]. Some wine?

MOTHER. He doesn't touch it.

FATHER. Good for him!   [*Pause. They are all standing*

BRIDEGROOM [*to the* BRIDE]. I'll come tomorrow.

BRIDE. At what time?

BRIDEGROOM. Five o'clock.

BRIDE. I'll be waiting for you.

BRIDEGROOM. Whenever I leave you, I feel a great emptiness and a kind of lump in my throat.

BRIDE. When you're my husband, you won't have that feeling any more.

BRIDEGROOM. That's what I tell myself.

MOTHER. Let's go. The sun won't wait. [*To the* FATHER] Are we agreed about everything?

FATHER. Agreed.

MOTHER [*to the* SERVANT]. Goodbye.

SERVANT. God be with you both.

> [*The* MOTHER *kisses the* BRIDE, *and they go out in silence*

MOTHER [*at the door*]. Goodbye, daughter.

> [*The* BRIDE *answers with a gesture*

FATHER. I'll come out with you.   [*They exit*

SERVANT. I'm dying to see the presents.

BRIDE [*sharply*]. Never mind that!

SERVANT. Oh, go on, show me them!

BRIDE. I don't want to.

SERVANT. Just the stockings at least. They say they're fancy, all of them. Please!

BRIDE. I said No, didn't I?

SERVANT. For goodness' sake! Don't, then. Anyone would think you didn't want to get married.

BRIDE [*biting her own hand furiously*]. O-o-o-h!

SERVANT. Oh, my pretty! What's wrong with you? Are you sorry to give up living here like a queen? Don't think about things that upset you. Why should you? You've no reason to. Let's look at the presents.   [*Takes up the box*

BRIDE [*seizing her by the wrists*]. Put it down.

SERVANT. A-a-h! Don't, girl!

BRIDE. Put it down, I said.

SERVANT. You've got more strength than a man.

BRIDE. Haven't I done a man's work? I wish I were a man!

SERVANT. Don't talk like that!

BRIDE. That's enough, didn't I say? Let's talk of something else.
                              [*The light is growing dim. Long pause*

SERVANT. Did you hear a horse last night?

BRIDE. At what time?

SERVANT. Three o'clock.

BRIDE. Must have been a stray from the herd.

SERVANT. No. It had a rider.

BRIDE. How do you know?

SERVANT. Because I saw him. He was standing at your window.
   It gave me a shock, I can tell you.

BRIDE. I suppose it was my fiancé? He sometimes goes by at
   that time.

SERVANT. No.

BRIDE. Did you see him?

SERVANT. Yes.

BRIDE. Who was it?

SERVANT. It was Leonardo.

BRIDE [*vehemently*]. That's a lie! A lie, I tell you!

   What would he be doing here?

SERVANT. Well, he came.

BRIDE. Shut your mouth! Damn your filthy tongue!
                              [*The sound of a horse is heard*

SERVANT [*at the window*]. Look. See for yourself. Was it him?

BRIDE. It was!

QUICK CURTAIN

ACT 2

SCENE 1

The verandah of the BRIDE's *house. A large door at the rear. It is night. The* BRIDE *enters wearing a white ruffled petticoat heavy with lace and embroidered edgings, and a white bodice which leaves her arms bare. The* SERVANT *is similarly dressed.*

SERVANT. I'll finish doing your hair out here.

BRIDE. It's unbearable in there with this heat.

SERVANT. In these parts it's never cool, even at sunrise.
[*The* BRIDE *sits on a low chair and looks at herself in a little hand mirror. The* SERVANT *dresses her hair*

BRIDE. My mother came from a place that had lots of trees. The land was so rich there.

SERVANT. And she was so happy!

BRIDE. But here she wasted away.

SERVANT. That was her fate.

BRIDE. We all waste away here, we women. Even the walls blaze with heat. Ooow! Don't pull so hard!

SERVANT. I'm just trying to get this wave right. I want it to fall over your forehead. [*The* BRIDE *looks at herself in the mirror*] Now you look really beautiful. Oooh!
[*She kisses her violently*

BRIDE [*unsmiling*]. Just get on with my hair.

SERVANT [*dressing her hair*]. Lucky you who are going to hold a man in your arms and kiss him and feel his weight on you!

BRIDE. That's enough!

SERVANT. And the best part will be when you wake up and feel him beside you, and he tickles your shoulders with his breath, just like the feather of a nightingale.

BRIDE [*forcefully*]. Will you stop it?

SERVANT. Good Lord, girl! What do you think a wedding is? That's what a wedding's about, that and nothing else. Is it nice things to eat? Is it bunches of flowers? No. It's a bed all shining and a man and a woman.

BRIDE. It's not right to talk about it.

SERVANT. That's as may be. But it's very enjoyable!

BRIDE. Or very painful.

SERVANT. I'm going to pin your wreath from here to here so that the blossoms will shine against your hair.

[*She tries on the spray of orange blossom**

BRIDE [*she looks at herself in the mirror*]. Give it me.

[*She takes the orange blossom, looks at it, and lets her head fall dejectedly*

SERVANT. Now what is it?

BRIDE. Leave me alone.

SERVANT. This is no time to start feeling sad! [*Brightly*] Give me the orange blossom. [*The* BRIDE *flings the wreath away*] Really! Don't you know you're asking for bad luck, throwing your wreath on the floor like that? Look up at me, go on! Don't you want to get married, is that it? Say so, then. You can still change your mind.

BRIDE [*she stands up*]. Black clouds. A cold wind blowing round my heart. Doesn't everyone feel it?

SERVANT. You love the boy.

BRIDE. I love him.

SERVANT. Yes, yes, I'm sure you do.

BRIDE. But it's such a big step to take.

SERVANT. It has to be taken.

BRIDE. I've given my word.

SERVANT. I'm going to do your wreath for you.

BRIDE [*she sits*]. Hurry up, they'll be here any minute.

SERVANT. They'll have been on their way for at least two hours.

BRIDE. How far is it from here to the church?

SERVANT. Five leagues going by the stream, twice that on the
road.

[*The* BRIDE *stands up, and the* SERVANT *is delighted
with her appearance*

SERVANT.   Oh, let the bride awaken
                on this her wedding day.
                And all the world's bright rivers
                shall bear your crown away.

BRIDE [*smiling*]. Come on.

SERVANT [*she kisses her excitedly and dances round her*].
                Oh, let her awaken
                to see the green spray
                of laurel in blossom.
                Oh, let her awaken
                to see on this day
                the boughs and the branches
                of laurel and bay.

                            [*There is a loud banging at the door*

BRIDE. Open the door! The first guests must be here.

                                            [*She exits*

        The SERVANT *opens the door and is surprised.*

SERVANT. You?

LEONARDO. Yes, me. Good morning.

SERVANT. The first to arrive!

LEONARDO. Wasn't I asked?

SERVANT. Yes.

LEONARDO. So here I am.

SERVANT. Where's your wife?

LEONARDO. I rode here. She's on her way.

SERVANT. You didn't see anyone else?

LEONARDO. I passed them on the horse.

SERVANT. You'll kill that poor beast going so fast.

LEONARDO. When he stops living, he'll be dead.   [*Pause*

SERVANT. Sit down. Nobody's up yet.

LEONARDO [*sitting down*]. Not the bride?

SERVANT. I'm just going to dress her.

LEONARDO. The bride! She must be very happy!

SERVANT [*changing the subject*]. How's the little one?

LEONARDO. Little one?

SERVANT. Your son.

LEONARDO [*remembering as if half asleep*]. Ah!

SERVANT. Are they bringing him?

LEONARDO. No.   [*Pause. Voices heard singing in the distance*

VOICES.   Oh, let the bride awaken
        on this her wedding day!

LEONARDO.   Oh, let the bride awaken
        on this her wedding day.

SERVANT. The guests. They're still some way off.

LEONARDO [*getting up*]. I suppose the bride will be wearing a big wreath, eh? It shouldn't be too big. Something a bit smaller would suit her better. Did the bridegroom bring the orange blossom for her to pin on her breast?

BRIDE [*appearing still in her petticoat with the wreath of orange blossom in place*]. Yes, he did.

SERVANT [*sternly*]. Don't come out like that!

BRIDE. What does it matter? [*Gravely*] Why did you ask if he brought the orange blossom? Are you trying to say something?

LEONARDO. Not at all. What would I be trying to say? [*Drawing closer*] You know me; you know there's nothing I *could* say. Tell me so. What have I ever been to you? Look back, refresh your memory. But a single yoke of oxen and a tumbledown hovel don't amount to much. That's what sticks in the gullet.

BRIDE. Why have you come?

LEONARDO. To see your marriage.

BRIDE. Just as I saw yours!

LEONARDO. A knot tied by you, the work of your two hands. I
can be killed but I won't be spat on. And gold, that shines so
bright, will sometimes spit.

BRIDE. That's not true!

LEONARDO. I'd best say nothing: I have blood in my veins, and
I don't want my voice ringing all round the hills.

BRIDE. Mine would ring louder.

SERVANT. You must stop this. [*To the* BRIDE] It's not right for
you to talk about what's gone before.

[*She looks anxiously at the doors*

BRIDE. She's right. I shouldn't even speak to you. But it makes
me wild that you should come here to look at me and spy on
my wedding and hint at things, asking about the orange blossom. Go and wait for your wife outside.

LEONARDO. Can't we even talk, you and I?

SERVANT [*angrily*]. No: you can't talk.

LEONARDO. Ever since I got married, night and day I've asked
myself who was to blame, and every time I think about it I
find some new thing to blame that swallows up the one before; but blame there is, always!

BRIDE. A man with a horse has more than enough knowledge
and experience to wear down a poor girl stuck in a desert. But
I have my pride. That's why I'm getting married. I shall shut
myself up with my husband, I shall be bound to love him, and
that will come before everything else.

LEONARDO. Pride won't be any help to you.

[*He draws nearer to her*

BRIDE. Don't come near me!

LEONARDO. Keeping quiet and burning inside is the worst punishment we can heap on ourselves. What good did it do me
to be proud and not look at you, and leave you to lie awake
night after night? None at all! All it did was throw blazing
coals over me! You think time heals and walls seal up, but it's
not true, it's not true. When something has got right deep into
you, there's nobody can root it out.

BRIDE [*trembling*]. I can't bear to listen to you. I can't bear to hear your voice. It's as if I'd drunk a whole bottle of anisette and fallen asleep on a quilt of roses. And it's tugging me forward; I know that I'm suffocating, but I still go on.

SERVANT [*pulling at* LEONARDO *by the lapels*]. You must go this minute!

LEONARDO. It's the last time I shall speak to her. There's no need to be afraid.

BRIDE. I'm out of my mind, the strain has rotted my heart, I know that, and here I am at peace just hearing him speak, just seeing his arms moving.

LEONARDO. I can't rest without telling you these things. I got married. Now you get married.

SERVANT [*to* LEONARDO]. She *is* getting married!

VOICES [*singing, nearer*].
> Oh, let the bride awaken
> on this her wedding day.

BRIDE. Let the bride awaken!   [*She runs off to her room*

SERVANT. The guests are here. [*To* LEONARDO] Don't you come near her again.

LEONARDO. Don't worry.
> [*He exits to the left. The day starts to dawn*

FIRST GIRL [*entering*].
> Oh, let the bride awaken
> on this her wedding day.
> Send round the serenaders,
> the windows hung with bay.*

VOICES. Let the bride awaken!

SERVANT [*whipping up excitement*].
> Oh, let her awaken
> to see the green spray
> of love that's in blossom.
> Oh, let her awaken
> to see on this day
> the boughs and the branches
> of laurel and bay! .

SECOND GIRL [*entering*].
>Oh, let her awaken,
>her hair all unbraided,
>her shift like the snow,
>her boots of fine leather
>all studded with silver,
>and jasmine on her brow.

SERVANT.
>Ah, lovely lass, the moon
>is peering out at last!

FIRST GIRL.
>Ah, handsome lad, best leave
>your hat in the olive-grove!

FIRST YOUTH [*entering, holding his hat up high*].
>Oh, let the bride awaken,
>for through the meadows weaving
>the wedding now draws near;
>its trays are dressed with dahlias,
>and blest new bread they bear.

VOICES. Let the bride awaken!

SECOND GIRL.
>The bride!
>She sets the white wreath on her head.
>The groom!
>He ties it with a golden thread.

SERVANT.
>The bride lies under the grapefruit tree,
>but she cannot get to sleep.

THIRD GIRL [*entering*].
>Under the orange tree the groom
>offers her cloth and spoon.

>*Enter three* GUESTS.

FIRST YOUTH.
>Sweet dove, awake:
>bells of shadow fly away
>as day begins to break.

GUEST. The bride so pure, so white,
the bride a maid today
tomorrow will be a wife.

FIRST GIRL.
Come down, dark beauty, come,
trailing your tail of silk.

GUEST. Come down, dark little one,
the morning dew rains chill.

FIRST YOUTH.
Señora, waken, señora,
orange blossom falls from the air.

SERVANT.
I want to embroider a tree for her;
red ribbons for branches I'll work.
And on each ribbon a cherub I'll weave
with 'Long may they Live!'

VOICES. Let the bride awaken.

FIRST YOUTH.
On this her wedding day!

GUEST.
On this your wedding morning
how finely dressed you'll be!
A mountain flower, you'll seem
a wife fit for a captain.

FATHER [*entering*].
A wife fit for a captain
the groom will bear away.
He comes now with his oxen for his treasure!

THIRD GIRL.
The bridegroom seems to be
a flower of gold.
Wherever he sets foot
carnations crowd.

SERVANT.
Oh, my lucky girl!

SECOND YOUTH.
> Let the bride awaken.

SERVANT.
> Oh, my lovely girl!

FIRST GIRL.
> From every window
> the wedding is calling.

SECOND GIRL.
> We want the bride.

FIRST GIRL.
> Come out, come out!

SERVANT.
> Ring out the bells,
> ring loud and clear!

FIRST YOUTH.
> She's coming out! She's coming now!

SERVANT.
> Strong as a bull
> the wedding is rising!

The BRIDE *appears. She is wearing a 1900-style black dress with panniers and a long train trimmed with pleated gauze and heavy lace. Fastened to her hair, which is dressed to fall over her forehead, is the wreath of orange blossom. Guitars begin to play. The* GIRLS *kiss the* BRIDE.

THIRD GIRL. What perfume did you put on your hair?

BRIDE [*laughing*]. None.

SECOND GIRL [*looking at the dress*]. The material is a dream.

FIRST GIRL. Here's the groom!

BRIDEGROOM [*entering*]. Greetings!

FIRST GIRL [*putting a flower behind his ear*].
> The bridegroom seems to be
> a flower of gold today.

SECOND GIRL.   Content and quiet joy
> are brimming in his eyes.
> > [*The* BRIDEGROOM *goes to join the* BRIDE

BRIDE. Why are you wearing those shoes?

BRIDEGROOM. They're more cheerful than black ones.

LEONARDO'S WIFE [*entering and kissing the* BRIDE]. Greetings!
[*They all chatter excitedly*

LEONARDO [*entering as if fulfilling a duty*].
          The morning of your marriage
          we crown you with a wreath.

LEONARDO'S WIFE.
          And gladden all the country round
          with the brightness of your hair.

          The MOTHER *and* FATHER *enter.*

MOTHER [*to the* FATHER]. So they're here too?

FATHER. They're family. Today is a day for forgiveness!

MOTHER. I'll hold my peace, but I'll not forgive.

BRIDEGROOM. With the wreath it's a joy to look at you!

BRIDE. Let's be off to the church!

BRIDEGROOM. Are you in such a hurry?

BRIDE. Yes. I long to be your wife and to be alone with you, and
to hear no other voice but yours.

BRIDEGROOM. That's what I want too!

BRIDE. And to see only your eyes. And for you to hold me tight.
So that even if my mother were to call me, my mother who
is dead, I couldn't ever tear myself away from you.

BRIDEGROOM. My arms are strong. I'm going to hold you close
for forty years together.

BRIDE [*dramatically, seizing his arm*]. For ever!

FATHER. Let's go now! Fetch the horses and carts!
          The sun is up.

MOTHER. Be sure to take care! Let no misfortune fall on us!
          [*The great door at the rear opens. They begin to
          leave*

SERVANT [*weeping*].
          When you go from your home,
          white maiden pure,

>   remember that you go
>   bright as a star.

FIRST GIRL.

>   With clothes and body clean she's led,
>   when from her home she goes to wed!
>   [*They continue to leave*

SECOND GIRL.

>   Now you go from your house
>   to church to be wed!

SERVANT.   Flowers are blown upon
>   the sandy ways!

THIRD GIRL.

>   Ah, girl so white and pure!

SERVANT.   Darkly blows the lace
>   of her veil.
>   [*They exit. Guitars, castanets, and tambourines are
>   heard.* LEONARDO *and his* WIFE *are left alone*

WIFE. Let's go.

LEONARDO. Where to?

WIFE. To the church. But you're not going on your horse. You're
going with me.

LEONARDO. In the cart?

WIFE. How else?

LEONARDO. I'm not the sort of man who rides in a cart.

WIFE. And I'm not the sort of woman who goes to a wedding
without her husband. I've had as much as I can stand.

LEONARDO. So have I!

WIFE. Why are you looking at me like that? You've a thorn in
each eye.

LEONARDO. Let's go!

WIFE. I don't know what's happening. But I keep thinking things
and I don't want to think. One thing I do know. I've been
thrown over. But I've got a child. And another one coming.
That's how it goes. The same fate as my mother. But I'll not
budge from here.   [*Voices are heard from outside*

VOICES.   When you leave for the church,
                 white maiden pure,
                 remember that you go
                 bright as a star.

WIFE [*weeping*].
                 Remember that you go
                 bright as a star!
That's how I left my home too, with the world at my feet.

LEONARDO [*getting up*]. Let's go.

WIFE. But you with me!

LEONARDO. Yes. [*Pause*] Get moving!   [*They go out*

VOICES.   When you leave for the church,
                 white maiden pure,
                 remember that you go
                 bright as a star.

SLOW CURTAIN

SCENE 2

The exterior of the BRIDE's *cave. Shades of white, grey, and
cold blue. Large prickly pears. Shadowy and silver tones.
Vistas of biscuit-coloured table-land, everything looking
hard like a landscape in traditional ceramics.*

SERVANT [*setting out glasses and trays on a table*].
                 On the wheel turned
                 went turning and turning
                 and on flowed the water;
                 now the wedding is here,
                 let the branches open wide
                 and let the moon stand radiant
                 at her white balcony.
[*raising her voice*] Lay the tablecloths!
[*with poetic delivery*]
                 The bride and groom sang,
                 went on singing and singing,
                 and on flowed the water.

> Now the wedding is here,
> bring out bright frosted fruits
> and let the bitter almonds
> with honey overflow.

[*raising her voice*] Get out the wine!

[*with poetic delivery*]

> Dressed fine as you are,
> fine girl of our land,
> see the water flow on.
> Now the wedding is here,
> draw back your skirts
> and keep to your house
> beneath your groom's wing.
> For the bridegroom's a dove
> with breast all afire,
> and the hushed fields await
> the fertile blood's shedding.
> On the wheel turned,
> went turning and turning,
> and on flowed the water.
> Now your wedding is here,
> let the water shine!

MOTHER [*entering with the* FATHER]. At last!

FATHER. Are we the first?

SERVANT. No. Leonardo and his wife got back a little while ago. They drove like the devil. His wife got here frightened to death. They covered the ground as fast as if they'd been on horseback.

FATHER. That one goes looking for trouble. He's got bad blood.

MOTHER. What kind of blood do you expect him to have? What his whole family has. It comes down from his great-grandfather who started off by killing, and it's spread through the whole rotten bunch of them; they're all handy with knives, they smile, but you can never trust them.

FATHER. Let's forget it.

SERVANT. How can she forget it?

MOTHER. I feel the hurt right to the tips of my veins. In all their faces I can see nothing but the hand that killed what was mine. You see how I am? Don't I seem mad to you? That's the madness that comes from not screaming out all that is bursting in my breast. Inside me I have a scream always straining to break out, so I have to beat it down and wrap it tight in my shawl. But the dead are taken from us, and we have to hold our peace. Then people find fault.

[She takes off her shawl

FATHER. Today is not the day when you should be remembering those things.

MOTHER. When the talk comes round to them, I have to say what I feel. And today more than ever. Because today I shall be left alone in my house.

FATHER. With the hope of new company.

MOTHER. That is my dream: to have grandchildren.   *[They sit*

FATHER. I want them to have many. This land needs strong arms that don't have to be paid. We have to keep up the battle against weeds, thistles, and lumps of rock that come from nowhere. And the strong arms have to belong to the owners, so that they'll punish the land and master it, and force the seeds to sprout. Plenty of sons, that's what we need.

MOTHER. And daughters too! Boys have to go with the wind. They've no choice but to carry weapons. Girls never go out into the street.

FATHER [*smiling*]. I think they'll have plenty of both.

MOTHER. My son will cover her well. He comes of good seed. His father could have had plenty of children with me.

FATHER. What I'd like is for it all to happen in one day. For them to have two or three men straight away.

MOTHER. But it's not like that. It takes a long time. That's why it's such a terrible thing to see one's blood spilt over the ground. A spring that pours away in a moment, after all the years we've put into it. When I got to my son, he was stretched out in the middle of the road. I wet my hands with his blood and licked them with my tongue. Because it was my blood. You don't know what that's like. The earth that was soaked in it I'd like to have set in crystal and topaz like a holy relic.

FATHER. Now you must live in hope. My daughter is broad-hipped and your son is strong.

MOTHER. That gives me hope.   [*They get up*

FATHER. Get the trays of wheat ready.*

SERVANT. They are ready.

LEONARDO'S WIFE [*entering with Leonardo*]. Good fortune go with them!

MOTHER. Thank you.

LEONARDO. Are there going to be fun and games?

FATHER. Not for long. People have to get away.

SERVANT. Here they are!

The guests begin to arrive in high-spirited groups. The BRIDE *and* GROOM *enter arm in arm.* LEONARDO *goes out.*

BRIDEGROOM. There's never been a wedding with so many people.

BRIDE [*downcast*]. Never.

FATHER. It was splendid.

MOTHER. Whole families came.

BRIDEGROOM. People who'd never been out of their houses.

MOTHER. Your father sowed good seed and you're reaping the harvest.

BRIDEGROOM. There were cousins of mine that I'd never even met.

MOTHER. All the people from the coast.

BRIDEGROOM [*gaily*]. They were scared of the horses.
                                        [*General conversation*

MOTHER [*to the* BRIDE]. What are you thinking about?

BRIDE. I'm not thinking about anything.

MOTHER. The blessings of marriage weigh heavy.

BRIDE. Like lead.   [*Guitars are heard*

MOTHER [*vigorously*]. They shouldn't be heavy. Light as a dove you should be.

BRIDE. Are you staying here tonight?

MOTHER. No. My house is empty.

BRIDE. You ought to stay!

FATHER [*to the* MOTHER]. Look at the dancing they've started up. Dances from down by the sea-shore.

> LEONARDO *returns and sits. His* WIFE *is standing stiffly behind him.*

MOTHER. They're my husband's cousins. Sturdy as rocks when it comes to dancing.

FATHER. I'm happy to see them. What a change for this old house!   [*He exits*

BRIDEGROOM [*to the* BRIDE]. Were you pleased with the orange blossom?

BRIDE [*looking fixedly at him*]. Yes.

BRIDEGROOM. It's all made of wax. Everlasting. I'd like you to have worn it all over your dress.

BRIDE. There's no need for that. [LEONARDO *exits to the right*

FIRST GIRL. Let's go and take out your pins.*

BRIDE [*to the* BRIDEGROOM]. I won't be long.

> [*She exits with the* GIRLS

WIFE. I hope you will be happy with my cousin.

BRIDEGROOM. I'm sure I shall.

WIFE. The two of you here; never going out, building a home. I wish I lived far away like this!

BRIDEGROOM. Why don't you buy some land? It's cheap on the hillside and better for bringing up children.

WIFE. We've no money. And the way things are going with us. . .!

BRIDEGROOM. Your husband's a good worker.

WIFE. Yes, but he's too fond of flitting about. Going from one thing to another. He's not a quiet man.

SERVANT [*to them both*]. Aren't you going to have anything? [*To the* WIFE] I'll wrap up some wine-cakes for your mother, she likes them so much.

BRIDEGROOM. Give her three dozen.

WIFE. No, no. Half a dozen will be plenty for her.

BRIDEGROOM. It's an occasion.

WIFE [*to the* SERVANT]. Where's Leonardo?

SERVANT. I haven't seen him.

BRIDEGROOM. He must be talking to people.

WIFE. I'm going to see!   [*She exits*

SERVANT [*looking at the dancing*]. That's so beautiful!

BRIDEGROOM. Why aren't you dancing?

SERVANT. I haven't been asked.

Two GIRLS *pass across the rear of the stage; during the whole of this scene there is a lively toing and froing in the background.*

BRIDEGROOM [*gaily*]. That shows they don't know what's what. Lively old girls like you dance better than the young ones.

SERVANT. Oh, so you're going to flirt with me, young man? What a family yours is! Red-blooded men! When I was a girl I saw your grandfather's wedding. What a man! It was like a mountain getting married.

BRIDEGROOM. I'm not so tall.

SERVANT. But you've got the same twinkle in your eyes. Where's the little one, then?

BRIDEGROOM. Taking off her wreath.

SERVANT. Ah! Listen. For a midnight snack, since you two won't be sleeping, I've put you some ham and two big glasses of old wine. In the bottom of the cupboard. In case you need it.

BRIDEGROOM [*smiling*]. I never eat at midnight.

SERVANT [*slyly*]. If you don't, the bride might.   [*Exits*

FIRST YOUTH [*entering with* SECOND YOUTH]. You must come and have a drink with us.

BRIDEGROOM. I'm waiting for the bride.

SECOND YOUTH. You'll have *her* with you in the wee small hours.

FIRST YOUTH. When it's best of all!

SECOND YOUTH. Just for a minute.

BRIDEGROOM. All right.

[*They exit. A hubbub of voices is heard*
The BRIDE *enters. From the opposite side two* GIRLS *come running to meet her.*

FIRST GIRL. Who did you give the first pin to, me or her?

BRIDE. I don't remember.

FIRST GIRL. It was to me, here.

SECOND GIRL. It was to me, in front of the altar.

BRIDE [*ill at ease, with a fierce inner conflict*]. I've no idea.

FIRST GIRL. It's just that I wish you'd. . .

BRIDE [*interrupting*]. And what's more I don't care. I've got a lot to think about.

SECOND GIRL. Sorry.

LEONARDO *crosses the rear of the stage.*

BRIDE [*seeing* LEONARDO]. And this is a very upsetting time.

FIRST GIRL. We wouldn't know about that!

BRIDE. You'll know when your time comes. It's not easy to take a step like this.

FIRST GIRL. Are you cross with us?

BRIDE. No. Forgive me.

SECOND GIRL. For what? But it's true that *both* the pins mean you'll be married, don't they?

BRIDE. Both of them.

FIRST GIRL. But still, one of us will be married before the other.

BRIDE. You want it so much?

SECOND GIRL [*coyly*]. Yes.

BRIDE. Why?

FIRST GIRL. Because, well. . .

> [*She embraces the* SECOND GIRL. *They both run off*

The BRIDEGROOM *enters and, very slowly, embraces the*
BRIDE from behind.

BRIDE [*with sudden shock*]. Stop that!

BRIDEGROOM. You're not scared of me?

BRIDE. Oh! So it was you?

BRIDEGROOM. Who else would it be? [*Pause*] Either your father
or me.

BRIDE. That's true!

BRIDEGROOM. Though your father wouldn't have held you so
tight.

BRIDE [*downcast*]. Of course not.

BRIDEGROOM. Because he's old.

> [*He draws her to him rather roughly*

BRIDE [*sharply*]. Leave me alone!

BRIDEGROOM. Why?   [*Lets her go*

BRIDE. Well. . . People can see us.

The SERVANT *recrosses the rear of the stage without looking*
at the BRIDE *and* GROOM.

BRIDEGROOM. So what? It's just been blessed.

BRIDE. Yes, but leave me alone. . . Later.

BRIDEGROOM. What's wrong with you? You seem scared!

BRIDE. Nothing's wrong. Don't go.

Enter LEONARDO'S WIFE.

WIFE. I don't want to intrude, but. . .

BRIDEGROOM. What is it?

WIFE. Has my husband been through here?

BRIDEGROOM. No.

WIFE. Only I can't find him, and the horse has gone from the
stable.

BRIDEGROOM [*lightly*]. He must have taken him off for a gallop.
                    [*The* WIFE *exits, still anxious*

                    The SERVANT *enters.*

SERVANT. You must both be very happy, with so many people
wishing you well.

BRIDEGROOM. I just wish it would all finish. The bride is a bit
tired.

SERVANT. What's all this about, my pet?

BRIDE. I feel as if something were banging inside my head.

SERVANT. A bride from these mountains has to be strong. [*To
the* BRIDEGROOM] You're the only one who can make her
better, because she belongs to you.   [*She runs off-stage*

BRIDEGROOM [*embracing the* BRIDE]. Let's go and dance for a
bit.   [*He kisses her*

BRIDE [*distressed*]. No. I'd like to lie down on the bed for a while.

BRIDEGROOM. I'll keep you company.

BRIDE. You won't! With all these people here? What would they
say? Just let me have a little rest.

BRIDEGROOM. If that's what you want! But don't be like this
tonight!

BRIDE [*at the door*]. Tonight I'll be fine.

BRIDEGROOM. That's what *I* want!

                    The MOTHER *appears.*

MOTHER. Son.

BRIDEGROOM. Where have you been?

MOTHER. In the middle of it all. Are you happy?

BRIDEGROOM. Yes.

MOTHER. Where's your wife?

BRIDEGROOM. Taking a little rest. It's a bad day for brides!

MOTHER. A bad day? The only good one. For me it was like
coming into an inheritance. [*The* SERVANT *enters, and crosses
towards the* BRIDE's *room*] It's ploughing the land, planting
new trees.

BRIDEGROOM. Are you going already?

MOTHER. Yes. I need to be in my own house.

BRIDEGROOM. Alone.

MOTHER. No, not alone. Not when my head is full of so many things, so many men, so much fighting.

BRIDEGROOM. But the fighting is finished now.

The SERVANT *enters quickly; she runs off upstage.*

MOTHER. As long as there's life, there's fighting.

BRIDEGROOM. I always do what you tell me!

MOTHER. Try to be warm and tender with your wife, and, if you see her getting above herself or moody, give her a caress that hurts a little: a tight hug or a bite, and then a gentle kiss. Nothing unpleasant, just enough to make her feel that you're the man, the master, the one who gives the orders. That's what I learned from your father. And since you don't have him, I have to be the one to teach you these strong ways.

BRIDEGROOM. I shall always do as you say.

FATHER [*entering*]. Where's my daughter?

BRIDEGROOM. She's inside.   [*The* FATHER *goes inside*

FIRST GIRL [*entering with the* FIRST YOUTH]. They want the bride and groom, we're going to dance the Wheel!*

FIRST YOUTH [*to the* BRIDEGROOM]. You're going to be the leader.

FATHER [*returning*]. She's not there!

BRIDEGROOM. No?

FATHER. She must have gone out on the balcony.

BRIDEGROOM. I'll go and see!   [*Exits*
                              [*Excited hubbub and the sound of guitars*

FIRST GIRL. They've started already!   [*Exits*

BRIDEGROOM [*returning*]. She isn't there!

MOTHER [*uneasily*]. Isn't she?

FATHER. Where can she have gone, then?

SERVANT [*entering*]. The little one, where is she?

MOTHER [*gravely*]. We don't know.   [*The* BRIDEGROOM *exits*

Three GUESTS *enter*.

FATHER [*dramatically*]. But isn't she in the dance?

SERVANT. She's not in the dance.

FATHER [*exploding*]. There are a lot of people there. Look, all of you!

SERVANT. I have looked.

FATHER [*heavily*]. Then where can she be?

BRIDEGROOM [*returning*]. No sign of her. Not anywhere.

MOTHER [*to the* FATHER]. What's going on? Where is your daughter?

Enter LEONARDO'S WIFE.

WIFE. They've run away! They've run away! She and Leonardo. On the horse. Off like the wind with their arms wrapped round each other!

FATHER. It's not true! Not my daughter!

MOTHER. Yes, your daughter! Bad child of a bad mother, and he's the same, he's just as bad. But now she's married to my son!

BRIDEGROOM. Let's go after them! Who's got a horse?

MOTHER. Who's got a horse ready now, who has a horse? I'll give him all I have—my eyes, my tongue even. . .

VOICE. There's one here.

MOTHER [*to her son*]. Go on! After them! [*He leaves with two* YOUTHS] No. Don't go. Those people are quick to kill and good at it. . .; but go, chase after them, and I'll be behind you!

FATHER. It can't be her. Perhaps she's thrown herself into the water tank.

MOTHER. It's the decent girls who throw themselves into the water, the ones who are still clean; not that one! But now she's married to my son. Two sides. There are two sides here now.

[*Everyone assembles on stage*] My family and yours. Out from here, all of you! Shake the dust from your shoes! We're going to help my son. [*The people divide into two groups*] Because he's got people all right: his cousins from the sea and all those who come from inland. Out of here! Take every road there is. It's come again: the hour of blood. Two sides. You with yours and I with mine. After them! After them!

CURTAIN

ACT 3

SCENE 1

A wood. It is night. Great moist tree trunks. A sombre atmosphere. Two violins are heard.

Enter three woodcutters.

FIRST WOODCUTTER. And have they found them?

SECOND WOODCUTTER. No. But they're looking for them everywhere.

THIRD WOODCUTTER. They'll soon get them.

SECOND WOODCUTTER. Shhh!

THIRD WOODCUTTER. What?

SECOND WOODCUTTER. They seem to be closing in on all sides at once.

FIRST WOODCUTTER. When the moon comes out they'll see them.

SECOND WOODCUTTER. They should have left them alone.

FIRST WOODCUTTER. The world's a big place. There's room for everyone.

THIRD WOODCUTTER. They'll kill them though.

SECOND WOODCUTTER. You have to follow your feelings. They were right to run away.

FIRST WOODCUTTER. They weren't being honest with each other; in the end the blood was too strong for them.

THIRD WOODCUTTER. Blood!

FIRST WOODCUTTER. You have to follow where your blood takes you.

SECOND WOODCUTTER. But blood that sees the light of day is drunk up by the earth.

FIRST WOODCUTTER. So be it. Better dead and drained of blood than alive and have it rotting.

THIRD WOODCUTTER. Quiet.

FIRST WOODCUTTER. What? Can you hear something?

THIRD WOODCUTTER. I can hear the crickets and the frogs, the night watching and waiting.

FIRST WOODCUTTER. But no sound of the horse.

THIRD WOODCUTTER. No.

FIRST WOODCUTTER. He'll be loving her now.

SECOND WOODCUTTER. Her body was meant for him and his for her.

THIRD WOODCUTTER. They're looking for them and they'll kill them.

FIRST WOODCUTTER. But first they'll have mingled their blood, they'll be like two empty jugs, two dried-up streams.

SECOND WOODCUTTER. There are thick clouds. The moon might easily not come out.

THIRD WOODCUTTER. The bridegroom will find them, with or without the moon. I saw him leave. Like a raging star. His face pale as ashes. In him showed the fate of all his family.

FIRST WOODCUTTER. His family of dead men lying in the street.

SECOND WOODCUTTER. That's right!

THIRD WOODCUTTER. Do you think those two will be able to break through the ring?

SECOND WOODCUTTER. It won't be easy. There are knives and shot-guns for ten leagues all around.

THIRD WOODCUTTER. He's riding a good horse.

SECOND WOODCUTTER. But he's carrying a woman.

FIRST WOODCUTTER. We're close to it now.

SECOND WOODCUTTER. A tree with forty branches. We'll soon cut it down.

THIRD WOODCUTTER. Now the moon's coming out. Let's hurry.

To the left a patch of bright light comes up.

FIRST WOODCUTTER.
    Ah, rising moon!
    Moon amid the big leaves.

SECOND WOODCUTTER.
    Load the blood with jasmine!

FIRST WOODCUTTER.
    Ah, lonely moon!
    Moon amid the green leaves!

SECOND WOODCUTTER.
    Silver on the bride's face.

THIRD WOODCUTTER.
    Ah, cruel moon!
    For love's sake, let the dark branch cast its shadow.

FIRST WOODCUTTER.
    Ah, mournful moon!
    For love's sake, let the dark branch cast its shade.

                      [They exit

*   In the bright light on the left appears the* MOON.
The MOON *is a young wood-cutter with a white face.*
*   The stage is bathed in intense blue light.*

MOON.   Round swan on the river,
            cathedral's eye,
            false dawn on the leaves
            am I; they shall not escape!
            Who's hiding? Who's sobbing
            in the valley's deep thicket?
            The moon leaves a knife
            abandoned in the air,
            a leaden ambush waiting,
            bent upon bloodshed and pain.
            Let me in! I come frozen
            by windows and walls!
            Open your rooftops and breasts
            to let me find warmth!
            I'm so cold! My pale embers
            of slumbering metal
            are seeking the crest of fire
            by mountain and street.
            But the snow carries me
            on its jasper-speckled back,

and I am drowned in pools
of water cold and hard.
So tonight there shall be
red blood for my cheeks
and for the reeds that cluster
round the broad feet of the wind.
No shade, no thicket let there be
to offer them escape!
For I must steal into some breast
where I can warm myself.
Some heart be mine!
Warm! that will spurt and flow
over the mountains of my breast;
let me come in; oh! Let me in!

[*To the branches*]

I want no shadows. Let my beams
find their way into every corner,
and among the dark tree trunks
let there be whispers of pale light
so that tonight there'll be
sweet blood for my cheeks
and for the reeds that cluster
round the broad feet of the wind.
Who's hiding? Out, I say!
No! They shall not escape!
For I shall make the horse shine out
a feverish diamond.

The MOON *disappears among the tree trunks, and the stage grows dark again. There appears an old woman completely covered in dark-green drapery. She has bare feet. Her face can hardly be seen between the folds of cloth. This character does not figure in the cast-list.*

BEGGAR WOMAN.
That moon has gone, and they are getting near.
They won't get past this place. The whispering river
and the whispering trees will smother
the shattered flight of their screams.
It must be here, and soon. I'm tired.

The coffers* are open and the white sheets
are waiting on the floor of the bedroom
for heavy bodies with torn throats.
Let no bird waken, let the breeze
gather their groans in her skirt
and fly with them over the black tree-tops
or bury them in the soft mud.
[*Impatiently*] Oh, that moon, that moon!

The MOON *reappears. The bright blue light returns.*

MOON.   They're coming closer now.
Some through the ravine and that one along the river.
I'm going to throw light on the stones. What do you need?

BEGGAR WOMAN.   Nothing.

MOON.
The wind is blowing harder now, and double-edged.

BEGGAR WOMAN.
Just throw light on the jacket and pick out the buttons;
the knives will know the road that they must take.

MOON.
But let them linger long in dying, that their blood
may slip its gentle hissing through my fingers.
See how my ashen valleys are waking,
impatient for that fountain's spurting jet!

BEGGAR WOMAN.
We mustn't let them past the stream. Be quiet!

MOON.
There they are!   [*Goes. The stage is left dark*

BEGGAR WOMAN. Quick! Plenty of light! Do you hear me?
They can't get away!

Enter the BRIDEGROOM *and* FIRST YOUTH. *The* BEGGAR
WOMAN *sits and covers herself with her cloak.*

BRIDEGROOM. This way.

FIRST YOUTH. You won't find them.

BRIDEGROOM [*vehemently*]. I *will* find them!

FIRST YOUTH. I don't think they came this way.

BRIDEGROOM. Yes, they did. I heard the sound of galloping just now.

FIRST YOUTH. It must have been a different horse.

BRIDEGROOM [*intensely*]. Listen. There's only one horse in the world, and this is it. Understand? Come with me, if you're coming, but don't talk.

FIRST YOUTH. It's just that I'd like...

BRIDEGROOM. Quiet. I know I'm going to catch them here. You see this arm? Well, it's not just my arm. It's my brother's arm, and my father's, and the arm of all my family that's dead. It's got so much strength it could pull up this tree by the roots if it wanted to. And let's hurry, because I can feel all my family's teeth sunk so deep into me here that I can hardly breathe.

BEGGAR WOMAN [*moaning*]. Ah!

FIRST YOUTH. Did you hear that?

BRIDEGROOM. Go over there and work round.

FIRST YOUTH. This is a hunt.

BRIDEGROOM. That's right. The greatest hunt there ever was.
      [*The* YOUTH *goes off. The* BRIDEGROOM *moves rapidly to the left, and stumbles over the* BEGGAR WOMAN: DEATH

BEGGAR WOMAN. Ah!

BRIDEGROOM. What do you want?

BEGGAR WOMAN. I'm cold.

BRIDEGROOM. Where are you going?

BEGGAR WOMAN [*continually moaning, like a beggar*]. Far away, over there...

BRIDEGROOM. Where have you come from?

BEGGAR WOMAN. From over there... very far away.

BRIDEGROOM. Have you seen a man and a woman rushing past on one horse?

BEGGAR WOMAN [*awakening*]. Wait a minute... [*She looks at him*] A handsome young man. [*She gets up*] But how much more handsome if he were sleeping.

BRIDEGROOM. Tell me, answer me, have you seen them?

BEGGAR WOMAN. Wait... What broad shoulders! Wouldn't you rather be lying on them instead of walking on the soles of your feet which are so small?

BRIDEGROOM [*shaking her*]. I asked if you'd seen them! Have they passed this way?

BEGGAR WOMAN [*forcefully*]. They have not passed; but they are coming from the hill. Can't you hear them?

BRIDEGROOM. No.

BEGGAR WOMAN. Don't you know the way?

BRIDEGROOM. I'll get there somehow.

BEGGAR WOMAN. I'll go with you. I know these parts.

BRIDEGROOM [*impatiently*]. Let's go then! Which way?

BEGGAR WOMAN [*dramatically*]. That way!

> [*They exit quickly. Distant sound of two violins which represent the forest*

The WOODCUTTERS *return. They carry axes on their shoulders. Slowly they move among the tree trunks.*

FIRST WOODCUTTER.
> Ah, rising death!
> Death amid the big leaves.

SECOND WOODCUTTER.
> Do not release the stream of blood.

FIRST WOODCUTTER.
> Ah, lonely death!
> Death amid the dry leaves.

THIRD WOODCUTTER.
> Do not strew flowers on the wedding.

SECOND WOODCUTTER.
> Ah, mournful death!
> For love's sake let the green branch grow.

FIRST WOODCUTTER.
> Ah, cruel death!
> For love's sake let the green branch be.

> [*They exit while still speaking*

LEONARDO *and the* BRIDE *appear.*

LEONARDO.
Be quiet!

BRIDE.
From here I will go on alone.
Leave me. I want you to go back.

LEONARDO.
Be quiet, I say.

BRIDE.   With your teeth,
with your hands, with whatever you may,
free my untarnished throat
from the metal of this chain,
and let me lie hidden away
there in my house of earth.
And, if you don't wish to kill me
as you'd kill a little snake,
put into these bride's hands of mine
the barrel of your gun.
Ah, what sorrow, what fierce fire
is leaping through my head!
Shivers of glass are spiking through my tongue!

LEONARDO.
We've done what can't be undone; quiet!
now they are close behind us
and I must take you with me.

BRIDE.
Then it must be by force!

LEONARDO.
By force? Who first
went down the stairs?

BRIDE.
I did.

LEONARDO.
            Who was it put
a new bridle on the horse?

BRIDE.

I did. That's true.

LEONARDO.   Whose hands
strapped spurs on to my boots?

BRIDE.

These hands that belong to you,
but which, when they see you, would like
to break the blue branches
and the rippling of your veins.
I love you! I love you! Leave me!
If it were in my power to kill you,
I should wrap you in a shroud
all edged with violets.
Ah! what sorrow, what fierce fire
is leaping through my head!

LEONARDO.

What shivers of glass are spiking through my tongue!
Because I did try to forget
and put a wall of stone
between your house and mine.
It's true. Don't you remember?
And when I saw you from afar
I threw sand in my eyes.
But then I'd mount my horse
and my horse would find your door.
The silver pins of your wedding
made my blood turn black,
and, when I slept, my dreams
would choke my flesh with weeds.
It's not I who am to blame;
The blame lies in the earth
and in that fragrance stealing
from your breasts and from your hair.

BRIDE.

Ah! what madness! I don't want
to share your table or your bed,

yet there's no moment in the day
when I don't want to be with you,
for you draw me and I follow,
and you tell me to go back
and I trail you through the air
like a wind-blown blade of grass.
I've left a good strong man
and all his family
with my wedding in full flow
and my bride's crown on my head.
On you the punishment will fall,
and I don't want it to be so.
Leave me alone! Go, run away!
There's no one in the world who will defend you.

LEONARDO.

The birds of dawn are calling
to each other in the trees.
The night is dying now
up there on the stony ridge.
Let's go to some dark hiding-place
where I can always love you,
for I don't care about the people
or the venom they cast at us.

                    [*He clasps her in a strong embrace*

BRIDE.

And I shall sleep at your feet
to watch over your dreams.
Naked, looking over the fields,
[*Intensely*] as if I were a bitch,
Because that's what I am! When I look at you,
your beauty makes me burn!

LEONARDO.

It's fire that lights a fire.
The same small flame will kill
two ears of corn that touch.
Come on!   [*He pulls at her*

BRIDE.   Where will you take me?

LEONARDO.

> Where those men cannot come
> who are surrounding us.
> Where I can look at you!

BRIDE [*sarcastically*].

> Drag me round the fairgrounds
> to make decent women grieve,
> so that the people see me
> with my wedding sheets displayed*
> like banners on the breeze.

LEONARDO.

> I too would want to leave you,
> if I thought as most men think.
> But I must go where you go.
> And you with me. Just try to step away. You see.
> By nails of moonlight we are fused,
> My loins; your hips.
>> [*The entire scene is violent, imbued with intense
>> sensuality*

BRIDE.

> Listen!

LEONARDO.

> They're coming.

BRIDE.   Run!

> It's right for me to die here
> with water over my feet
> and thorns upon my head.
> And for the leaves to weep for me,
> a ruined woman and a virgin still.

LEONARDO.

> Be quiet. They're coming.

BRIDE.   Go now!

LEONARDO.

> Don't speak. Don't let them hear us.
> You first. Let's go, I say.   [*The* BRIDE *hesitates*

BRIDE.
Both together!

LEONARDO [*embracing her*].
As you will.
If they part us, it will be
because I am dead.

BRIDE.   And I too will be dead.
[*They go out in each other's arms*

The MOON *appears very slowly. The stage takes on an intense
blue light. The two violins are heard. Suddenly two long
piercing screams ring out and the music of the two violins is
cut off. At the second scream the* BEGGAR WOMAN *appears
and stands with her back to the audience. She opens her
cloak and stands centre-stage like a great bird with vast
wings. The* MOON *stops in its course. The curtain falls in
absolute silence.*

FINAL SCENE

*A white room with arches and thick walls. To the right
and left white stairs. At the rear a great arch and wall
of the same colour. The floor too should be gleaming white.
This simple room will have the monumental feeling of a
church. There is no shade of grey, no shadow, not even what
is needful to create perspective.*

Two GIRLS *dressed in dark blue are winding a skein of red
wool. A* LITTLE GIRL *is watching.*

FIRST GIRL.
Oh, wool, will you tell me,
now what would you make?

SECOND GIRL.
A dress all of jasmine,
and cloth paper-thin.
At four o'clock born and
at ten o'clock dead.

A thread of this wool makes
a chain for your feet,
and for bitter laurel
a tightening knot.

LITTLE GIRL [*singing*].
  Were you at the wedding?

FIRST GIRL.
  No.

LITTLE GIRL.
  Neither was I!
  What can have happened
  among the vineshoots?
  What can have happened
  under the olive branch?
  What happened
  that no one came back?
  Were you at the wedding?

SECOND GIRL.
  We've told you we weren't.

LITTLE GIRL [*leaving*].
  And neither was I!

SECOND GIRL.
  Oh, wool, will you tell me
  of what would you sing?

FIRST GIRL.
  Of wounds that are waxen,
  of myrtle in blight,
  of sleep in the morning
  and watching at night.

LITTLE GIRL [*in the doorway*].
  Of how the thread stumbles
  on stones made of flint.
  How mountains, blue mountains,
  allow it to pass.
  Running, running, running,

it comes at the last
to handle a knife and
to cut off the bread.   [*She goes out*

SECOND GIRL.
Oh, wool, will you tell me
now what would you say?

FIRST GIRL.
The lover is silent
and crimson the groom.
On the mute shore-line
I saw them laid down.

                    [*She stops and gazes at the skein*

LITTLE GIRL [*appearing at the door*].
Running, running, running,
the thread will reach here.
All covered in clay
I feel them draw near.
Bodies stretched stiffly
in ivory sheets.   [*She leaves*

    LEONARDO'S WIFE *and* MOTHER-IN-LAW *appear.*
        They are in a state of anguish.

FIRST GIRL.
Are they coming?

MOTHER-IN-LAW [*harshly*].
                    We don't know.

SECOND GIRL.
So what about the wedding?

FIRST GIRL.   Tell me.

MOTHER-IN-LAW [*curtly*].   No.

WIFE.
I want to go back, I want to know everything.

MOTHER-IN-LAW [*forcefully*].
You, to your house.
Brave and alone in your house.
To grow old and to weep.

But with the door shut tight.
No one ever. Dead or alive.
We shall nail up the windows.
And let the rains fall and the nights fall
on the bitter weeds.

WIFE.
What can have happened?

MOTHER-IN-LAW.   No matter.
Hide your face with a veil.
Your children are your children,
that's all. On the bed
place a cross of ashes
where once his pillow lay.   [*They go out*

BEGGAR WOMAN [*at the door*].
A crust of bread, girls.

LITTLE GIRL.   Go away!
                         [*The* GIRLS *huddle together*

BEGGAR WOMAN.
Why?

LITTLE GIRL. Because you whine: go away.

FIRST GIRL [*to the* LITTLE GIRL].   Be quiet!

BEGGAR WOMAN.
I might have asked for your eyes! A cloud
of birds is following me. Do you want one?

LITTLE GIRL.
I want to go home!

SECOND GIRL [*to the* BEGGAR WOMAN].
                    Don't mind her!

FIRST GIRL.
Did you come by the stream?

BEGGAR WOMAN.
I came that way.

FIRST GIRL [*timidly*].   Can I ask you something?

BEGGAR WOMAN.
>   I saw them; soon they'll be here: two torrents
>   still at last among the big rocks,
>   two men at the horse's feet.
>   Dead in all the beauty of the night.
>   [*With joy*] Dead, yes, dead.

FIRST GIRL.
>   Quiet, old woman, quiet!

BEGGAR WOMAN.
>   Torn flowers their eyes, and their teeth
>   two fistfuls of snow frozen hard.
>   The two of them fell, and the bride is coming back
>   with blood-soaked skirt and hair.
>   Covered with two blankets they're coming
>   on the shoulders of tall young men.
>   So it was; just that. It was right.
>   Over the flower of gold, filthy sand.
>> [*She leaves. The* GIRLS *bow their heads and make
>> their way out, rhythmically*

FIRST GIRL.
>   Filthy sand.

SECOND GIRL.   Over the flower of gold.

LITTLE GIRL.
>   Over the flower of gold
>   they're bringing the dead from the stream.
>   Dark-skinned the one,
>   dark-skinned the other.
>   What shadowy nightingale flies lamenting
>   over the flower of gold!
>> [*She leaves. The stage is left empty*

> *The* MOTHER *appears with a woman* NEIGHBOUR.
> *The* NEIGHBOUR *is weeping.*

MOTHER. Stop it.

NEIGHBOUR. I can't.

MOTHER. Stop it, I said. [*At the door*] Is there nobody here? [*She raises her hands to her forehead*] It's my son who should be answering me. But now my son is an armful of withered flowers. Now my son is a dark voice beyond the mountains. [*Furiously, to the* NEIGHBOUR] Will you stop it? I want no weeping in this house. Your tears come only from your eyes, but mine will come when I'm alone, from the soles of my feet, from my very roots, and they will burn hotter than blood.

NEIGHBOUR. You come to my house; don't stay here.

MOTHER. Here. Here is where I want to be. At peace. They're all dead now. At midnight I shall sleep, and guns and knives won't terrify me now. Other mothers will look out of their windows, lashed by the rain, to watch for the faces of their sons. I won't. I shall make out of my dreams a cold ivory dove that will carry camellias of frost to the graveyard. No, no: it's not a graveyard; it's a bed of earth, a resting-place that wraps them round and rocks them in the sky.

Enter a woman in black who goes over to the right and kneels down.

[*To the* NEIGHBOUR]. Take your hands from your face. We have terrible days ahead of us. I don't want to see anybody. The earth and I. My weeping and I. And these four walls. Ah! Ah!   [*She sits, overcome*

NEIGHBOUR. Have pity on yourself.

MOTHER [*tossing back her hair*]. I must be calm. [*She sits down*] Because the neighbours will come and I don't want them to see me so poor. So poor! A woman without even one son she can press to her lips.

The BRIDE *appears. She is without her orange blossom and wearing a black cloak.*

NEIGHBOUR [*going up to the* BRIDE, *furiously*]. Where are you going?

BRIDE. I'm coming here.

MOTHER [*to the* NEIGHBOUR]. Who is it?

NEIGHBOUR. Don't you see?

MOTHER. That's why I ask. Because I must not see who she is, if I'm not to sink my teeth in her throat. You snake! [*She*

moves dangerously towards the BRIDE, *then controls herself.
To the* NEIGHBOUR] Look at her! There she stands and she's
crying, and I'm calm and not tearing her eyes out. I don't
understand myself. Can it be that I didn't love my son? But
what about his good name? Where's his good name now?

[*She strikes the* BRIDE, *who falls to the floor*

NEIGHBOUR. For God's sake!   [*She tries to separate them*

BRIDE [*to the* NEIGHBOUR]. Let her do it. I came so that she
would kill me, and I'd be taken away with the two of them.
[*To the* MOTHER] But not with your hands; with iron hooks,
with a sickle, hard, hard, so that they break on my bones. Let
her do it! I want her to know that I'm pure: mad I may be,
but they can bury me and not a single man will have seen
himself in the whiteness of my breasts.

MOTHER. Quiet, quiet; why should I care about that?

BRIDE. Because I went with the other one, I went with him! [*In
anguish*] You'd have gone too, you'd have done the same. I
was a woman on fire, I was blistered everywhere, inside and
out, and your son was a drop of cool water that I hoped
would give me children, land, health; but the other one was
a dark river, clogged with branches, which sent me the sound
of its reeds and its murmuring song. I was running along with
your son, who was like a little boy, all cold water, and the
other one sent after me hundreds of birds that crowded my
path and left frost on my wounds, the wounds of a poor
wilting woman, a girl fondled by fire. I didn't want it to
happen, believe me, I didn't want it. Your son was what I
wanted and I didn't deceive him, but the other one's arm
swept me away like the surge of the sea, like the butt of a
mule, and would always have swept me away, always, always,
even if I'd been an old woman and all the sons of your son
had grabbed me by the hair to hold me back.

Enter a woman NEIGHBOUR.

MOTHER. So she's not to blame and neither am I!
[*Sarcastically*] Who is then? It's a flabby, weak, sleepless sort
of woman who throws away her wedding wreath to seek out
a bed-space warmed by another woman!

BRIDE. Hush, hush! Take your revenge on me; here I am! See how soft my throat is; it will be easier for you than cutting a dahlia in your garden. But that, no, never! I'm still pure, as pure as a little girl new-born. And strong enough to prove it to you. Light the fire. We'll put our hands in it: you for your son, I for my body. You'll be the first to pull back.

Enter another woman NEIGHBOUR.

MOTHER. What is your good name to me? What is your death to me? What does anything matter to me? Blessed be the wheat, for my sons lie beneath it; blessed be the rain, for it wets the faces of the dead. Blessed be God, for He lays us side by side that we may rest.

Enter another woman NEIGHBOUR.

BRIDE. Let me weep with you.

MOTHER. Weep. But by the door.

Enter the LITTLE GIRL. *The* BRIDE *remains by the door, the* MOTHER *centre stage.*

WIFE [*entering and moving over to the left*].
He was a fine-looking horseman,
    a snowdrift now.
He rode by fairground and mountain
    and women's arms.
Now the moss of night's darkness
    crowns his brow.

MOTHER.
A sunflower to your mother,
    mirror of the earth;
a cross of bitter rosebay*
    be placed on your breast;
the sheet that is your cover
    be made of shining silk,
and water run like tears
    between your quiet hands.

WIFE.
Ah, four boys are coming now,
    their shoulders aching!

BRIDE.
>   Ah, four young men are bearing
>   cold death through the air!

MOTHER. Neighbours.

LITTLE GIRL [*at the door*]. They're bringing them now.

MOTHER.
>   Always the same.
>   The cross, the cross.

WOMEN.
>   Sweet the nails,
>   sweet the cross,
>   sweet the name
>   of Jesus.

BRIDE. May the cross protect the living and the dead.

MOTHER.
>   Neighbours: with a knife,
>   with a little knife,
>   on a day appointed, between two and three,
>   the two love-driven men killed each other.
>   With a knife.
>   With a little knife
>   that hardly fits into the hand;
>   but which neatly enters
>   the astonished flesh
>   and stops at the place
>   where lies trembling, enmeshed,
>   the dark root of the scream.

BRIDE.
>   And this is a knife,
>   a little knife
>   that hardly fits into the hand;
>   a fish without river or scales,
>   so that on a day appointed, between two and three,
>   with this knife
>   two fine men are left
>   with yellowing lips.

MOTHER.

> It hardly fits into the hand,
> but it coldly enters
> the astonished flesh,
> and there it stops, in the place
> where lies trembling, enmeshed,
> the dark root of the scream.

[*Kneeling on the floor, the* NEIGHBOURS *weep*

CURTAIN

YERMA

A Tragic Poem in Three Acts
and Six Scenes

(1934)

CHARACTERS

Yerma*
Juan
María
Victor
Pagan Old Woman
First Girl
Second Girl
First Washerwoman
Second Washerwoman
Third Washerwoman
Fourth Washerwoman
Fifth Washerwoman
Sixth Washerwoman
Elder Sister
Younger Sister
Dolores
First Old Woman
Second Old Woman
First Woman
Second Woman
Male Mask
Female Mask
First Man
Second Man
Third Man
Boy
Shepherd and little boy, pilgrims, crowd.

ACT 1

SCENE 1

When the curtain rises, YERMA *is asleep with a sewing-basket at her feet. The stage is bathed in a strange, dreamlike light.*

A shepherd enters on tiptoe with his eyes fixed on YERMA. *He is leading by the hand a little boy dressed in white. The clock strikes. As the shepherd exits, the light becomes that of a bright Spring morning.* YERMA *wakes up.*

VOICE [*singing off-stage*].
> Hushaby, hushaby, we shall build
> a little wooden hut in the middle of the field.
> Our little hut will be three feet wide,
> and all of us will creep inside.

YERMA. Juan. Can you hear me? Juan.

JUAN [*off-stage*]. Just coming.

YERMA. It's time to go.

JUAN [*entering*]. Have the oxen gone by?

YERMA. Yes, they have.

JUAN. See you later. [*He makes to leave*

YERMA. Why don't you have a glass of milk?

JUAN. What for?

YERMA. You work hard, and your body isn't strong enough for heavy work.

JUAN. When a man keeps himself lean and dry, he gets as tough as steel.

YERMA. But you don't. When we got married you weren't like this. Your face is so white now you'd think the sun never shone on it. I'd like to see you swimming in the river, and climbing on to the roof* of the house when the rain is streaming down. Twenty-four months we've been married, and you get sadder and sadder, thinner and thinner, as if you were growing backwards.

JUAN. Have you finished?

YERMA [*getting up*]. Don't take it the wrong way. If *I* were not well, I'd be pleased if you took care of me. 'My wife isn't well; I'm going to kill this lamb and make her a nourishing stew. My wife isn't well; I'll save this chicken fat to rub on her chest; I'll take her this sheepskin to keep the cold from her feet.' That's how I am. That's why I take good care of you.

JUAN. And I'm grateful.

YERMA. But you won't let me take care of you.

JUAN. Because there's nothing wrong with me. All these things are only in your mind. I work hard. As the years pass, I'll get older.

YERMA. As the years pass... You and I here and the years passing.

JUAN [*smiling*]. That's right. And very snug we shall be. The farm's doing well, and we've no children to run away with the money.

YERMA. We've no children... Juan!

JUAN. What?

YERMA. I do love you, don't I?

JUAN. Of course you do.

YERMA. I know girls who were frightened and burst into tears the first time they slept with their husbands. Did I cry the first time we slept together? Wasn't I singing when I turned back the fine linen sheets? And didn't I say: 'Don't these bedclothes smell just like apples?'

JUAN. That's what you said!

YERMA. My mother cried because I didn't mind leaving her. And really I didn't! Nobody was happier to get married than I was. And even so...

JUAN. Be quiet!

YERMA. And even so...

JUAN. Be quiet! It's hard enough for me to keep hearing people say...

YERMA. No. I don't want to hear what they say. I can see for myself that can't be true. . . The rain falling on the rocks makes them soft in time, and then they grow wild mustard which people say is no use. It's no use, wild mustard, but I can still see it waving its yellow flowers in the breeze.

JUAN. We must just wait!

YERMA. Yes, and love each other, and want it to happen!
[YERMA *hugs and kisses her husband: it is she who takes the initiative*

JUAN. If you need anything, just tell me and I'll bring it. You know I don't like you going out.

YERMA. I never go out.

JUAN. It's best for you to be here.

YERMA. Yes.

JUAN. The street is for people with nothing to do.

YERMA [*gloomily*]. That's right.

The husband leaves, and YERMA *moves towards her sewing, passes her hand over her belly, raises her arms in a graceful yawn, and sits down to sew.*

YERMA [*singing*].
Where have you come from, my darling child?
'Down from the peak of the cold so wild.'
What is it you're seeking, my darling child?
'The warmth of your dress, that's so soft and mild.'
[*She threads her needle*
Let the branches dance in the sun's bright glance
and the fountains leap for joy.

[*As if talking to a child*]

Out in the yard the dog is barking;
up in the trees the wind is singing;
the oxen are lowing to their drover;
and moonbeams through my hair are weaving.
From so far away, child, what is it you need? [*Pause*
'On the mountains of your white breasts to feed.'
Let the branches dance in the sun's bright glance
and the fountains leap for joy! [*Sewing*

I answer, my child, yes, let it be.
I am torn and broken for your sake,
and still this empty womb must ache
where your first cradling is to be.
Oh, when, my child, will you come to me?   [*Pause*
'When your flesh with jasmine shall scented be.'
Let the branches dance in the sun's bright glance
and the fountains leap for joy!

> YERMA *goes on singing.* MARÍA *enters, carrying a bundle of cloth.*

Where've you been?

MARÍA. To the shop.

YERMA. To the shop, so early?

MARÍA. If I'd had my way, I'd have waited at the door till it opened. Can't you guess what I've been buying?

YERMA. Coffee for breakfast, I suppose, sugar, and bread.

MARÍA. No. I've bought lace, three lengths of linen, ribbons, and coloured wool to make tassels. My husband had the money and he gave it to me himself.

YERMA. You're going to make yourself a blouse.

MARÍA. No, it's because. . . What do you think?

YERMA. What?

MARÍA. Because it's happened.

> [*Her eyes are lowered.* YERMA *gets up and stands looking at her admiringly*

YERMA. After five months!

MARÍA. Yes.

YERMA. You're quite sure?

MARÍA. Of course I am.

YERMA [*with curiosity*]. And how do you feel?

MARÍA. I don't know. Disturbed, anxious.

YERMA. Anxious. [*Holding her tight*] But. . . when it happened? . . . Tell me. . . You weren't anxious then, you were happy?

MARÍA. Yes, happy.

YERMA. I expect you were singing, weren't you? I sing. You were... Tell me.

MARÍA. Don't ask me. Have you ever held a live bird in your hand?

YERMA. Yes.

MARÍA. It's the same... but it's right inside your blood.

YERMA. How beautiful!   [*She looks at* MARÍA, *lost in wonder*

MARÍA. I'm so confused. I don't know anything.

YERMA. About what?

MARÍA. About what I'm supposed to do. I'll have to ask my mother.

YERMA. Why her? She's old, she'll have forgotten all about that sort of thing. Don't tire yourself walking too much, and when you breathe, breathe gently as if you were holding a rose between your teeth.

MARÍA. You know, they say that later on it kicks you gently with its little feet.

YERMA. And that's when you feel most love for it, when you say to yourself, that's my child!

MARÍA. I can't help feeling embarrassed about it all.

YERMA. What does your husband say about it?

MARÍA. Nothing.

YERMA. Does he love you very much?

MARÍA. He doesn't say anything, but he snuggles up to me and his eyes tremble like two green leaves.

YERMA. Did he know when you...?

MARÍA. Yes.

YERMA. How did he know?

MARÍA. I don't know how. But on our wedding night he kept saying it to me, over and over, with his mouth pressed against my cheek; so that now my baby seems like a shining white dove that he slipped into my ear.

YERMA. You're so lucky!

MARÍA. But you know more about these things than I do.

YERMA. What good does it do me?

MARÍA. That's true. Why should that be? Of all the girls who got married when you did, you're the only one.

YERMA. That's how it is. There's still time, of course. Elena took three years, and some women years ago in my mother's day took much longer, but the two years and twenty days that I've been waiting is too long. I don't think it's right that I should waste away in this place. I often walk barefoot in the yard, just to tread on the earth, I don't know why. If I carry on like this, I shall turn into a nasty woman.

MARÍA. Now look here, you silly thing. You talk as if you were old already. You listen to me! With things like this no woman should start feeling sorry for herself. My mother's sister had a baby when she was forty, and you've never seen such a beautiful boy!

YERMA [eagerly]. Tell me the things he did.

MARÍA. He howled like a young bull, as loud as a thousand grasshoppers all chirping at once, he peed all over us and pulled our plaits, and by the time he was four months old he was scratching us all over our faces.

YERMA [laughing]. But they don't hurt, those things.

MARÍA. Oh, don't they!

YERMA. Pooh! I've seen my sister feed her baby with her nipples all cracked and sore, and it was really painful for her, but it was a good, wholesome pain, it kept her healthy.

MARÍA. They do say you suffer a lot with children.

YERMA. That's not true. It's only weak and feeble mothers who say that, the sort who are always whining. Why do they have children? It's not meant to be a bed of roses. We have to suffer so that we can see them grow. I think it drains us of half the blood in our veins. But that's good, it's healthy, it's beautiful. Every woman has enough blood for four or five children, and when she doesn't have them it turns to poison, and that's what's going to happen to me.

MARÍA. I don't know why I feel so strange.

YERMA. I've always heard it scares you the first time.

MARÍA [*timidly*]. I wonder whether... You're so good at sewing, do you think...?

YERMA [*taking up the bundle*]. Let's see. I'll cut out two little dresses for you. What's this for?

MARÍA. That's for the nappies.

YERMA. Right. [*She sits down*

MARÍA. Well, I'll be going, then.
[*She draws close, and* YERMA *lovingly places her hands on* MARÍA'*s belly*

YERMA. Don't run over the cobblestones in the street.

MARÍA. 'Bye now. [*She kisses* YERMA *and exits*

YERMA. Come back soon.
[YERMA *is left as we found her at the beginning of the scene. She takes up the scissors and starts cutting*

VICTOR *enters.*

YERMA. Hello, Victor.

VICTOR [*he is a thoughtful man, steady and dignified*]. Where's Juan?

YERMA. Out in the fields.

VICTOR. What's that you're sewing?

YERMA. I'm making some nappies.

VICTOR [*smiling*]. Well, well!

YERMA [*laughing*]. I'm going to trim them with lace.

VICTOR. If it's a girl, you'll give her your name.

YERMA [*trembling*]. What do you mean?

VICTOR. I'm very happy for you.

YERMA [*almost choking*]. No... They're not for me. They're for María's baby.

VICTOR. Well, perhaps you'll feel like following her example. What this house needs is a child.

YERMA [*in anguish*]. That's what it needs!

VICTOR. Well, do something about it. Tell your husband not to think about work so much. He's keen to make money and he will, but who's he going to leave it to when he dies? I'm going out with the sheep. Tell Juan to collect the two he bought from me, and, about the other thing—tell him to dig deeper!

[*He goes, smiling*

YERMA [*passionately*]. That's right: dig deeper!

[YERMA *rises thoughtfully, moves to where* VICTOR *was standing and inhales deeply as if breathing in mountain air. Then she crosses to the other side of the room as if looking for something, and from there returns to her chair and takes up the sewing again. She begins to sew, then stops, staring into the distance*

YERMA.

I answer, my child, yes, let it be.
I am torn and broken for your sake,
and still this empty womb must ache
Where your first cradling is to be.
Oh, when, my child, will you come to me?
'When your flesh with jasmine shall scented be.'

CURTAIN

SCENE 2

The countryside. Enter YERMA. *She is carrying a basket. Enter the* PAGAN OLD WOMAN.

YERMA. Good-day.

PAGAN WOMAN. Good-day to you, pretty one. Where are you going?

YERMA. I've been taking my husband his food. He's working in the olive grove.

PAGAN WOMAN. Have you been married long?

YERMA. Three years.

PAGAN WOMAN. Any children?

YERMA. No.

PAGAN WOMAN. Pooh! They'll come along.

YERMA [*with anxious eagerness*]. Do you think so?

PAGAN WOMAN. Why not? [*She sits*] I've been taking his food to my husband too. He's old. He still works. I've got nine sons, like nine bright suns in the sky they are, but no daughters at all, so here I am always toing and froing across the river.

YERMA. You live on the other side, then?

PAGAN WOMAN. Yes. By the windmills. What family are you from?

YERMA. I'm Enrique the shepherd's daughter.

PAGAN WOMAN. Ah! Enrique the shepherd. I knew him. Good folk, they are. Get up, toil away, eat a few loaves of bread, and then die. No fun and games, no nothing. Holidays are for other people. Brought up to make no noise. I could have married an uncle of yours. But, oh, no! I've always been a woman with her skirts flying, I always went straight for the slice of melon, the feasting, the icing on the cake. Many's the time I've stuck my head into the street in the small hours thinking I heard guitars coming and going, but it was only the wind. [*She laughs*] You'll have a good laugh at me. I've had two husbands and fourteen children, five of them died, but there's nothing sad about me and I've a mind to go on living for a long time yet. What I say is, look at the fig-trees, see how long they last! Houses, how long they last! It's only us poor cursed women who get ground to dust for nothing at all.

YERMA. I'd like to ask you something.

PAGAN WOMAN. Let's look at you. [*She looks closely*] I know what you're going to ask me. There's not a word to be said about things like that.   [*She gets up*

YERMA [*stopping her*]. Why not? After hearing you speak I feel I can trust you. I've been wanting to talk about things with an older woman for a long time. Because I have to know. I have to. And you can tell me...

PAGAN WOMAN. What?

YERMA [*lowering her voice*]. You know what it is. Why am I barren? Am I to spend the best years of my life looking after the fowls or ironing dainty curtains to put up at my little window? No. You just tell me what I have to do and I'll do it, whatever it is, even if you tell me to stick needles into the tenderest part of my eyes.

PAGAN WOMAN. Me? I don't know what to tell you. I just used to lie on my back and start singing. Babies pour out like water. Ah! You've got a beautiful body, anyone can see that. Just walk down the street and the stallions will start neighing. Ah! Leave me in peace, girl, don't make me speak. There are a lot of things in my head that I don't want to say.

YERMA. Why not? With my husband I talk about nothing else.

PAGAN WOMAN. Tell me, then. Do you go for your husband?

YERMA. What do you mean?

PAGAN WOMAN. Do you love him? Do you want to be in his arms?

YERMA. I don't know.

PAGAN WOMAN. Do you start trembling when he gets near you? Do you get lost in a dream when he brings his lips close to yours? Tell me.

YERMA. No. I've never felt like that.

PAGAN WOMAN. Never? Not even when you were dancing?

YERMA [*remembering*]. Perhaps. . . Just once. . . When Victor. . .

PAGAN WOMAN. Yes, go on.

YERMA. He put his arm round my waist, and I couldn't say a word to him because I couldn't speak. Another time—it was Victor again; when I was fourteen—he was a big, strong boy; he picked me up in his arms to get across a ditch, and I started trembling so much my teeth chattered. But then I've always been very modest.

PAGAN WOMAN. And with your husband. . .?

YERMA. With my husband it's not the same. My father gave him to me and I took him. Gladly. That's the absolute truth. Then the moment I got engaged to him I began to think... about having children. And I could see myself in his eyes. Yes, but what I saw was myself very tiny and easy to handle, just as if I myself were my own little girl.

PAGAN WOMAN. Just the opposite of me. Perhaps that's why you haven't had a baby yet. Men have to give us pleasure, girl. They have to let down our hair and quench our thirst from their own mouths. That's what makes the world go round.

YERMA. Your world, not mine. I think about many things, all sorts of things, and I'm quite sure that my child is meant to make those things come true. It was for his sake that I first gave myself to my husband, and it's so that he can be born that I go on giving myself, but I never do it for pleasure.

PAGAN WOMAN. And so you're left empty!

YERMA. No, not empty, because I'm filling up with hatred. You tell me, am I the one who's to blame? Are you supposed to want a man just for being a man and for nothing else? If that's all, what are you going to think in bed when he leaves you staring miserably up at the ceiling while he turns his back on you and goes to sleep? Am I supposed to go on thinking about him or about the glorious new life that might come out of my body? I don't know, but you tell me; for pity's sake, tell me!   [*She falls to her knees*

PAGAN WOMAN. Ay, a flower in full bloom you are; such a beautiful creature! Let me be. Don't make me say any more. I don't want to talk to you any more. They're matters of honour, these things, and I don't like to damage anyone's honour. You'll find out. You're too innocent, that's your trouble.

YERMA [*sadly*]. Country girls like me find every door closed against them. All we get are hints and gestures because they say that all these things are not for us to know. And you're the same, you won't speak either; you put on the airs of a doctor who knows it all, and then you won't give water to a woman who's dying of thirst.

PAGAN WOMAN. A different kind of woman, one who was at peace with herself, I would speak to. But not to you. I'm old, and I know what I'm talking about.

YERMA. God help me, then.

PAGAN WOMAN. No, not God. God's never meant anything to me. When are people like you going to understand that there's no such thing? It's men you have to look to for help.

YERMA. Why do you tell me that? Why?

PAGAN WOMAN [*going*]. Though there ought to be a God all the same, if only a little tiny one, to strike down those men with rotten seed who turn the fields of joy into a swamp.

YERMA. I don't know what you mean.

PAGAN WOMAN [*on her way*]. Well, it's all clear enough to me. Don't give way to sadness. Let your hope be strong. You are still very young. What do you expect me to do about it?

[*She goes*

Two GIRLS *enter.*

FIRST GIRL [*to* YERMA]. We keep finding people, everywhere we go.

YERMA. With all the work to be done the men are in the olive groves, and we have to take them their food. Only the old folk are indoors.

SECOND GIRL. Are you going back to the village?

YERMA. That's where I'm going.

FIRST GIRL. I must rush. I left the little one asleep and there's no one at home.

YERMA. Then get going, girl. Children can't be left on their own. There aren't any pigs there?

FIRST GIRL. No. But you're quite right. I'll hurry back.

YERMA. Go on. That's how accidents happen. I expect you've left the door locked.

FIRST GIRL. Of course.

YERMA. Yes, but girls like you don't realize what small children are like. Things that seem quite harmless to us can be fatal to them. A needle, a drink of water.

FIRST GIRL. You're right. I'll run. I just don't think about things.

YERMA. Off you go.   [FIRST GIRL *runs off*

SECOND GIRL. If you had four or five, you wouldn't talk like that.

YERMA. Why not? I'd be the same if I had forty.

SECOND GIRL. Anyway we have a more peaceful life without them, you and I.

YERMA. I don't.

SECOND GIRL. Well, I do. All that trouble! My mother, though, she never stops feeding me herbs and things to make me have them, and in October we're going to the Saint,* the one who gives them to you, so they say, if you pray really hard. My mother will do all the praying. I won't.

YERMA. Why did you get married?

SECOND GIRL. Because they arranged it. All women get married. If we carry on like this, the only ones left single will be little girls, I tell you, and anyway you're a wife in all but name long before you go to church. It's just the old women who fuss about these things. I'm nineteen and I don't like cooking or washing clothes. So what happens? I have to spend all day doing what I don't like. And all for what? What does my husband have to be my husband for? Because we don't do anything now we didn't do before we got married. It's just the stupid ideas old people have.

YERMA. Be quiet, don't talk like that.

SECOND GIRL. *You*'ll say I'm mad too. The mad girl! The mad girl! [*She laughs*] I'll tell you the only thing I've learned in this life: everyone's stuck inside their houses doing things they don't like. It's so much better out in the street. Me, I go off down to the stream, I climb up and ring the bells, sometimes I even treat myself to a glass of anisette.

YERMA. You're just a child.

SECOND GIRL. All right, but I'm not mad.   [*She laughs*

YERMA. Does your mother live at the top end of the village?

SECOND GIRL. Yes.

YERMA. In the last house?

SECOND GIRL. Yes.

YERMA. What's her name?

SECOND GIRL. Dolores. Why do you want to know?

YERMA. No reason.

SECOND GIRL. You must have a reason for asking.

YERMA. Not really. It was just something to say.

SECOND GIRL. Suit yourself. Look, I'm going to take my husband his food. [*She laughs*] Who'd have thought I'd come to that? Shame I can't still call him my sweetheart! Don't you think? [*She goes off, laughing gaily*] Goodbye!

VICTOR'S VOICE [*singing*].

    Why do you sleep alone, shepherd?
    Why do you sleep alone?
    You'd do better to lie
    in my blanket of wool.
    Why do you sleep alone?

YERMA.

    You'd do better to lie
    in my blanket of wool.
    Why do you sleep alone?

VICTOR'S VOICE.   [YERMA *is listening*

    Your blanket is dark stone, shepherd,
    your shirt the frost of dawn;
    with the grey sedge of winter
    at night your bed is strewn.

    The oak-trees rib the ground, shepherd,
    where your pillow lies;
    the woman's voice you hear, shepherd,
    is the water's broken voice.

    What draws you to the hill, shepherd,
    with bitter herbs overgrown?
    Some child that will not let you rest?
    The wild broom and its thorn.

    [YERMA *makes to exit, and comes up against* VICTOR *as he enters*

VICTOR [*cheerfully*]. So where's this beautiful creature off to?

YERMA. Was that you singing?

VICTOR. It was.

YERMA. Wonderful! I'd never heard you sing.

VICTOR. Hadn't you?

YERMA. You've got a powerful voice. It fills your mouth and streams out like a torrent.

VICTOR. I'm a happy man.

YERMA. Yes, you are.

VICTOR. And you are a sad woman.

YERMA. It's not my nature; but things have made me sad.

VICTOR. And your husband is sadder than you.

YERMA. He is, yes. He was born dry.

VICTOR. He's always been the same. [*Pause.* YERMA *is sitting down*] Have you been taking him his food?

YERMA. Yes. [*She looks at him. Pause*] What's that you've got?
                                          [*She points to his face*

VICTOR. Where?

YERMA [*she gets up and draws close to him*]. Here... on your cheek... like a burn.

VICTOR. It's nothing...

YERMA. I thought it was.   [*Pause*

VICTOR. It must be the sun.

YERMA. Perhaps...
            [*Pause. The silence grows more intense and, without their making the slightest movement, a strong tension is established between them*

YERMA [*trembling*]. Listen.

VICTOR. What?

YERMA. Can't you hear the sound of crying?

VICTOR [*listening*]. No.

YERMA. I thought I heard a child crying.

VICTOR. Yes?

YERMA. Very close. It was a kind of muffled cry.

VICTOR. There are always a lot of children around here; they come to steal fruit.

YERMA. No. It's the voice of a tiny child.   [*Pause*

VICTOR. I can't hear anything.

YERMA. It must be in my head.
> [*She looks intently at* VICTOR *and he looks at her in the same way, then slowly turns his eyes away from her as if in fear*

JUAN *enters.*

JUAN. What are you doing here still?

YERMA. Talking.

VICTOR [*leaving*]. Goodbye, then.

JUAN. You ought to be in the house.

YERMA. I got delayed.

JUAN. I don't see what delayed you.

YERMA. I stopped to hear the birds singing.

JUAN. Oh, did you? That's just the way to start people talking.

YERMA [*aggressively*]. Juan, just what are you thinking?

JUAN. It's not you I'm worried about. It's other people.

YERMA. To hell with other people.

JUAN. Don't swear. It's not nice in a woman.

YERMA. If only I could be a woman.

JUAN. Let's leave it there. Go home.   [*Pause*

YERMA. All right. Shall I expect you?

JUAN. No. I shall be watering all night.* There's not much water coming through. It's my turn to use it till the sun comes up, I've got to stop anyone else from stealing it. You go to bed and go to sleep.

YERMA [*dramatically*]. I'll go to sleep!   [*She exits*

CURTAIN

ACT 2

SCENE 1

The rushing stream where the village women do their washing. The WASHERWOMEN *are ranged on various levels. They are heard singing before the curtain rises.*

WOMEN.　　　In the stream's cool water
　　　　　　I will wash your lace.
　　　　　　Like jasmine warm and glowing
　　　　　　the smile that lights your face.

FIRST WOMAN. I'm not one for gossiping myself.

THIRD WOMAN. But here everyone gossips.

FOURTH WOMAN. And there's nothing wrong with that.

FIFTH WOMAN. If a woman wants a good name, she has to earn it.

FOURTH WOMAN.
　　　　　　In the soil I planted thyme;
　　　　　　　it grew all by itself.
　　　　　　She who values her good name:
　　　　　　　she'd best behave herself.　　　*[Laughter*

FIFTH WOMAN. That's what they're saying, anyway.

FIRST WOMAN. Yes, but nobody ever knows for certain.

FOURTH WOMAN. What we do know is that the husband has got his two sisters to move in with them.

FIFTH WOMAN. The spinsters?

FOURTH WOMAN. Yes. They used to watch over the church, and now they'll be watching over their sister-in-law. *I* couldn't live with them.

FIRST WOMAN. Why not?

FOURTH WOMAN. They'd give you the creeps. They're like those great plants you suddenly find sprouting over graves. They've got candle-grease smeared all over them. And they're all turned in on themselves. I can just see them cooking their food in the oil for the altar lamps.

THIRD WOMAN. Are they in the house yet?

FOURTH WOMAN. Since yesterday. Now the husband can go out to his fields again.

FIRST WOMAN. Will somebody please tell me what happened?

FIFTH WOMAN. The night before last she spent out on the door-step in the freezing cold.

FIRST WOMAN. But why?

FOURTH WOMAN. She can't bear to stay inside her house.

FIFTH WOMAN. That's how they are, those barren women. Instead of making lace or apple jam they like climbing up on to the roof or walking barefoot by the river.

FIRST WOMAN. What right have you got to say things like that? She hasn't got any children, but it's not her fault.

FOURTH WOMAN. If a woman wants children, she has them. The trouble with the namby-pamby, wishy-washy spoilt ones is that they're not made to have stretch-marks on their bellies.

[*Laughter*

THIRD WOMAN. Then they cover themselves with powder and paint and sprigs of oleander, and go chasing after a man who's not their husband.

FIFTH WOMAN. That's the truth of it.

FIRST WOMAN. But have any of you seen her with another man?

FOURTH WOMAN. Not us, but other people have.

FIRST WOMAN. It's always other people!

FIFTH WOMAN. Twice, they say.

SECOND WOMAN. And what were they doing?

FOURTH WOMAN. Talking.

FIRST WOMAN. Talking's not a sin.

FOURTH WOMAN. There's such a thing in this world as a way of looking. That's what my mother used to say. A woman looking at roses isn't the same as a woman looking at a man's thighs. Well, she looks at him.

FIRST WOMAN. At who?

FOURTH WOMAN. A man. Do you hear? Get it into your head. Do you want me to say it louder? [*Laughter*] And when she's not looking at him, because she's by herself, because she hasn't got him in front of her, she sees him in her head.

FIRST WOMAN. That's not true.   [*Uproar*

FIFTH WOMAN. And what about her husband?

THIRD WOMAN. He might as well be deaf. He never stirs himself; he's like a lizard lying in the sun.   [*Laughter*

FIRST WOMAN. It would all come right if only they had children.

SECOND WOMAN. It's what comes of people not being content with their lot.

FOURTH WOMAN. That house becomes more like hell with every hour that passes. She and the sisters keep their lips tight shut, and spend the whole day whitewashing the walls, scouring the copper, cleaning the windows, and polishing the floors. And the more the house sparkles, the hotter it burns inside.

FIRST WOMAN. It's all his fault, not hers. When a man doesn't give his wife children, he should watch out for trouble.

FOURTH WOMAN. It's her fault for having a tongue like a flint.

FIRST WOMAN. What the devil's got into you to make you talk like that?

FOURTH WOMAN. And who the hell gave you the right to tell me what to do?

FIFTH WOMAN. Quiet!   [*Laughter*

FIRST WOMAN. I'd like to stick a knitting-needle through every wagging tongue.

FIFTH WOMAN. Shut up!

FOURTH WOMAN. And I'd like to stick one through the breast of every two-faced female.

FIFTH WOMAN. Quiet. The sisters are here, look.

Whispering. Enter YERMA'S *two* SISTERS-IN-LAW. *They are dressed as if in mourning. They set about their washing amid a heavy silence. Sheep-bells can be heard.*

FIRST WOMAN. Are the shepherds going now?

THIRD WOMAN. Yes, the flocks are all leaving.

FOURTH WOMAN [*inhaling*]. I love the smell of sheep.

THIRD WOMAN. You do?

FOURTH WOMAN. Why shouldn't I? The smell of what belongs
to you. The way I love the smell of the red mud the river
brings down in winter.

THIRD WOMAN. Daft, I call it.

FIFTH WOMAN [*looking*]. The flocks are all moving together now.

FOURTH WOMAN. A great flood of wool. Sweeping everything
along with it. If the green wheat-stalks had eyes, they'd tremble to see it getting nearer.

THIRD WOMAN. Look at the sheep running! Like a horde of
enemy soldiers!

FIRST WOMAN. Now they've all gone, there's not one flock left
behind.

FOURTH WOMAN. Let's see. . . No. . . Oh, yes, there's one still to
come.

FIFTH WOMAN. Which is that?

FOURTH WOMAN. Victor's.
                           [*The two* SISTERS *straighten up and look*

FOURTH WOMAN [*singing*].
    In the stream's cool water
    I will wash your lace.
    Like jasmine warm and glowing
    the smile that lights your face.
    In that small jasmine snowfall
    I want to live always.

FIRST WOMAN.
    Weep, oh weep for the barren wife:
    the wife whose breasts are sand!

FIFTH WOMAN.
    Oh, tell me whether
    your man's seed sends
    the water singing
    through your shift.

FOURTH WOMAN.

> Your shift is a ship
> of silver and wind
> along the shore.

FIRST WOMAN.

> My baby's white linen
> I've come to wash
> and teach the water
> like crystal to flash.

SECOND WOMAN.

> My man comes down the mountain
> to eat with me.
> He brings for me a single rose:
> I give him three.

FIFTH WOMAN.

> My man came over the plain
> to sup with me.
> I'll wrap the burning coals he brought
> in myrtle leaves.

FOURTH WOMAN.

> My man comes flying through the air
> to sleep with me.
> I am gillyflowers red,
> a red gillyflower he.

FIRST WOMAN.

> Flower with flower shall be joined
> when summer dries the reaper's blood.

FOURTH WOMAN.

> And bellies welcome sleepless birds
> when winter trembles at the door.

FIRST WOMAN.

> Between our sheets we shall make moan.

FOURTH WOMAN.

> And we shall sing!

FIFTH WOMAN.

> When our men come to us
> with garlands and with bread.

FOURTH WOMAN.
> Because there will be arms entwined together.

SECOND WOMAN.
> Because a blaze of light will shatter in our throats.

FOURTH WOMAN.
> Because the branches' stem will fill with sweetness.

FIRST WOMAN.
> And windy canopies will overhang the mountains.

SIXTH WOMAN [*appearing at the summit of the falls*].
> So that a child may fuse as one
> the crystal shards of dawn.

FIRST WOMAN.
> And in our bodies we have branches,
> raging branches made of coral.

SIXTH WOMAN.
> So that there may be rowers
> on the waters of the sea.

FIRST WOMAN.
> A little child, a child!

SECOND WOMAN.
> And doves outstretch their wings and beaks.

THIRD WOMAN.
> A crying child, a son.

FOURTH WOMAN.
> The men come on like wounded stags.

FIFTH WOMAN.
> Rejoice, rejoice, rejoice
> for the belly roundly swollen beneath the smock!

SECOND WOMAN.
> Rejoice, rejoice, rejoice
> for the navel's tender cup of wonderment!

FIRST WOMAN.
> But weep, oh weep for the barren wife,
> the wife whose breasts are sand!

FOURTH WOMAN.
    Let her shine!

FIFTH WOMAN.
    Let her run!

FOURTH WOMAN.
    Let her shine again!

THIRD WOMAN.
    And sing!

SECOND WOMAN.
    And hide!

THIRD WOMAN.
    And sing again!

SIXTH WOMAN.
    My child bears in his apron
    the light of a new dawn.

ALL THE WOMEN IN CHORUS.
    In the stream's cool water
    I will wash your lace.
    Like jasmine warm and glowing
    the smile that lights your face.
    Ha! Ha! Ha!
        [*They agitate the clothes rhythmically and beat them*

CURTAIN

SCENE 2

YERMA's *house. It is growing dark.* JUAN *is seated.
The two* SISTERS *are standing.*

JUAN. You say she hasn't been out long? [*The* ELDER SISTER
shakes her head] She'll be fetching water. But you know very
well I don't like her going out alone. [*Pause*] You can lay the
table.   [*The* YOUNGER SISTER *exits*
The bread I eat is well earned, I tell you. [*To his* SISTER] I had
a tough day yesterday. I was pruning the apple trees, and as
it was getting dark I started wondering why I should sweat so

hard over it if I can't put a single apple in my own mouth. I've had enough. [*He wipes his hand over his face. Pause*] She's still not back. . . One of you should have gone with her, that's what you're here for, eating at my table and drinking my wine. My life is outside on the land, but my good name is in this house. And my good name is your good name as well. [*The* SISTER *bows her head*] Don't be upset. [YERMA *enters with two pitchers. She stops in the doorway*] You've been to the well?

YERMA. To get cool water to have with our meal. [*The other* SISTER *exits*] How are things on the land?

JUAN. I was pruning trees yesterday.

[YERMA *puts down the pitchers. Pause*

YERMA. You're staying tonight?

JUAN. I have to watch the sheep. You know that's the boss's job.

YERMA. Yes, I know. You don't need to tell me again.

JUAN. Every man has his life to get on with.

YERMA. And every woman hers. I'm not asking you to stay. I've got everything I need here. Your sisters keep a close watch on me. Here I eat fresh bread, and cheese, and roast lamb; and out on the hills your sheep eat grass wet with dew. I think you can live in peace.

JUAN. To live in peace you have to be easy in your mind.

YERMA. And you're not?

JUAN. No, I'm not.

YERMA. Adjust your sights.

JUAN. Don't you know the kind of man I am? The sheep in the fold, and the women in their houses. You go out too much. Haven't you heard me say that from the beginning?

YERMA. That's fine. The women in their houses. As long as the houses are not tombs. As long as the chairs get broken and the bedlinen gets worn out. But here it's not like that. Every night when I lie down I find a bed that's newer, more bright and gleaming than ever, as if it had just been delivered from town.

JUAN. You know yourself that I have a right to complain. That I have good reason to be on my guard.

YERMA. On guard against what? I don't do anything you can take exception to. I live completely under your thumb, and my suffering I keep locked up inside me. And it will get worse with every day that passes. Let's leave it alone. I'll bear my cross as best I can, but don't question me. If I could suddenly turn into an old woman with a mouth like a crumpled flower, I could give you a smile and cheerfully share my life with you. But now, just leave me alone with my pain.

JUAN. When you talk like that I don't understand you. I don't deprive you of anything. I send to the villages around for the things you like. I've got my faults, but I want to live with you in peace and quiet. I want to be able to sleep away from the house and know that you're sleeping too.

YERMA. But I don't sleep. I can't sleep.

JUAN. Is it because there's something you're wanting? Tell me. Answer me.

YERMA [*meaningfully and looking intently at her husband*]. Yes, there is something I want.   [*Pause*

JUAN. Always the same thing. It's over five years now. I've almost put it out of my mind.

YERMA. But I'm not you. Men have a whole other life: their animals, their trees, their talk among themselves; for women there's no life except having babies and bringing them up.

JUAN. Everyone's not the same. Why don't you take in one of your brother's children? I've no objection.

YERMA. I don't want to bring up other women's children. I'm sure my arms would freeze, just holding them.

JUAN. You drive yourself crazy, brooding over this the whole time; your mind is not where it should be; you're just determined to bang your head against a stone wall.

YERMA. And a wicked thing it is that it should be a stone wall, when it ought to be a basket of flowers and fresh water.

JUAN. Being with you makes a man uneasy, restless. When there's nothing to be done you should resign yourself.

YERMA. I didn't come to these four walls to resign myself. When I have a handkerchief tied round my head to keep my mouth shut and my hands bound together in my coffin, that's when I'll resign myself.

JUAN. So what do you want to do?

YERMA. I want to drink water, but there's no glass and no water; I want to climb up the mountain, but I've no feet; I want to embroider my petticoats, but I can't find any thread.

JUAN. The trouble is you're not a proper woman, and you're trying to ruin a man who's too easy-going.

YERMA. I don't know who I am. Let me go out and breathe. Not once have I ever let you down.

JUAN. I don't like people pointing me out. That's why I want to see that door kept shut and everyone inside their own house.

One of the SISTERS *enters slowly and moves towards a cupboard.*

YERMA. Talking to people is not a sin.

JUAN. But it can look like one. [*The other* SISTER *enters and makes for the pitchers from which she fills a jug. He lowers his voice*] I can't handle this kind of thing. When they start talking to you, keep your mouth shut and remember you're a married woman.

YERMA [*astonished*]. Married!

JUAN. And that every family has its good name, which it's everyone's duty to protect. [*The* SISTER *with the jug exits, slowly*] But that good name lives right where the blood races inside us; it's shadowy, remember, and easily destroyed. [*The other* SISTER *exits with a large dish, moving almost as if in a procession*] Forgive me. [YERMA *looks at her husband; he looks up and meets her gaze*] Although, the way you're looking at me, I shouldn't be asking you to forgive me, I should be forcing you to do what I want and locking you up, because that's how a husband is meant to behave.

The two SISTERS *appear in the doorway.*

YERMA. Please don't say any more. Leave it alone.   [*Pause*

JUAN. Let's eat. [*The* SISTERS *exit*] Did you hear?

YERMA [*sweetly*]. You go and eat with your sisters. I'm not hungry yet.

JUAN. Just as you like.   [*He exits*

YERMA [*as if in a dream*].
      Ah! great meadow sown only with grief!
      Ah! door that is barred against beauty!
      I seek a child to suffer, and the air
      offers me dahlias from the sleeping moon.
      These, my twin fountains of warm milk,
      throb in the thickness of my flesh
      like hoofbeats, like two pulsing steeds
      that thresh the branches of my pain.
      Blind breasts beneath my dress!
      Doves without eyes, without whiteness!
      Ah! how the pain of my imprisoned blood
      drives nails like stinging wasps into my neck!
      Yet surely you will come, my love, my child,
      for water yields its salt, the earth its fruit,
      and in our bellies we hold tender sons
      just as the clouds are bearers of sweet rain.
                             [*She looks towards the door*
María! Why are you hurrying past my door?

MARÍA [*entering with a child in her arms*]. When I have the little one with me, I do—because it always makes you cry!

YERMA. Yes, you're right.   [*She takes the child and sits*

MARÍA. It makes me sad to see you so jealous.   [*She sits*

YERMA. It's not jealousy I suffer from, it's poverty.

MARÍA. Don't complain.

YERMA. How can I help complaining when I see you and all the other women blossoming within, and see myself so useless with all that beauty around me?

MARÍA. But you have other things. You could still be happy, if you'd only listen to me.

YERMA. A country woman who doesn't have children is as useless as a bunch of thorns; she's a bad woman, I tell you, for
all that I'm one of those Godforsaken, barren wretches. [MARÍA
holds out her arms for the child] Take him; he's happier with
you. I just don't have a mother's hands, I suppose.

MARÍA. Why do you say that?

YERMA [*getting up*]. Because I'm sick of it, sick of having hands
and not being able to use them as they were meant to be used.
Because I feel hurt, hurt and utterly humiliated to see corn
always ripening, springs always giving water, sheep giving birth
to lambs by the hundred, bitches the same, and the whole
countryside, it seems, standing up to show me its sweet, sleepy
offspring, while here I feel two hammer-blows instead of my
baby's lips.

MARÍA. I don't like to hear you talk like that.

YERMA. You women who have children can't think about us
who are without. You're always cool and unaware, like people swimming in fresh water who have no idea what it's like
to be thirsty.

MARÍA. I don't like saying the same thing over and over again.

YERMA. My longing keeps growing as my hopes fade away.

MARÍA. That's terrible.

YERMA. I shall end up believing I'm my own child. I often go
down at night to feed the oxen, which I never used to do
because it's man's work, and when I walk through the sheds
in the dark my footsteps sound like a man's.

MARÍA. Every living creature has a purpose.

YERMA. In spite of everything he goes on wanting me. You see
what my life is?

MARÍA. How do you get on with the sisters?

YERMA. I'll be drawn and quartered before I'll say one word to
them.

MARÍA. What about your husband?

YERMA. It's three against one.

MARÍA. What do they think?

YERMA. They imagine things, as people do when they don't have a clear conscience. They believe I could fall for another man, and they don't understand that, even if I did, I come from a family that puts honour before everything. Stones in my path, that's what they are. But what they don't know is that, if I choose, I can turn into a raging torrent that will sweep away the lot of them.

One of the SISTERS *enters, and exits carrying a loaf of bread.*

MARÍA. All the same, I do believe your husband still loves you.

YERMA. My husband gives me board and lodging.

MARÍA. What a hard time you're having, what a lot of problems; but remember the sufferings of our Lord.

> [*They are in the doorway*

YERMA [*looking at the child*]. He's woken up.

MARÍA. He'll start singing in a minute.

YERMA. He's got your eyes, did you know that? Have you noticed? [*Weeping*] He's got your eyes!

> [YERMA *gently pushes* MARÍA, *who leaves in silence*

YERMA *goes over to the door by which her husband left.*

The SECOND GIRL *appears.*

SECOND GIRL. Pssst!

YERMA [*turning*]. What?

SECOND GIRL. I waited till she'd gone. My mother's expecting you.

YERMA. Is she alone?

SECOND GIRL. Two neighbours are there.

YERMA. Tell them to wait for a bit.

SECOND GIRL. Aren't you scared? You're really going?

YERMA. I'm going all right.

SECOND GIRL. Rather you than me!

YERMA. Tell them to wait for me however late it gets.

Enter VICTOR.

VICTOR. Is Juan in?

YERMA. Yes.

SECOND GIRL [*covering up*]. Right, I'll bring the blouse then.

YERMA. Whenever you like. [*The* GIRL *exits*] Sit down.

VICTOR. I'm all right as I am.

YERMA [*calling*]. Juan!

VICTOR. I've come to say goodbye.

YERMA [*a slight shiver passes through her, but she recovers her coolness*]. You're going to live with your brothers?

VICTOR. That's what my father wants.

YERMA. He must be very old now.

VICTOR. Yes, very old.   [*Pause*

YERMA. You're right to seek fresh fields.

VICTOR. All fields are the same.

YERMA. No. I'd like to get far away from here.

VICTOR. It's no different. The same wool on the same sheep.

YERMA. For men that's true, but for us women it's different. I've never heard a man say when he was eating, 'Aren't these apples good!' You do what you have to do without even noticing the little pleasures of life. I can tell you, I've come to loathe the water in this well.

VICTOR. Perhaps you're right.   [*The stage is in soft shadow*

YERMA. Victor.

VICTOR. Yes?

YERMA. Why are you going away? Everyone here is fond of you.

VICTOR. I've done the right things.   [*Pause*

YERMA. You've done the right things. When you were a strong young lad, you lifted me up in your arms once; don't you remember? We never know how things are going to turn out.

VICTOR. Everything changes.

YERMA. Some things don't change. There are things locked away behind closed doors that can't change because nobody hears them.

VICTOR. That's the way it is.

The YOUNGER SISTER *appears, and slowly makes her way to the outer door, where she remains still, lit by the last rays of daylight.*

YERMA. But, if they suddenly broke out and screamed, they'd echo round the whole world.

VICTOR. It wouldn't do any good. The water in the ditch, the sheep in their pen, the moon in the sky, and man at his plough.

YERMA. It's hard when we can't learn from what the old folk have to teach us!

   [*The long, melancholy sound of the shepherds' horns is heard*

VICTOR. The sheep.

JUAN [*entering*]. Are you off already?

VICTOR. I want to get through the pass before daybreak.

JUAN. Any complaints?

VICTOR. No. You paid a good price.

JUAN [*to* YERMA]. I've bought his sheep.

YERMA. Have you?

VICTOR [*to* YERMA]. They're yours now.

YERMA. I didn't know.

JUAN [*pleased*]. That's right.

VICTOR. Your husband's going to make his fortune.

YERMA. The labourer gets the fruit he cares about.

   [*The* SISTER *in the doorway withdraws into the house*

JUAN. We haven't got room for so many sheep.

YERMA [*darkly*]. The land is vast.   [*Pause*

JUAN. I'll go with you as far as the stream.

VICTOR. I wish this house every blessing.

   [*He holds out his hand to* YERMA

YERMA. May God hear what you say! Be happy!

> [VICTOR *starts to leave, but when* YERMA *makes a slight movement he turns back*

VICTOR. Did you say something?

YERMA [*with great intensity*]. I said, Be happy!

VICTOR. Thank you.

> [*They go.* YERMA *is left in anguish, looking at the hand she gave to* VICTOR. *Then she moves swiftly to the left and picks up a shawl*

> *The* SECOND GIRL *enters and covers* YERMA's *head without speaking.*

SECOND GIRL. Let's go.

YERMA. Let's go.   [*They leave stealthily*

> *The stage is almost dark. The* ELDER SISTER *enters with an oil lamp which brightens the stage by no more than its natural light. She moves to the edge of the stage, looking for* YERMA. *The shepherds' horns can be heard.*

ELDER SISTER [*softly*]. Yerma!

> *The* YOUNGER SISTER *enters. They look at each other and move towards the outer door.*

YOUNGER SISTER [*more loudly*]. Yerma!   [*She goes out*

ELDER SISTER [*also going to the door, and calling imperiously*]. Yerma!

> [*She goes out. Sound of hooting owls and shepherds' horns. The stage is very dark*

CURTAIN

ACT 3

SCENE 1

The house of DOLORES, *the wise woman. It is just before dawn. Enter* YERMA *with* DOLORES *and two* OLD WOMEN.

DOLORES. You've been brave.

FIRST OLD WOMAN. When you want something enough, you find the strength you need.

SECOND OLD WOMAN. But it was so dark in the graveyard.

DOLORES. Many's the time I've said those prayers in the graveyard with women longing for a baby, and they were all of them frightened. Except you.

YERMA. I'm here because of what will come of it. I don't think you're the kind who would deceive people.

DOLORES. I'm not. May my tongue crawl with ants, like the mouths of the dead, if I've ever told a lie. The last time I said the prayer was with a beggar-woman who'd been barren longer than you, and her belly grew so ripe and sweet she had two babes down by the river because she hadn't time to get herself to the houses, and she brought them herself wrapped in a cloth for me to see to them.

YERMA. And she managed to walk here all the way from the river?

DOLORES. She did. With her shoes and her petticoats all soaked in blood. . . but her face was shining.

YERMA. And she came to no harm?

DOLORES. What harm should she come to? God is God.

YERMA. Yes, of course. She could come to no harm. She only had to take hold of the little ones and wash them in the running water. Animals lick them clean, don't they? It wouldn't disgust me to do that with my baby. I have this idea that women who've just given birth are sort of lit up inside, and their babies lie asleep on them for hours and hours listening to the stream of warm milk filling their breasts for them to suck, for them to play with till they don't want any more and they turn their heads away—'a little drop more, my little one'— and in the end the baby's face and the mother's breast are covered with white splashes.

DOLORES. Now you will have a child. I promise you.

YERMA. I will have one because I must. Or else the world makes no sense. Sometimes, when I feel sure I never will. . . never. . . something like a wave of fire sweeps up through my feet, and everything around seems empty, and the men walking in the street, and the bulls, and the stones all seem made of cotton wool. And I ask myself: 'Why have they been put here?'

FIRST OLD WOMAN. Of course, it's natural for a married woman to want children, but, if they don't come, why break your heart over it? What matters in this life is to let the years carry you along. Oh, I'm not blaming you. You saw how I joined in the prayers. But what have you got to offer a son, what broad acres, what wealth and ease, what silver spoon?

YERMA. I don't think about the future; I think about now. You are old, and you see everything like a book you've read right through. All I can think about is that I'm parched and shackled. I want to hold my child in my arms so that I can sleep in peace, and—listen to this and don't be shocked by what I'm going to say—even if I knew that in time my son would torment me and hate me and drag me through the streets by the hair, I'd still be full of joy when he was born, because it's much better to weep over a real live man who sticks a knife into you than over this phantom I've had weighing on my heart for year after year.

FIRST OLD WOMAN. You're too young to listen to good advice. But, while you're waiting for God's grace, you should take comfort in the love of your husband.

YERMA. Ah! Now you've touched the deepest wound in my body.

DOLORES. Your husband is a good man.

YERMA [getting up]. He's a good man! Yes, he's a good man! Does that help? I wish he were a bad man. But he's not. He takes his sheep out to graze, and he counts his money at night.

When he covers me, he does his duty, but I feel his loins cold as if he had a corpse for a body. I've always felt there was something revolting about a hot-blooded woman, but at those moments I just wish I were a mountain of fire!

DOLORES. Yerma!

YERMA. I'm not a shameless wife; but I do know that it takes a man and a woman to have children. Oh, if I could only have them all by myself!

DOLORES. Remember, it's hard on your husband too.

YERMA. It isn't hard on him. He doesn't want children.

FIRST OLD WOMAN. Don't say that!

YERMA. I can see by the look in his eyes; he doesn't want them, and that's why he doesn't give them to me. I don't love him, I don't love him, and yet he's my only hope of salvation. For my own good name and my family's. My only hope of salvation.

FIRST OLD WOMAN [*fearfully*]. It'll be getting light soon. You ought to go home.

DOLORES. They'll be driving the flocks out any minute, and you'd best not be seen alone.

YERMA. It's been a relief to say all that. How many times do I recite the prayers?

DOLORES. The laurel prayer twice, and at midday the one to St Anne.* When you feel you're pregnant, bring me the bushel of wheat you promised.

FIRST OLD WOMAN. It's beginning to get light over the mountains. Go now!

DOLORES. They'll start opening their front doors in a minute; you'd better go round by the water.

YERMA [*disheartened*]. I don't know why I came!

DOLORES. Are you sorry you did?

YERMA. No!

DOLORES [*agitated*]. If you're afraid, I'll go with you as far as the corner.

FIRST OLD WOMAN [*uneasily*]. It will be broad daylight by the time you get to your door.   [*Voices are heard*

DOLORES. Quiet!   [*They listen*

FIRST OLD WOMAN. It's nobody. God go with you.
          [YERMA *moves towards the door, but at that moment
          there's a knock on it. The three women freeze*

DOLORES. Who's there?

JUAN'S VOICE. It's me.

YERMA. Open the door.   [DOLORES *hesitates*
     Are you going to open it or not?
                              [*Murmuring voices are heard*
          JUAN *appears, with the two* SISTERS.

YOUNGER SISTER. There she is.

YERMA. Here I am.

JUAN. What are you doing in this place? If I could shout it
     aloud, I'd rouse the whole village and let them all see what's
     been happening to the good name of my house; but I have to
     choke it back and keep quiet because you are my wife.

YERMA. If I could shout it aloud, then so would I, and even
     rouse the dead to witness how clean and innocent I am.

JUAN. No! Don't talk like that! I can stand anything, but not
     that. You make a fool of me, you muddle me up, and, because
     I'm only a simple man who works on the land, I can't cope
     with your cunning ways.

DOLORES. Juan!

JUAN [*to* DOLORES *and the* OLD WOMEN]. You keep out of this.

DOLORES [*forcefully*]. Your wife has done nothing wrong.

JUAN. She's been doing wrong ever since the day we got mar-
     ried. Looking at me with eyes like needles, lying awake all
     night beside me, with her eyes wide open and breathing wicked
     sighs all over my pillow.

YERMA. Be quiet!

JUAN. And I can't take any more of it. You'd have to be made
     of bronze to live with a woman who wants to poke her fingers
     right into your heart and goes out at night from her house,
     looking for what, I ask you. Tell me, what does she go looking

for? The streets are full of men. You don't go out on the streets to pick flowers.

YERMA. I won't let you say another word. Not one. You and your people, you think you're the only ones who look after your good name; you ought to know that my family has never had anything to hide. Come here, come close to me and smell my clothes; closer! See if you find a trace of any smell but your own, anything which isn't from your body. Stand me naked in the middle of the square and spit on me. Do what you want with me, I'm your wife, but don't you dare label me any man's woman but yours.

JUAN. I'm not the one who does that; you do it yourself by the way you behave, and the village is beginning to say so. They're beginning to say so loud and clear. When I go up to a group of people, they stop talking; when I take flour to the buyer's, everyone stops talking; and even when I wake up in the night, out in the fields, the branches of the trees seem to stop talking.

YERMA. I don't know why the air turns spiteful and blows down the corn, when you can see the corn is good!

JUAN. And I don't know what a woman goes looking for out of her house at all hours.

YERMA [*in a burst of emotion, clinging to her husband*]. It's you I'm looking for. I'm looking for you. It's you I go looking for, day and night, and never find any shade where I can breathe. It's your blood I long for, your help I need.

JUAN. Get away.

YERMA. Don't push me away: love me and want what I want.

JUAN. Stop it.

YERMA. See how alone I am. Like the moon roaming the sky in search of itself. Look at me!   [*She looks at him*

JUAN [*he looks at her and pushes her away roughly*]. Once and for all, get away from me.

DOLORES. Juan!   [YERMA *falls to the floor*

YERMA [*crying out*]. When I went out to pick my carnations, I ran into a stone wall. Ay! Ay! Against that wall I'm doomed to smash my head to pieces!

JUAN. Quiet. Let's go.

DOLORES. Oh, my God!

YERMA [*shouting*]. A curse on my father for giving me his blood
that could have fathered a hundred children! A curse on my
blood that goes hammering on the walls in search of them!

JUAN. Quiet, I said!

DOLORES. There are people coming. Keep your voice down.

YERMA. I don't care. At least let my voice be free. Now that I'm
going to sink into the deepest darkness of the pit. [*She gets up*]
At least let this one beautiful thing come out of my body and
let it fill the air.   [*Voices are heard*

DOLORES. They're coming this way.

JUAN. Be quiet.

YERMA. Yes. That's right. Be quiet. Don't worry.

JUAN. Let's go. Quickly!

YERMA. That's how it is. That's how it's to be. It's no use my
wringing my hands. To want something in your head is one
thing. . .

JUAN. Quiet!

YERMA [*softly*]. To want something in your head is one thing,
but it's another thing when your body—damn the body!—
won't do what you want. That's how it's fated to be, and I'm
not going to fight bare-handed against the ocean. That's how
it has to be. From now on let my mouth be dumb.

                                                  [*She goes out*

RAPID CURTAIN

FINAL SCENE

*The vicinity of a shrine, high up in the mountains. In the
foreground some cartwheels and blankets form* YERMA's
crude tent. WOMEN *enter, bringing offerings to the shrine.
They are barefoot. On stage is the lively* PAGAN OLD WOMAN
from Act 1.

SONG [*heard before the curtain rises*].

>   I could never see your body
>   before you were wed.
>   Now you're married I shall find you.
>   I could never see your body
>   before you were wed.
>   I'll strip you naked when I find you,
>   a pilgrim now and wed,
>   when in the dark the clock strikes twelve.

PAGAN WOMAN [*mischievously*]. Have you drunk the holy water yet?

FIRST WOMAN. Yes.

PAGAN WOMAN. And now you're going to see him in there?

SECOND WOMAN. We have faith in him.

PAGAN WOMAN. You come to ask the Saint for children, and what happens? Every year more and more men come on their own to join the pilgrimage. I wonder what goes on?

[*She laughs*

FIRST WOMAN. Why are you here if you've no faith?

PAGAN WOMAN. To watch. I love to watch it all. And to look after my son. Last year two men killed each other over one of the barren wives, and I want to keep an eye on things. But, when it comes down to it, I'm here because I feel like being here.

FIRST WOMAN. May God forgive you!   [*The* WOMEN *exit*

PAGAN WOMAN [*sarcastically*]. May God forgive you!

[*She goes*

Enter MARÍA *and the* FIRST GIRL.

FIRST GIRL. Has she come, then?

MARÍA. That's the cart over there. I had a hard job getting them to come. For the past month she hasn't got up from her chair. She scares me. She's got some idea in her head; I don't know what it is, but it's something bad, that's for sure.

FIRST GIRL. I came with my sister. She's been coming for eight years and nothing's happened.

MARÍA. A woman has children if she's meant to have them.

FIRST GIRL. That's what I say.   [*Voices are heard*

MARÍA. I've never liked this pilgrimage. Let's go down to the threshing-floors, that's where everyone is.

FIRST GIRL. Last year, when it got dark, some lads started mauling my sister's breasts.

MARÍA. You hear nothing but wicked talk for miles around this place.

FIRST GIRL. I saw over forty barrels of wine stacked behind the hermitage.

MARÍA. There's a river of single men flowing down these mountains.

Voices are heard. YERMA *enters with six* WOMEN *on their way to the church. They are barefoot and carrying twisted candles. Night is beginning to fall.*

MARÍA.   Lord, let the rose bloom;
              let it not lie in shadow.

SECOND WOMAN.
              In her withered flesh
              let the yellow rose bloom.

MARÍA.   And in the womb of thy handmaiden
              the dark flame of the earth.

CHORUS.   Lord, let the rose bloom;
              let it not lie in shadow.   [*They kneel*

YERMA.   In Heaven there are gardens
              with rose-trees full of joy.
              All among the rose-trees
              one wondrous rose
              like a ray of dawn.
              An archangel guards it
              with wings of storm
              and death-dealing eye.
              All about its leaves
              streams of warm milk play,
              sprinkling the faces
              of the quiet stars.

Lord, let thy rose open
in my withered flesh.   [*They stand up*

SECOND WOMAN.

Lord, cool with thy hand
the fire in her cheeks.

YERMA.   O hear thy penitent
on holy pilgrimage.
Open thy rose in my flesh,
though it be fraught with thorns.

CHORUS.   Lord, let the rose bloom;
let it not lie in shadow.

YERMA.   In my withered flesh
thy wondrous rose.   [*They exit*

Four GIRLS *run on stage from the left with long streamers in
their hands, and exit. From the right come three more with
long ribbons, looking back over their shoulders; they also
exit. There is a kind of crescendo of voices on stage with the
sound of cowbells and harness bells. On an upper level the
seven* GIRLS *appear, waving their ribbons towards the left.*

*The noise increases, and two masked mummers come on,
one as a male, the other as a female. They are wearing large
folk masks. The* MALE *is clutching a bull's horn in his hand.*

*They are in no way grotesque, but singularly beautiful and
redolent of pure earthiness. The* FEMALE *is shaking a necklace
of large bells.*

CHILDREN. The devil and his wife! The devil and his wife!

*The rear of the stage fills with people who shout and cheer
the dancers on. It has grown very dark.*

FEMALE.

In the river in the mountains
the unhappy wife was bathing,
and creeping up her body
went shining snails of water.
The sand along the shore
and the breezes of the morning
put fire into her laughter
and a quivering in her shoulders.

Ah! naked to the wide world
was the maiden in the stream.

BOY.   Ah! how she was lamenting!

FIRST MAN.
Ah! starved she was of love
amid the water and the wind!

SECOND MAN.
Let her name the man she hopes for!

FIRST MAN.
Let her name the man she waits for!

SECOND MAN.
Sad the dryness of her belly
and her colour that is lost!

FEMALE.
When night comes I shall tell,
when night comes clear.
When night comes to the pilgrimage
I'll tear my petticoats apart.

BOY.   And all at once night fell.
Ah! how it fell!
See how dark it is,
the mountain waterfall.

                                          [The sound of guitars is heard

MALE [*getting up and brandishing his horn*].
How pale she is, how white,
the unhappy wife!
Ah! how she moans amid the branches!
You shall be poppy and carnation red
when the man's cloak lies outspread.

                                          [He draws nearer

If you have come on the pilgrimage
to ask that your womb may flower,
don't dress yourself in a mourning veil
but a shift of smoothest linen.
Go walking alone behind the walls
where the fig-trees crowd together,

and bear my body that's of the earth
till the first pale cry of dawn.
Ah! how she shines!
Ah! how she shone!
Ah! how the wedded woman shifts and sways!

FEMALE.

Ah! how love decks her out
with garlands and bright crowns,
while darts of flashing gold
strike deep into her breast!

MALE.   Seven times she cried aloud,
nine times she rose upright;
and fifteen times they joined as one
the jasmine to the orange.

THIRD MAN.

On with the horn, the horn!

SECOND MAN.

On with the rose and the dance.

THIRD MAN.

Ah! how the wedded woman shifts and sways!

MALE.   On this pilgrimage
the man will have his way.
Husbands are bulls,
the man will have his way.
The pilgrim women are like flowers
for the stronger man to pluck.

BOY.   On with the breeze, the breeze!

SECOND MAN.

On with the branches, on!

MALE.   Come and see how she shines,
the woman that was bathing.

THIRD MAN.

She bends like a reed.

BOY.   She wilts like a flower.

MEN.   Little girls, away now!

MALE.   Let the dance catch fire!
And the gleaming body blaze
of the wife washed clean.
[*They dance off smiling and clapping their hands. They sing*
In heaven there are gardens
with rose-trees of joy.
All among the rose-trees
one wondrous rose.

Two GIRLS *pass by again, shouting.*
Enter the cheerful PAGAN OLD WOMAN.

PAGAN WOMAN.   We'll see if you let us get some sleep tonight.
But it won't be that sort of night.

YERMA *enters.*

You! [YERMA *is downcast and says nothing*] Tell me, what did
you come for?

YERMA.   I don't know.

PAGAN WOMAN.   Don't you believe in it? What about your
husband?
[YERMA *shows signs of exhaustion; she behaves like one tormented by an obsession*

YERMA.   He's over there.

PAGAN WOMAN.   What is he doing?

YERMA.   Drinking. [*Pause. She puts her hand to her forehead*]
Ay!

PAGAN WOMAN.   Ay, ay! Let's have less moaning and more spirit.
I couldn't tell you anything before, but now I can.

YERMA.   And what can you tell me that I don't know already?

PAGAN WOMAN.   What can't be kept secret any longer. What's
screaming out from the rooftops. It's your husband that's to
blame. Do you hear me? You can cut off my hands if I tell a
lie. Look at his father, and his grandfather, and his great-
grandfather—a poor sort of breed, every one of them. Heaven
and earth had to come together before they could father a
child. They're all made of spit. But your people are different.

You've got brothers and sisters and cousins for a hundred miles around. See what a curse has fallen on a lovely girl like you.

YERMA. A curse. The ears of corn swamped in poison.

PAGAN WOMAN. But you've got a pair of legs to walk out of your house.

YERMA. To walk out?

PAGAN WOMAN. When I saw you on the pilgrimage, my heart turned over. Women come here to find another man, and the Saint works the miracle. My son is sitting behind the shrine, waiting. My house needs a woman. Join up with him and we'll all three live together. My son has good blood in his veins. Like me. You'll find the smell of babies there still, if you come to my house. Your bed of ashes will turn to bread and salt for your little ones. Go on! Never mind what people say. As for your husband, we've got the guts and the weapons to stop him even crossing the road.

YERMA. Stop, stop! That's not the answer! I'd never do that. I can't go looking for another man. Do you suppose I could give myself to anyone else? What price do you put on my honour? Water can't run uphill and the full moon can't come out at midday. Get away from me. I'll carry on as I am. Did you really think I could submit to another man? That I'd beg him like a slave for what is my right? Know who I am, so that you'll never speak to me again. I'm not on the hunt.

PAGAN WOMAN. A thirsty woman is grateful for water.

YERMA. I'm like a parched field big enough to be ploughed by a thousand yoke of oxen, and what you're offering me is a tiny glass of water from the well. My pain strikes deeper than the flesh.

PAGAN WOMAN [*forcefully*]. Go on as you are, then. It's your choice. Like the thistles in the dry lands, all prickly and withered.

YERMA [*vehemently*]. Withered, yes, I know that! Withered! You don't have to ram it down my throat. Don't gloat over it like little children over some poor creature in its death throes. Ever since I got married, that word has been going round and round in my head, but this is the first time I've heard it spoken, the first time I've had it thrown in my face. The first time I've realized that it's the truth.

PAGAN WOMAN. I've no pity for you, none. I'll find another woman for my son.

> [*She goes. A great chorus of pilgrims is heard singing in the distance. As* YERMA *moves over to the cart, her husband appears from behind it*

YERMA. You were there?

JUAN. I was there.

YERMA. Spying?

JUAN. Spying.

YERMA. And you heard everything?

JUAN. Yes.

YERMA. What of it? Leave me alone, go and sing with the rest.

> [*She sits on the blankets*

JUAN. It's time I had my say as well.

YERMA. Say it, then.

JUAN. And time I complained.

YERMA. What about?

JUAN. About the bitterness I have in my throat.

YERMA. And what about the bitterness I have in my bones?

JUAN. I can't bear it a moment longer—this constant wailing over things that are shadowy, things that have nothing to do with real life, phantoms floating in the air.

YERMA [*with dramatized astonishment*]. Things that have nothing to do with real life, you say? Phantoms, you say?

JUAN. Things that haven't happened, and that you and I have no control over.

YERMA [*violently*]. Go on! Go on!

JUAN. Things that don't matter to me. Do you hear? They don't matter to me. At last I have to tell you straight. What matters to me is what I can hold in my hands, what my eyes can see.

YERMA [*straightening up on her knees, desperately*]. That's it! That's it! That's what I wanted to hear from your own lips. The truth doesn't make itself felt when it's inside you, but how huge it is, how it screams when it moves outside and raises its arms. It doesn't matter to him! At last I've heard him say it!

JUAN [*drawing closer to her*]. Believe me, this is how it had to be. Listen to me. [*He puts his arms round her to raise her to her feet*] A lot of women would be happy with the life you have. Without children life is sweeter. I'm happy not having them. We've no reason to feel guilty.

YERMA. Then what did you want from me?

JUAN. You yourself.

YERMA [*frenziedly*]. That's right! You wanted a home, peace and quiet, and a woman. And that's all. Is that true, what I'm saying?

JUAN. It's true. Like any man.

YERMA. And what about the rest? What about your son?

JUAN [*vehemently*]. Didn't you hear me say it doesn't matter to me? Stop questioning me! Must I shout it in your ear before you can get it into your head and lead a quiet life at last?

YERMA. And you've never thought about your son when you've seen me longing for him?

JUAN. Never.   [*They are both on the ground*

YERMA. And I'm not to go on hoping he will come?

JUAN. No.

YERMA. And neither will you?

JUAN. Neither will I. Resign yourself.

YERMA. Withered!

JUAN. And let's live in peace. The two of us, contentedly, pleasantly. Hold me close!   [*He puts his arms round her*

YERMA. What is it you want?

JUAN. I want you. Just you. In the moonlight you look so beautiful.

YERMA. You want me in the same way that you want to eat a pigeon.

JUAN. Kiss me... like this.

YERMA. Like that I never will. Never.

> [YERMA *cries out and grips her husband's throat. He falls backward. She squeezes his throat until she has killed him. The pilgrims' chorus begins*

YERMA. Withered, withered, but sure of it. Now I know for certain that it's true. And I'm alone. [*She gets up. People start to gather*] Now I shall rest easy without startling myself awake to see if my blood gives promise of new blood. My body barren now and for ever. What do you want to know? Don't come near me, I have killed my son. With my own hands I've killed my son!

> [*A group of people gathers upstage. The pilgrims' chorus can be heard*

CURTAIN

THE HOUSE OF
BERNARDA ALBA

A Drama about the Women who
Live in the Villages of Spain

(1936)

CHARACTERS

Bernarda, aged 60
María Josefa (Bernarda's mother), aged 80
Angustias (Bernarda's daughter), aged 39
Magdalena (Bernarda's daughter), aged 30
Amelia (Bernarda's daughter), aged 27
Martirio (Bernarda's daughter), aged 24
Adela (Bernarda's daughter), aged 20
Poncia, aged 60
Maid, aged 50
Prudencia, aged 50
Beggar Woman
Little Girl
First Woman
Second Woman
Third Woman
Fourth Woman
Girl
Women Mourners

The author gives notice that these three acts are intended as a photographic document.

ACT 1

A whiter-than-white inner room of BERNARDA's *house.*
Thick walls. Arched doorways with hessian curtains edged
with tassels and flounces. Rush-bottomed chairs. Pictures
of nymphs or legendary kings in unrealistic landscapes.
It is summer. A great shadowy silence pervades the stage.
When the curtain rises the stage is empty. Sound of
tolling bells.

The MAID *enters.*

MAID. I've got those bells tolling right inside my head.

PONCIA [*entering, eating bread and spiced sausage*]. More than
two hours they've been moaning away. Priests have come from
all the villages around. The church looks lovely. Before they'd
got through the first anthem Magdalena fainted.

MAID. She's the one who'll miss him most.

PONCIA. She's the only one their father loved. Ay! Thank God
we've got the place to ourselves for a bit. I came back for
something to eat.

MAID. If Bernarda could see you!

PONCIA. Just because she's not eating she'd like us all to starve.
Giving her orders! Bossing everyone about! But I've fooled
her. I've been into her sausage-jar.

MAID [*with sad longing*]. Can't you give me some for my little
girl, Poncia?

PONCIA. Help yourself, and grab a handful of chickpeas while
you're about it. Today she won't notice.

VOICE [*within*]. Bernarda!

PONCIA. There's the old woman. You're sure she can't get out?

MAID. I double-locked the door.

PONCIA. But you have to put the bar across as well. She's got
fingers like five skeleton keys.

VOICE. Bernarda!

PONCIA [*shouting*]. She's coming! [*To the* MAID] Give the whole place a good clean. If Bernarda doesn't see everything gleaming, she'll yank out the few hairs I've got left.

MAID. What a woman!

PONCIA. She lords it over everyone around her. She'd sit on your heart and watch you die for a whole year and never once wipe that cold smile off her blasted face. Scrub those dishes, get them clean!

MAID. My hands are bleeding from so much scrubbing.

PONCIA. She has to be the cleanest, the most respectable, the most superior. Her poor husband's earned a good rest.

[*The bells stop*

MAID. Have all the relations come?

PONCIA. Hers have. His people hate her. They came to view the body and say a prayer over him, that's all.

MAID. Are there enough chairs?

PONCIA. Plenty. They can sit on the floor. Since Bernarda's father died, people have stopped coming into this house. She doesn't like to be seen in her own little kingdom. To hell with her!

MAID. She's been good to you.

PONCIA. Thirty years washing her sheets, thirty years eating her left-overs, sleepless nights when she's got a cough, days on end peeping through the shutters to spy on the neighbours and pass on the gossip to her; never a secret that we haven't shared between us, but damn and blast her all the same, may she roast in hell!

MAID. Poncia!

PONCIA. I'm a good dog, though: I bark when she tells me to, and I snap at beggars' heels when she sets me on them; my sons work on her land, and now both of them are married, but one day I'll have had enough.

MAID. And then...

PONCIA. And then I shall shut myself up in a room with her and spit at her for a whole year without stopping: 'This is for this, Bernarda, this for that, and this for the other,' till she looks like a lizard squashed to bits by little boys, which is what she is, her and all her tribe. She's welcome to her life, I say. Five girls she's left with, five ugly daughters, and barring Angustias, the eldest, her child by her first husband who's got some money of her own, the rest—lots of frills, lots of linen petticoats, but bread and grapes is all they can expect to inherit.

MAID. I wish I had what they've got!

PONCIA. All we have is our hands, and a hole in God's earth to look forward to.

MAID. That's the only land they give to people like us, who've got nothing.

PONCIA [*at the cupboard*]. There are specks on this glass.

MAID. Soap won't shift them, or dishcloths or anything.

[*The bells ring*

PONCIA. They're getting to the end. I'm going over to listen. I love the way the priest sings. In the 'Our Father' his voice went up and up, higher and higher, like a pitcher slowly filling with water. Of course, it cracked in the end, but it's glorious to hear him. Mind you, there's nobody like the old sexton; Treecleaver they called him. He sang at the mass for my mother, God rest her soul. The walls trembled, and when he reached the Amen you'd have thought a wolf had got into the church. [*Imitating him*] AME—EE—N!! [*She has a fit of coughing*

MAID. You'll strain your windpipe.

PONCIA. I'd sooner strain something else!

[*She exits, laughing*
[*The* MAID *gets on with her cleaning. The bells ring*

MAID [*imitating the tune*]. Ding, ding, dong. Ding, ding, dong. God have mercy on him.

BEGGAR WOMAN [*entering with a* LITTLE GIRL]. Praise be to God!

MAID. Ding, ding, dong. Many years may it be before we join him! Ding, ding, dong.

BEGGAR WOMAN [*loudly, rather irritated*]. Praise be to God!

MAID [*irritated*]. For ever and ever!

BEGGAR WOMAN. I've come for the leftovers. [*The bells cease*

MAID. The way to the street is out through that door. Today I'm getting the leftovers.

BEGGAR WOMAN. Oh, come on, you've got a man to look after you. We're all alone, me and my little girl.

MAID. Dogs are all alone too, and they manage.

BEGGAR WOMAN. They always give them to me.

MAID. Get out of here! Who said you could come in? Leaving your footmarks on my floor! [*They leave. She goes on with her cleaning*] Floors shone with oil, cupboards and plant-stands and steel beds; a bitter pill to swallow for those of us who live in hovels with one plate and one spoon. I only hope one day there'll be none of us left to tell the tale! [*The bells start ringing again*] Yes, yes, clang away! They can put you in a coffin with gold inlay and silken slings to carry it! You'll still end up just the same as me! Rot you, Antonio María Benavides, stiff in your broadcloth suit and high boots. Rot you! You won't be lifting up my skirts again behind your stable door!

From the rear of the stage WOMEN MOURNERS *begin to enter two by two with large black shawls, black skirts, and black fans. They come in slowly until they fill the stage.*

MAID [*starting to wail*]. Ay, Antonio María Benavides, never again will you see these walls or eat the bread of this house! Of all your servants I'm the one who loved you most. [*Tearing her hair*] Must I go on living now that you are gone? Must I go on living?

When the two hundred women have all entered, BERNARDA *and her five* DAUGHTERS *appear.* BERNARDA *is leaning on a stick.*

BERNARDA [*to the* MAID]. Be quiet!

MAID [*weeping*]. Bernarda!

BERNARDA. Less wailing and more work. You should have got the whole place cleaner, ready for the mourners. Get out. You don't belong here. [*The* MAID *goes, sobbing*] The poor are like animals. You'd think they were made out of different ingredients.

FIRST WOMAN. The poor feel their afflictions just the same.

BERNARDA. Give them a plateful of chickpeas and they soon forget them.

GIRL [*timidly*]. We can't live without eating.

BERNARDA. At your age you should hold your tongue in front of your elders.

FIRST WOMAN. You be quiet, my girl.

BERNARDA. I've never let anyone tell me what's what. Sit down.
[*They sit. Pause*

BERNARDA [*loudly*]. Magdalena, don't cry. If you want to cry, get under your bed. Do you hear me?

SECOND WOMAN [*to* BERNARDA]. Have you started on the threshing?

BERNARDA. Yesterday.

THIRD WOMAN. The sun beats down like lead.

FIRST WOMAN. It's years since I've known it so hot.
[*Pause. They all fan themselves*

BERNARDA. Is the lemonade ready?

PONCIA [*entering with a large tray full of little white mugs that she hands round*]. Yes, Bernarda.

BERNARDA. Give some to the men.

PONCIA. They're drinking it in the yard.

BERNARDA. They can leave the way they came in. I don't want them tramping through here.

GIRL [*to* ANGUSTIAS]. Pepe el Romano was with the men in church.

ANGUSTIAS. Yes, he was.

BERNARDA. His mother was there. She saw his mother. She didn't see Pepe and neither did I.

GIRL. I thought. . .

BERNARDA. I tell you who *was* there, the widower from Darajalí. Sitting next to your aunt. We all saw him all right.

SECOND WOMAN [*aside, softly*]. She's wicked, she's really evil.

THIRD WOMAN [*aside, softly*]. She's got a tongue like a knife.

BERNARDA. The only man women should look at in church is the priest, and that's only because he's in skirts. When they look around it's a bit of trouser-comfort they're after.

FIRST WOMAN [*softly*]. Frustrated old lizard!

PONCIA [*muttering*]. All twisted and knotted up with wanting it herself!

BERNARDA [*striking the floor with her stick*]. Praise be to God!

ALL [*crossing themselves*]. For ever blessed and praised.

BERNARDA.   Rest in peace, in the holy
             company of saints.

ALL. Rest in peace.

BERNARDA.   With St Michael the archangel
             and his sword of justice.

ALL. Rest in peace.

BERNARDA.   With the key that opens every lock
             and the hand that closes every door.

ALL. Rest in peace.

BERNARDA.   With all the blessed ones
             and the little lights of the field.

ALL. Rest in peace.

BERNARDA.   With our holy charity
             and all souls by land and sea.

ALL. Rest in peace.

BERNARDA. Grant rest to thy servant Antonio María Benavides and give him the crown of thy sacred glory.

ALL. Amen.

BERNARDA [*stands and sings*]. Requiem aeternam dona eis, Domine.

ALL [*standing and chanting in the Gregorian style*]. Et lux perpetua luceat eis.*   [*They cross themselves*

FIRST WOMAN. God grant you good health to pray for his soul.
                                           [*They are filing out*

THIRD WOMAN. You shall not lack a fresh-baked loaf.

SECOND WOMAN. Nor a roof for your daughters.

> [*They all pass in front of* BERNARDA *and exit.*
> ANGUSTIAS *leaves by another door, the one
> that leads into the yard*

FOURTH WOMAN. May the corn of your marriage-harvest never
fail you.*

PONCIA [*entering with a purse*]. From the men, this bag of money
to say prayers for him.

BERNARDA. Thank them and give them a glass of brandy.

GIRL [*to* MAGDALENA]. Magdalena.

BERNARDA [*to* MAGDALENA, *who is bursting into tears*]. Shhh!
[*She bangs with her stick. All the women exit. When they
have gone she addresses them*] Back home to your caves all of
you and pull to pieces everything you've seen today. I hope it
will be many a year before you cross my threshold again.

PONCIA. You've nothing to complain about. The whole village
came.

BERNARDA. Yes, to fill my house with the stink of their greasy
linen and the poison of their tongues.

AMELIA. Mother, don't talk like that!

BERNARDA. That's the only way to talk in this damned riverless
place, this village full of wells where every time you drink the
water you're afraid it might be poisoned.

PONCIA. Look what they've done to the floor!

BERNARDA. You'd think a herd of goats had been over it. [PONCIA
cleans the floor] Give me a fan, girl.

ADELA. Here you are.

> [*She gives her a round fan decorated with red and
> green flowers*

BERNARDA [*flinging the fan to the floor*]. Is that the sort of fan
to give to a widow? Give me a black one and have some
respect for your father's memory.

MARTIRIO. Take mine, mother.

BERNARDA. What about you?

MARTIRIO. I don't feel hot.

BERNARDA. Well, you'd better find yourself another because you're going to need it. We've eight years mourning ahead of us, and while it lasts no breath of air from the street is going to get into this house. It's going to be as if we'd bricked up the doors and windows. That's how it was in my father's house and in my grandfather's before him. You can pass the time embroidering your trousseaus. I've got twenty bolts of linen in the chest for you to make sheets and pillowcases. Magdalena can embroider them.

MAGDALENA. I'm not interested.

ADELA [*sharply*]. If you don't want to embroider them, they'll stay plain. So yours will look better.

MAGDALENA. I'm not doing mine any more than I'm doing yours. I know I'm not going to get married. I'd rather carry sacks to the mill. Anything rather than sit in this dark room day after day.

BERNARDA. That's what being a woman's all about.

MAGDALENA. Then damn all women.

BERNARDA. What I say goes in this house. You can't go running to your father any more. A needle and thread for females; a mule and a whip for the man. That's the way of it for people born to a certain position in life.   [ADELA *exits*

VOICE. Bernarda, let me out!

BERNARDA [*shouting*]. You can let her out now!

The MAID *enters.*

MAID. I've had a hard job holding her. Eighty years old, and your mother's as strong as an oak.

BERNARDA. It runs in the family. My grandmother was the same.

MAID. More than once while the funeral was going on I had to gag her with an empty sack because she wanted to shout to you to bring her some dishwater to drink if nothing else, and a lump of dogmeat, which is what she says you give her.

MARTIRIO. She's a wicked old woman.

BERNARDA [*to the* MAID]. Put her in the yard to cool off.

MAID. She took her rings and the amethyst earrings out of the box; she put them on, and told me she wanted to get married.
                                             [*The* DAUGHTERS *laugh*

BERNARDA. Go with her and see she doesn't go near the well.

MAID. Don't worry, she won't jump in!

BERNARDA. It's not that. If she's there, the neighbours can see her from their windows.   [*The* MAID *exits*

MARTIRIO. We'd better go and change.

BERNARDA. Yes, but don't take off your headscarves. [ADELA *enters*] Where's Angustias?

ADELA [*sardonically*]. I saw her peering through the crack in the gate. The men had just left.

BERNARDA. And what were you doing by the gate, may I ask?

ADELA. I went to see if the hens had laid.

BERNARDA. But the men at the funeral must have gone by now!

ADELA [*pointedly*]. There were some still standing around outside.

BERNARDA [*furiously*]. Angustias! Angustias!

ANGUSTIAS [*entering*]. Yes, mother, what do you want?

BERNARDA. What were you looking at? And who?

ANGUSTIAS. Nobody.

BERNARDA. Is it fitting for a woman of your class to go running after a man on the day of her father's funeral? Answer me! Who were you looking at?   [*Pause*

ANGUSTIAS. I...

BERNARDA. Yes, you!

ANGUSTIAS. Nobody.

BERNARDA [*advancing on her with her stick*]. You slippery, sugary little humbug!   [*Strikes her*

PONCIA [*rushing to* BERNARDA]. Bernarda, calm down!
                                             [*She restrains her*
                                             [ANGUSTIAS *is weeping*

BERNARDA. Get out of here, all of you! [*The* DAUGHTERS *exit*

PONCIA. She did it without realizing what she was doing; it was quite wrong of her, of course. I was really shocked to see her sneaking off to the yard! Then she went and stood by a window, listening to the conversation the men were having, which as usual was not fit to be heard.

BERNARDA. That's what they come to funerals for! [*Curiously*] What were they talking about?

PONCIA. They were talking about Paca la Roseta. Last night they tied her husband up in a cowshed, and her they slung over a horse and carried off to the top of the olive grove.

BERNARDA. And how did she take that?

PONCIA. Oh, she didn't object. They say she went with her breasts hanging out, and Maximiliano held her as if he was playing a guitar. Dreadful!

BERNARDA. And what happened?

PONCIA. What you'd expect to happen. It was almost daylight when they came back. Paca la Roseta had her hair down and a crown of flowers on her head.

BERNARDA. She's the only bad woman we have in the village.

PONCIA. Because she doesn't come from here. She's from a long way off. And the men who went with her, their folk are from other parts too. The men from here wouldn't do such a thing.

BERNARDA. No, but they enjoy watching it, and talking about it, and licking their chops over such a thing happening.

PONCIA. They were talking about a lot of other things as well.

BERNARDA [*shifting her gaze somewhat fearfully*]. What things?

PONCIA. Things I'd be ashamed to repeat.

BERNARDA. And my daughter heard them?

PONCIA. Of course she did!

BERNARDA. She's just like her aunts, that one: all pale and greasy they were, and making sheep's eyes at any piddling little barber that buttered them up. What a deal of suffering and struggling it takes to get people to behave decently and show a little civilized self-control!

PONCIA. Well, your daughters have reached their years of discretion. They give you precious little to worry about. Angustias must be way over thirty by now.

BERNARDA. Thirty-nine to be precise.

PONCIA. Well, just think. And she's never had a sweetheart.

BERNARDA [*furious*]. No, none of them has ever had a sweetheart, and they don't need one. They can do very well without.

PONCIA. I didn't mean to upset you.

BERNARDA. There's no one worthy of them within a hundred miles of here. The men of these parts are not in their class. Do you want me to let them go to some farmhand?

PONCIA. You should have moved somewhere else.

BERNARDA. I see, to put them on the market!

PONCIA. No, Bernarda, just to make a change... Of course, in other places *they*'d be the poor ones!

BERNARDA. You just hold your spiteful tongue!

PONCIA. It's impossible to talk to you. Can we be frank with each other or can't we?

BERNARDA. No, we can't. You're my servant and I pay you. That's all!

Enter the MAID.

MAID. Don Arturo is here. He's come to sort out the legacies.

BERNARDA. Right! [*To the* MAID] You can go outside and start whitewashing. [*To* PONCIA] And you can start putting away all the dead man's clothes in the big chest.

PONCIA. Some of the things we could give...

BERNARDA. Nothing! Not a single button! Not even the handkerchief we used to cover his face!

> [*She exits slowly, leaning on her stick, with a last look back at her servants. They leave after her*

Enter AMELIA *and* MARTIRIO.

AMELIA. Have you taken your medicine?

MARTIRIO. For all the good it will do me.

AMELIA. But you have taken it?

MARTIRIO. I've no faith in things, but I still do them, regular as clockwork.

AMELIA. You've been more lively since the new doctor came.

MARTIRIO. I don't feel any different.

AMELIA. Did you notice? Adelaida wasn't at the funeral.

MARTIRIO. I knew she wouldn't be. Her young man won't let her go out, not even on to the doorstep. She used to be always laughing; now she doesn't even put powder on her face.

AMELIA. It's hard to know whether it's better to be engaged or not.

MARTIRIO. It's the same either way.

AMELIA. What causes the trouble is all this scandal-mongering that will never let us be. Adelaida must really have been through it.

MARTIRIO. She's scared of Mother. Mother's the only one who knows the true story of her father and how he got his land. Every time she comes here Mother keeps needling her with it. In Cuba Adelaida's father killed his first wife's husband so that he could marry her himself. When they came here, he deserted her and ran off with another woman who already had a daughter; then he took up with the daughter—Adelaida's mother—and married her when the second wife went mad and died.

AMELIA. And why isn't the monster in gaol?

MARTIRIO. Because with things like that men always cover up for each other and nobody can prove anything.

AMELIA. But Adelaida's not to blame for any of that.

MARTIRIO. No, but history repeats itself. I can see that everything always follows the same dreadful pattern. So she'll have the same fate as her mother and her grandmother, both of them wife to the man who fathered her.

AMELIA. How awful!

MARTIRIO. It's better never to set eyes on a man. I've always been frightened of them, ever since I was a child. I used to watch them in the yard, yoking the oxen and heaving sacks of wheat, shouting and stamping their feet, and I was always afraid of growing up, scared that they'd suddenly fling their arms round me. God made me weak and ugly so that they'd have nothing to do with me.

AMELIA. Don't say that! Enrique Humanes was after you, and he found you attractive.

MARTIRIO. That was just gossip. I stayed at the window once in my nightdress till it was daylight because he sent word by his farmhand's daughter that he was going to come, and he never came. It was all just talk. Then he married another girl with more money than me.

AMELIA. And as ugly as sin!

MARTIRIO. What do they care about ugliness! All they care about is land, teams of oxen, and a docile little bitch who'll dish up their food.

AMELIA [*sighing*]. Aaah!

Enter MAGDALENA.

MAGDALENA. What are you doing?

MARTIRIO. Nothing. We're here, that's all.

AMELIA. Where've you been?

MAGDALENA. All round the house. Just to stretch my legs. I was looking at the pictures Grandma embroidered, the little poodle and the black man wrestling with the lion, that we liked so much when we were little. Those were happier times! A wedding went on for ten days and people didn't go in for nasty gossiping. It's more refined now. Brides wear a white veil like in the big towns and we drink bottled wine, but we fester inside over what people might be saying about us.

MARTIRIO. God knows what went on in those days!

AMELIA [*to* MAGDALENA]. Your shoelace is undone.

MAGDALENA. Well?

AMELIA. You'll trip over it and fall down.

MAGDALENA. One mouth less to feed!

MARTIRIO. Where's Adela?

MAGDALENA. Well now! She put on the green dress she made to wear on her birthday, out she went to the yard and started yelling: 'Chickens, chickens, look at me!' I had to laugh.

AMELIA. Just as well Mother didn't see her!

MAGDALENA. Poor little thing! The youngest of us all and she still nurses her dreams. I'd give a lot to see her happy.

Pause. ANGUSTIAS *crosses the stage carrying some towels.*

ANGUSTIAS. What time is it?

MARTIRIO. It must be twelve by now.

ANGUSTIAS. As late as that?

AMELIA. It's just about to strike.   [*Exit* ANGUSTIAS

MAGDALENA [*knowingly*]. Have you heard?

[*Indicating* ANGUSTIAS

AMELIA. No.

MAGDALENA. Oh, come on!

MARTIRIO. I don't know what you're talking about.

MAGDALENA. You two know more about it than I do, always with your heads together like two little lambs and keeping it all to yourselves. I mean about Pepe el Romano.

MARTIRIO. Ah!

MAGDALENA [*mimicking her*]. Ah! It's all round the village already. Pepe el Romano wants to marry Angustias. He was roaming round the house last night, and I don't think it'll be long before he sends someone to speak for him.

MARTIRIO. I'm so pleased! He's a fine man.

AMELIA. Me too. Angustias has a lot to offer.

MAGDALENA. You're not pleased, either of you.

MARTIRIO. Magdalena! Really!

MAGDALENA. If he were interested in Angustias for herself, for Angustias as a woman, I'd be pleased; but what interests him is the money. Angustias is our sister I know, but here within these four walls we may as well admit that she's old and sickly and that she's always been the least attractive of any of us. I mean, if she looked like a scarecrow when she was twenty, what does she look like now that she's forty!

MARTIRIO. Don't talk like that. Luck comes to those who least expect it.

AMELIA. There's no getting away from it, she's right. Angustias has her father's money, she's the only rich woman in the house; and so, now that our father's dead and the estate is being shared out, they're coming for her.

MAGDALENA. Pepe el Romano is twenty-five and he's the best catch for miles around. The natural thing would be if he were after you, Amelia, or little Adela who is only twenty, but not that he should come asking for the dreariest one in the house, a woman who talks through her nose like her father before her.

MARTIRIO. Perhaps that's what he likes!

MAGDALENA. What a delicious little hypocrite you are!

MARTIRIO. May God forgive us!

Enter ADELA.

MAGDALENA. Have the chickens had a good look at you, then?

ADELA. So what was I supposed to do?

AMELIA. If Mother sees you, she'll tear your hair out!

ADELA. I had such dreams about that dress. I was going to wear it the day we were planning to eat water-melons down by the pump. There wouldn't have been another to compare with it.

MARTIRIO. It is a lovely dress.

ADELA. And it suits me so well. It's the best Magdalena's ever made.

MAGDALENA. What did the chickens think of it?

ADELA. They presented me with a set of fleas that had a good go at my legs!   [*Laughter*

MARTIRIO. What you could do is dye it black.

MAGDALENA. The best thing you can do is give it to Angustias for her wedding with Pepe el Romano!

ADELA [*with suppressed emotion*]. But Pepe el Romano. . .

AMELIA. Hadn't you heard?

ADELA. No.

MAGDALENA. Well, you know now!

ADELA. But it's impossible!

MAGDALENA. Money makes everything possible.

ADELA. Is that why she went out of here after the funeral to go and peep through the gate? [*Pause*] And that man could actually bring himself to. . .

MAGDALENA. Why not? What wouldn't he do?   [*Pause*

MARTIRIO. What are you thinking, Adela?

ADELA. What I'm thinking is that this period of mourning has come upon me at the time in my life when I'm least able to stand it.

MAGDALENA. You'll soon get used to it.

ADELA [*breaking into angry tears*]. No, no, I won't get used to it. I don't want to be shut in. I don't want my body to moulder like yours. I don't want the whiteness of my skin to fade away in these rooms! Tomorrow I'm going to put on my green dress and I'm going out into the street for a walk. I want to go out!

The MAID *enters.*

MAGDALENA [*sternly*]. Adela!

MAID. Poor girl! She feels the loss of her father!   [*She exits*

MARTIRIO. Stop it!

AMELIA. We're all in it together.   [ADELA *calms down*

MAGDALENA. The maid almost heard you.

MAID [*reappearing*]. Pepe el Romano is coming down the street!
          [AMELIA, MARTIRIO, *and* MAGDALENA *are galvanized into action*

MAGDALENA. Let's go and see him!   [*They rush out*

MAID [*to* ADELA]. Aren't you going?

ADELA. It's of no interest to me.

MAID. He'll be coming round the corner, so the window of your room will be a better place to see him.   [*She exits*
              [ADELA *hesitates. After a moment she quickly exits
              too in the direction of her room*

                        Enter BERNARDA *and* PONCIA.

BERNARDA. Damned legacies!

PONCIA. What a lot of money for Angustias!

BERNARDA. Yes.

PONCIA. And a lot less for the others.

BERNARDA. You've already said that to me three times and I've chosen not to reply. A lot less, yes, a great deal less. Don't go on reminding me.

            Enter ANGUSTIAS, *her face heavily powdered.*

BERNARDA. Angustias!

ANGUSTIAS. Mother.

BERNARDA. Have you had the audacity to put powder on your face? Have you had the audacity even to wash your face on the day of your father's funeral?

ANGUSTIAS. He wasn't my father. Mine died a long time ago. Have you forgotten he existed?

BERNARDA. You owe more to this man, your sisters' father, than you do to your own. Thanks to him your cup is overflowing.

ANGUSTIAS. That remains to be seen.

BERNARDA. If only out of common decency. Out of respect!

ANGUSTIAS. Mother, please let me go.

BERNARDA. Let you go? When I've wiped that powder off your face. Soft-soaping hypocrite! Jezebel! Just like your aunts! [*She roughly wipes off the powder with her handkerchief*] Now get out!

PONCIA. Don't be so harsh, Bernarda!

BERNARDA. My mother may be mad, but I've still got my wits about me, and I know perfectly well what I'm doing.

Enter the other DAUGHTERS.

MAGDALENA. What's going on?

BERNARDA. Nothing's going on.

MAGDALENA [*to* ANGUSTIAS]. If it's the will you're arguing about, you've got more money than any of us; you might as well keep the lot.

ANGUSTIAS. You just put a peg on your tongue!

BERNARDA [*striking the floor with her stick*]. Don't any of you imagine you're going to get the better of me! Till the day I go out of this house feet first, what I say goes—for me and for all of you.

Voices are heard, and MARÍA JOSEFA, *Bernarda's mother, enters. She is a very old woman, decked out with flowers on her head and breast.*

MARÍA JOSEFA. Bernarda, where's my mantilla? I don't want any of you to have any of my things. Not my rings, nor my black moiré dress, nothing. Because none of you are going to get married. Not one of you! Bernarda, give me my pearl choker!

BERNARDA [*to the* MAID, *who has followed* MARÍA JOSEFA]. Why did you let her in here?

MAID [*trembling*]. She got away from me!

MARÍA JOSEFA. I got away because I want to get married, because I want to get married to a fine handsome man from the sea-shore; the men of these parts won't have anything to do with women.

BERNARDA. Be quiet, mother!

MARÍA JOSEFA. No, no, I won't be quiet. I hate the sight of these spinster women, dying to get married, eating their hearts out. I want to go back to my village. Bernarda, I want a real man, so that I can be married and be happy!

BERNARDA. Lock her up!

MARÍA JOSEFA. Let me go out, Bernarda!

[*The* MAID *takes hold of* MARÍA JOSEFA

BERNARDA. Help her, all of you.

[They all seize the old woman

MARÍA JOSEFA. I want to get away from here! Bernarda! I want to get married down by the sea, down by the sea!

QUICK CURTAIN

ACT 2

A white inner room in BERNARDA's *house. The doors on the left lead to the bedrooms. Bernarda's* DAUGHTERS, *except for* ADELA, *are sitting on low chairs, sewing.* MAGDALENA *is embroidering.* PONCIA *is with them.*

ANGUSTIAS. I've cut the third sheet.

MARTIRIO. That'll be for Amelia.

MAGDALENA. Angustias, do I put Pepe's initials on as well?

ANGUSTIAS [*brusquely*]. No.

MAGDALENA [*calling out*]. Adela, aren't you coming?

AMELIA. I expect she's lying down.

PONCIA. There's something wrong with that girl. She seems restless, shaky, scared—as if she had a lizard between her breasts!

MARTIRIO. What's wrong with her is exactly the same as what's wrong with all of us.

MAGDALENA. All of us except Angustias.

ANGUSTIAS. *I* feel fine, and whoever doesn't like it can go to blazes.

MAGDALENA. Of course, you've always been known for your lovely figure and your exquisite manners.

ANGUSTIAS. Fortunately, I shall soon be getting out of this hell.

MAGDALENA. Perhaps you won't!

MARTIRIO. Let's change the subject.

ANGUSTIAS. And, let me tell you, you get further by having gold in your purse than dark eyes in your face.

MAGDALENA. Carry on, it's in one ear and out the other as far as I'm concerned.

AMELIA [*to* PONCIA]. Open the outside door, will you, and see if we can get some cool air in here.   [PONCIA *does so*

MARTIRIO. Last night I couldn't get to sleep for the heat.

AMELIA. Nor could I!

MAGDALENA. I got up to cool off. There was a black storm cloud, it even rained a few drops.

PONCIA. The earth hadn't stopped giving off heat at one in the morning. I got up too. Angustias was still at the window talking to Pepe.

MAGDALENA [*ironically*]. So late! What time did he go?

ANGUSTIAS. Magdalena, why do you need to ask if you saw him?

AMELIA. He must have gone at about half past one.

ANGUSTIAS. Yes, he did. And how do *you* know?

AMELIA. I heard him coughing, and I heard the sound of his pony moving off.

PONCIA. But I heard him go at about four o'clock!

ANGUSTIAS. That couldn't have been him.

PONCIA. I'm sure it was.

MARTIRIO. I thought so too.

MAGDALENA. That's very strange!   [*Pause*

PONCIA. Hey, Angustias, what did he say to you the first time he came to the window?

ANGUSTIAS. Nothing. What do you think he said? Just this and that.

MARTIRIO. It really is very peculiar that two people who've never met should suddenly get together at the bars of a window, and there they are, engaged!

ANGUSTIAS. Well, it didn't bother me.

AMELIA. I'd feel a bit funny about it.

ANGUSTIAS. No, you wouldn't, because when a man goes to the window bars he already knows from all the go-betweens who've been fetching and carrying that he's going to be accepted.

MARTIRIO. All right, but he's still got to ask you.

ANGUSTIAS. Of course!

AMELIA [*with curiosity*]. So how did he ask you?

ANGUSTIAS. Nothing special: 'You know I'm interested in you, I need a good, modest wife and you're the one for me if you're agreeable.'

AMELIA. I find these things so embarrassing!

ANGUSTIAS. So do I, but they have to be gone through.

PONCIA. Did he say anything else?

ANGUSTIAS. Yes, he did all the talking.

MARTIRIO. What about you?

ANGUSTIAS. I couldn't have said anything. My heart was practically in my mouth. It was the first time I'd been alone at night with a man.

MAGDALENA. And such a gorgeous man!

ANGUSTIAS. He's not bad-looking.

PONCIA. That's how it is with people who have some education and know how to speak and say things and wave their hands about. . . The first time my husband, Evaristo the Finches, came to my window. . . Ha, ha, ha!

AMELIA. What happened?

PONCIA. It was very dark. I saw him coming, and, when he got to me, he said: 'Good evening.' 'Good evening,' I said, and we didn't say another word for more than half an hour. I was sweating all over. Then Evaristo got closer and closer as if he was going to squeeze himself through the bars, and he said very softly: 'Come here, let me feel you!'
       [*They all laugh.* AMELIA *jumps up and looks out at one of the doors*

AMELIA. Lord! I thought Mother was coming.

MAGDALENA. We'd have got it in the neck!
       [*They go on laughing*

AMELIA. Shhh! She'll hear us.

PONCIA. After that he behaved himself. Instead of taking to other things, he took to breeding finches till the day he died. You unmarried women might as well know that a fortnight after the wedding the man moves from the bed to the table and then from the table to the local bar. And if the woman doesn't go along with it she's left to rot in a corner weeping her heart out.

AMELIA. You went along with it.

PONCIA. I could handle him all right!

MARTIRIO. Is it true you hit him a few times?

PONCIA. Yes, and once I nearly poked his eye out!

MAGDALENA. That's how all women should be!

PONCIA. I'm from the same school as your mother. He said something or other to me one day, and I took the pestle to his finches and killed the lot for him.   [*They laugh*

MAGDALENA [*calling*]. Adela, pet, this is too good to miss!

AMELIA. Adela!   [*Pause*

MAGDALENA. I'll go and find her.   [*She exits*

PONCIA. She's not well, that child.

MARTIRIO. That's a fact, she hardly sleeps.

PONCIA. What does she do, then?

MARTIRIO. How do I know what she does?

PONCIA. You must know better than I do, sleeping in the room next to hers.

ANGUSTIAS. She's eaten up with envy.

AMELIA. Don't exaggerate.

ANGUSTIAS. You can tell from her eyes. They're beginning to take on the look of a madwoman.

MARTIRIO. Don't talk about madness. This is the one place where that word must never be spoken.

Enter MAGDALENA *and* ADELA.

MAGDALENA. You weren't asleep, then?

ADELA. I don't feel well.

MARTIRIO [*insinuatingly*]. Because you didn't sleep last night?

ADELA. Yes.

MARTIRIO. Well, then?

ADELA [*vehemently*]. Leave me alone! It's none of your business whether I sleep or not. My body's my own to do as I like with.

MARTIRIO. It's only that I'm concerned about you.

ADELA. Concerned or curious. Weren't you sewing, all of you? Well, get on with it. I wish I were invisible, so that I could walk round the house without you all wanting to know where I'm going!

MAID [*entering*]. Bernarda wants you. The man with the lace is here.

    [*They go. As she leaves,* MARTIRIO *looks hard at* ADELA

ADELA. Stop staring at me. If you like, I'll make you a present of my bright young eyes, and my back so that you can get rid of that hump you've got; but just look the other way when I go by.   [*Exit* MARTIRIO

PONCIA. Adela, she is your sister, and she's the one who loves you most of all!

ADELA. She follows me everywhere. Sometimes she peeps into my room to see if I'm asleep. She won't let me breathe. And always: 'Such a shame about that pretty face! Such a shame about that body which will never belong to anyone!' Well, she's wrong! My body will be given to whoever I choose!

PONCIA [*significantly and softly*]. To Pepe el Romano you mean, don't you?

ADELA [*taken aback*]. What are you talking about?

PONCIA. You heard what I said, Adela.

ADELA. Be quiet.

PONCIA [*loudly*]. Do you think I haven't noticed?

ADELA. Don't talk so loud!

PONCIA. Smother those thoughts!

ADELA. What do you know?

PONCIA. Old women like me can see through walls. Where do you go when you get up in the night?

ADELA. It's a pity you're not blind!

PONCIA. I've got eyes all over my head and my hands when it comes to this sort of thing. But I just can't work out what you're up to. Why did you stand there practically naked with the light burning and the window open the second time Pepe came by to speak to your sister?

ADELA. That's not true!

PONCIA. Stop behaving like a child! Leave your sister alone, and, if you do fancy Pepe el Romano, just control yourself. [ADELA *bursts into tears*] Anyway, who says you can't be his wife? Your sister Angustias is not a healthy woman. The first child will finish her. She's narrow-hipped, she's old, and I know enough about it to tell you she'll be dead soon enough. Then Pepe will do what all the widowers do in these parts: he'll marry the youngest and prettiest girl, and that's you. Nourish that hope, or else put him out of your mind, but don't go against God's law.

ADELA. Be quiet!

PONCIA. I won't be quiet.

ADELA. Mind your own business. You nosey, treacherous old bitch!

PONCIA. I'll be on your tail like your own shadow.

ADELA. Instead of cleaning the house and going to bed to pray for your dead, you have to root around like an old sow for what goes on between men and women so you can slobber over it.

PONCIA. I keep watch; to make sure people don't spit as they go past the door of this house.

ADELA. You've grown very fond of my sister all of a sudden!

PONCIA. I'm not all that devoted to any of you, but I do want to live in a respectable house. I don't want to be smirched in my old age!

ADELA. You can keep your advice. It's too late now. You won't stop me, you're only a servant; not even my mother's going to stop me from quenching this fire I feel blazing in my legs and my mouth. What can you say about me? That I shut myself in my room and won't open the door? That I don't sleep? I'm cleverer than you! See if you can catch the hare: she won't fall into your hands.

PONCIA. Don't you defy me. Don't you defy me, Adela! Because I can give the alarm, set the lights blazing and the bells ringing.

ADELA. You can put four thousand yellow flares all round the walls of the yard. What has to happen will happen, and nobody can stop it.

PONCIA. That man really means so much to you!

ADELA. So much! When I look into his eyes, I feel I'm slowly drinking his blood.

PONCIA. I can't bear to listen to you.

ADELA. Well, you *will* listen to me! I was afraid of you. But now I'm stronger than you are.

Enter ANGUSTIAS.

ANGUSTIAS. Arguing as usual!

PONCIA. What do you expect? She wants me to go to the shop in all this heat and bring her Lord knows what.

ANGUSTIAS. Did you get me that bottle of perfume?

PONCIA. The most expensive one. And the powder. I put them on the table in your room.   [*Exit* ANGUSTIAS

ADELA. Just keep your mouth shut!

PONCIA. We'll see about that.

Enter MARTIRIO, AMELIA, *and* MAGDALENA.

MAGDALENA [*to* ADELA]. Have you seen the lace?

AMELIA. What we chose for Angustias' bridal sheets is so beautiful.

ADELA [*to* MARTIRIO, *who is holding some lace*]. What's that for?

MARTIRIO. It's for me. For a petticoat.

ADELA [*sarcastically*]. You must have a sense of humour.

MARTIRIO [*pointedly*]. It's for me to see. *I* don't have to show myself off to anyone.

PONCIA. Nobody sees a woman in her petticoat.

MARTIRIO [*pointedly, looking at* ADELA]. Sometimes they do! But I love underwear. If I were rich, I'd always wear the best Holland linen. It's one of the few pleasures I have left.

PONCIA. This lace is lovely for babies' bonnets and christening gowns. I could never afford it for mine. Now we'll see if Angustias uses it for hers. If she starts a family, you'll all be sewing from morning to night.

MAGDALENA. I've no intention of sewing a single stitch.

AMELIA. Much less looking after someone else's children. Look at the women down the lane, their whole lives sacrificed to four little snivellers.

PONCIA. They're better off than you are. At least they have a good laugh down there, and you can hear the kids biffing each other.

MARTIRIO. You'd better go and work for them, then.

PONCIA. No. I've made my bed here and I'll have to lie on it.
    [A jingling of little bells is heard as though through
    several thicknesses of wall

MAGDALENA. It's the men going back to work.

PONCIA. It's just struck three.

MARTIRIO. In this heat!

ADELA [as she sits]. Oh, if we could only go out to the fields like them!

MAGDALENA [as she sits]. Each class has to do what's prescribed for it.

MARTIRIO [as she sits]. That's how it is!

AMELIA [as she sits]. Ay!

PONCIA. There's no place happier than the fields at this time of year. Yesterday morning the reapers arrived. Forty or fifty fine-looking lads.

MAGDALENA. Where are they from this year?

PONCIA. A long way away. From up in the mountains. Full of fun. Tanned dark as trees. Shouting and throwing stones! Last night a woman came to the village dressed in sequins and dancing to an accordion, and fifteen of them made a deal with her to go with them to the olive-grove. I stood apart and watched. The one who fixed it with her was a boy with green eyes, as trim as a sheaf of wheat.

AMELIA. Is that true?

ADELA. I can't believe it!

PONCIA. Another of those women came, years ago now, and I gave my eldest boy money myself so that he could go with her. Men need that sort of thing.

ADELA. They get away with everything.

AMELIA. The worst punishment is to be born a woman.

MAGDALENA. Not even our eyes are our own.

> [*Distant singing is heard, coming closer*

PONCIA. It's them. Lovely songs they sing.

AMELIA. They're going out now to the reaping.

> [*Tambourines and rattles* are heard. There is a pause in the conversation. The women all listen in a silence shot through with sunlight*

CHORUS.
> The reapers are going to cut the corn,
> going to see that the ears are shorn;
> the girls who are watching them this fine day
> will find that their hearts have been swept away.

AMELIA. The heat doesn't bother them.

MARTIRIO. They reap in the blazing sun.

ADELA. I'd like to be a reaper so that I could come and go. That's the way to forget what's eating us away.

MARTIRIO. What have you got that you want to forget?

ADELA. We all have our private griefs.

MARTIRIO [*profoundly*]. All of us!

PONCIA. Shhh! Quiet!

CHORUS [*very far off*].
> Open your doors and windows wide,
> you girls who in this village bide:
> the reapers want you to throw them posies
> to trim their hats with bright red roses.

PONCIA. Lovely song!

MARTIRIO [*nostalgically*].
> Open your doors and windows wide,
> you girls who in this village bide...

ADELA [*passionately*].
> ...The reapers want you to throw them posies
> to trim their hats with bright red roses.

> > [*The singing fades into the distance*

PONCIA. Now they're turning the corner.

ADELA. Let's go and see them from the window in my room!

PONCIA. See you don't open it too wide, they might give it a push to find out who's looking.

> [ADELA, MAGDALENA, *and* PONCIA *go out.* MARTIRIO *remains seated on the low chair with her head in her hands*

AMELIA [*going to her*]. What's the matter?

MARTIRIO. The heat makes me feel ill.

AMELIA. Is that all it is?

MARTIRIO. I'm just longing for it to be November, for rainy days, for frost; anything but this endless summer.

AMELIA. It will pass, and then come round again.

MARTIRIO. I know! [*Pause*] What time did you go to sleep last night?

AMELIA. I don't know. I sleep like a log. Why do you ask?

MARTIRIO. No reason, but I thought I heard voices in the yard.

AMELIA. Voices?

MARTIRIO. Very late.

AMELIA. Weren't you frightened?

MARTIRIO. No. I've heard them before, on other nights.

AMELIA. We should protect ourselves. Couldn't it be the farmhands?

MARTIRIO. The farmhands come at six.

AMELIA. A little untamed mule, perhaps.

MARTIRIO [*muttering, very pointedly*]. Exactly! A little untamed mule.

AMELIA. We must warn everyone.

MARTIRIO. No, no! Don't say anything. Perhaps it's just a funny feeling I have.

AMELIA. Perhaps.   [*Pause.* AMELIA *makes to leave*

MARTIRIO. Amelia.

AMELIA [*at the door*]. What?   [*Pause*

MARTIRIO. Nothing.   [*Pause*

AMELIA. Why did you call me back?   [*Pause*

MARTIRIO. I didn't mean to. I spoke without thinking. [*Pause*

AMELIA. Go and lie down for a while.

ANGUSTIAS [*bursting angrily on to the stage so as to create a great contrast with the preceding interchange pregnant with silences*]. Where is the picture of Pepe I had under my pillow? Which of you has got it?

MARTIRIO. Nobody's got it.

AMELIA. Not even if Pepe were a silver St Bartholomew.*

Enter PONCIA, MAGDALENA, *and* ADELA.

ANGUSTIAS. Where is that picture?

ADELA. What picture?

ANGUSTIAS. One of you has hidden it.

MAGDALENA. You have the nerve to say that?

ANGUSTIAS. It was in my room, and it's not there now.

MARTIRIO. Don't you think it might have got out into the yard during the night? Pepe likes wandering around in the moonlight.

ANGUSTIAS. Don't try to be funny with me. When he comes, I'll tell him.

PONCIA. Don't do that: it's sure to turn up!

                    [*Looking at* ADELA

ANGUSTIAS. I'd love to know which one of you has got it!

ADELA [*looking at* MARTIRIO]. Somebody has! But it's certainly not me.

MARTIRIO [*pointedly*]. Oh no, of course not!

BERNARDA [*entering with her stick*]. What's this uproar going on in my house, and right in the middle of the afternoon heat when everyone's quiet? The neighbours must have their ears glued to the walls.

ANGUSTIAS. They've taken my fiancé's picture.

BERNARDA [*fiercely*]. Who has? Who?

ANGUSTIAS. They have!

BERNARDA. Which one of you? [*Silence*] Answer me! [*Silence. To* PONCIA] Go and search their rooms. Look in the beds.

[*Exit* PONCIA

This is what comes of giving you too much rein. But I'll make you sorry! [*To* ANGUSTIAS] Are you sure?

ANGUSTIAS. Yes.

BERNARDA. Have you looked everywhere?

ANGUSTIAS. Yes, mother.

[*They are all standing in an embarrassed silence*

BERNARDA. At the end of my days you're making me drink the bitterest poison a mother can swallow.

[*To* PONCIA *as she enters*]. You can't find it?

PONCIA. Here it is.

BERNARDA. Where was it?

PONCIA. It was...

BERNARDA. Speak out. Don't be afraid.

PONCIA [*wonderingly*]. Between the sheets of Martirio's bed.

BERNARDA [*to* MARTIRIO]. Is that true?

MARTIRIO. Yes, it is!

BERNARDA [*bearing down on* MARTIRIO *and hitting her with her stick*]. Damn your eyes, you sly puss, you troublemaker!

MARTIRIO [*fiercely*]. Don't you hit me, mother!

BERNARDA. I'll hit you as much as I like!

MARTIRIO. Only if I let you! Do you hear me? Get back!

PONCIA. Don't be disrespectful to your mother.

ANGUSTIAS [*taking hold of* BERNARDA]. Leave her alone. Please!

BERNARDA. There's not even a tear in those eyes of yours.

MARTIRIO. I'm not going to cry just to please you.

BERNARDA. Why did you take the picture?

MARTIRIO. Can't I play a joke on my sister? What else would I want it for?

ADELA [*breaking out, filled with jealousy*]. It wasn't a joke, you've never liked playing games. It was something else building up inside you, bursting to get out. Why don't you make a clean breast of it?

MARTIRIO. Be quiet and don't force me to speak, because, if I do, the walls will cling together in shame.

ADELA. There's no limit to the lies a wicked tongue will think up!

BERNARDA. Adela!

MAGDALENA. You're mad, both of you.

AMELIA. Inflicting your wicked thoughts on us.

MARTIRIO. There are those who do things even more wicked.

ADELA. Till they end up stripped naked and the river sweeps them away.

BERNARDA. Depraved creature!

ANGUSTIAS. It's not my fault that Pepe el Romano chose me.

ADELA. For your money.

ANGUSTIAS. Mother!

BERNARDA. Quiet!

MARTIRIO. For your acres and your orchards.

MAGDALENA. That's the truth of it!

BERNARDA. Quiet, I say. I saw the storm coming, but I didn't think it would break so soon. Ay, what a torrent of hatred you've unleashed on my heart! But old age hasn't caught up with me yet, and I've got five chains to bind you with besides this house my father built, so that not even the grass outside will hear of my humiliation. Get out of here! [*They leave.* BERNARDA *sits down desolately.* PONCIA *is standing, leaning against the wall.* BERNARDA *recovers, bangs on the floor with her stick, and says*] I must make them feel the weight of my hand. Bernarda, just you remember that's your duty.

PONCIA. May I speak?

BERNARDA. Go on. I'm sorry you heard all that. It's never good to let an outsider in on family matters.

PONCIA. What I've seen, I've seen.

BERNARDA. Angustias must be married at once.

PONCIA. That's right, she must be got away from here.

BERNARDA. Not her, him!

PONCIA. Yes, *he* must be got away from here. Good thinking.

BERNARDA. I'm not thinking. There are things that can't and shouldn't be thought. I give orders, that's all.

PONCIA. Do you think he'll be willing to go?

BERNARDA [*getting up*]. What's going on in that head of yours?

PONCIA. Of course, it's Angustias he'll marry!

BERNARDA. Go on. I know you well enough to see you've got the knife sharpened for me.

PONCIA. I never expected to hear a warning called a murder.

BERNARDA. Have you got something to warn me about?

PONCIA. I make no accusations, Bernarda. All I say is: open your eyes and you'll see for yourself.

BERNARDA. What will I see?

PONCIA. You've always been quick. You've always seen from miles away when people were up to no good. I've often thought you must be a mind-reader. But with your own children it's a different story. In this case you're blind.

BERNARDA. Do you mean Martirio?

PONCIA. Let's say Martirio... [*Probing*] Now why would she have hidden the picture?

BERNARDA [*trying to shield her daughter*]. She said it was a joke, didn't she? What other reason could there be?

PONCIA [*mockingly*]. You really believe that's what it was?

BERNARDA [*vehemently*]. It's not what I believe. It's the truth!

PONCIA. All right. It's your own daughter we're talking about. But supposing it was the girl over the road, what would you think then?

BERNARDA. Now you're going to stick the knife in.

PONCIA [*relentlessly cruel*]. No, Bernarda: there's something very serious going on here. I don't want to put the blame on you, but you've never given your daughters any freedom. Martirio falls in love easily, no matter what you say. Why didn't you let her marry Enrique Humanes? On the very day he was going to come to her window you sent and stopped him: why?

BERNARDA [*fervently*]. I'd do it again a thousand times over! My blood and the blood of the Humanes will never be mingled as long as I live. His father was a farmhand.

PONCIA. And this is what you get for putting on such airs and graces!

BERNARDA. If I put on airs it's because I can afford to. And you can't because you know very well where you came from.

PONCIA [*with hatred*]. There's no need to remind me! I'm old now. I've always been grateful for your protection.

BERNARDA [*drawing herself up*]. It doesn't look like it!

PONCIA [*with hatred masked by sweetness*]. Martirio will put all this behind her.

BERNARDA. It will be the worse for her if she doesn't. I don't believe that's the 'something very serious' that you say is going on here. But there's nothing going on here. It's only what you'd like to see! And, if something did go on here one day, you can be sure it wouldn't be known outside these four walls.

PONCIA. I'm not so sure about that! There are other folk in the village who can read people's secret thoughts from a distance.

BERNARDA. Wouldn't you just love to see me and my daughters on our way to the whorehouse!

PONCIA. We none of us know what's in store for us!

BERNARDA. I know what's in store for me. And for my daughters. As to the whorehouse, we can leave that to a certain woman no longer with us...

PONCIA [*fiercely*]. Bernarda, respect my mother's memory!

BERNARDA. Then don't you plague me with your evil thoughts!
[*Pause*

PONCIA. It'll be better for me to keep well out of it.

BERNARDA. That's what you should do. Get on with your work and keep your mouth shut. That's the duty of those who work for a living.

PONCIA. But I can't. Don't you think Pepe would be better off married to Martirio or—yes, why not?—to Adela?

BERNARDA. No, I do not.

PONCIA [*pointedly*]. Adela. She's the one who's really made for Pepe.

BERNARDA. Things never fall out the way we'd like them to.

PONCIA. But it's very hard for them to deny their true feelings. For Pepe to be with Angustias doesn't seem right to me, nor to other people, nor even to the air around us. Perhaps they'll get what they want in the end!

BERNARDA. There you go again! You sneak up on me and fill my mind with nightmares. I won't let myself understand what you're saying, because, if I fully grasped what you mean, I'd have to dig my nails into you.

PONCIA. It wouldn't be the end of the world.

BERNARDA. Luckily, my daughters respect me; they've never gone against my will.

PONCIA. That's very true. But the moment you let them loose they'll go flying up to the rooftops.

BERNARDA. And I'll hurl stones at them till they come down.

PONCIA. You're unbeatable, of course.

BERNARDA. I've never been one for half-measures.

PONCIA. It's funny, though! You wouldn't believe that at her age Angustias could be so keen on her future husband. And he seems just as struck with her! Yesterday my eldest boy told me that at half past four in the morning, when he went down the street with his oxen, they were still talking!

BERNARDA. At half past four!

ANGUSTIAS [*entering*]. That's not true!

PONCIA. That's what I was told.

BERNARDA [*to* ANGUSTIAS]. Well?

ANGUSTIAS. Pepe has been going at one o'clock for over a week now. May God strike me dead if I'm lying.

MARTIRIO [*entering*]. I've heard him go at four too.

BERNARDA. Did you see him with your own eyes?

MARTIRIO. I didn't like to show myself. You talk at the window that looks out on the lane now, don't you?

ANGUSTIAS. I talk at my bedroom window.

ADELA *appears at the door.*

MARTIRIO. Then how. . .

BERNARDA. What's going on here?

PONCIA. You'd better not find out! But it's obvious that at four in the morning Pepe was still talking at some window of your house.

BERNARDA. Do you know that for certain?

PONCIA. In this life no one knows anything for certain.

ADELA. Mother, don't listen to her! She only wants to ruin us all.

BERNARDA. I'll get at the truth, you'll see! If people in this village think they can bear false witness, they'll have a tough nut to reckon with. This business is not to be talked about. Sometimes other folk stir up a wave of filth to ruin us.

MARTIRIO. I'm not given to telling lies.

PONCIA. And there *is* something going on.

BERNARDA. Nothing is going on. I wasn't born with my eyes shut. Now I'll make sure they stay wide open till the day I die.

ANGUSTIAS. I have the right to know.

BERNARDA. You don't have any rights except to do what you're told. No one's going to push me around. [*To* PONCIA] And you keep your nose stuck in your own family's business. Here nobody's going to take a step from now on without my knowing it.

MAID [*entering*]. There's a big crowd at the top of the street, and all the neighbours are out on their doorsteps!

BERNARDA [*to* PONCIA]. Run and find out what's going on. [*The women run towards the door*] Where are *you* going? I always knew you were the kind of women who'd spy out of windows when they were supposed to be in mourning. Into the yard, all of you!

> [*They exit and so does* BERNARDA. *Distant voices are heard*

> MARTIRIO *and* ADELA *appear and stand listening, but not daring to venture in from the doorway.*

MARTIRIO. You can think yourself lucky I chose to keep quiet.

ADELA. There are things I could have said too.

MARTIRIO. What could you say? Wanting is one thing; doing is another.

ADELA. Doing is for the woman who finds a way and gets on with it. You wanted to all right, but you couldn't do it.

MARTIRIO. You won't go on much longer.

ADELA. I'll have it all!

MARTIRIO. I'll tear you out of his arms.

ADELA [*pleading*]. Martirio, leave me alone!

MARTIRIO. Some hope!

ADELA. He wants to live with me!

MARTIRIO. I saw how he was holding you!

ADELA. I didn't want to let him. I felt as if a rope were pulling me.

MARTIRIO. I'll see you dead first!

MAGDALENA *and* ANGUSTIAS *appear. The crowd noises grow louder.* PONCIA *enters at the same time as* BERNARDA.

PONCIA. Bernarda!

BERNARDA. What's happening?

PONCIA. Librada's daughter, the one who's not married, had a baby; no one knows who the father is.

ADELA. A baby?

PONCIA. And to hide her shame she killed it and put it under a pile of rocks. But then some dogs, with more feeling than a lot of creatures, pulled it out, and, as if the hand of God were guiding them, they laid it on her doorstep. Now the people mean to kill her. They're dragging her down the street, and the men are rushing along the pathways and out of the olive-groves, shouting so loud the fields are trembling.

BERNARDA. Good, let them all come with their mattocks and olive-staves; let them all come and kill her.

ADELA. No, no, not kill her, no!

MARTIRIO. Yes, and let's go out and join them, all of us.

BERNARDA. Let her pay the price for trampling on her own decency.

> [*From outside comes the sound of a woman shrieking and a great uproar*

ADELA. I hope they let her get away! Don't you go out there!

MARTIRIO [*looking at* ADELA]. Let her pay the price!

BERNARDA [*in the archway*]. Finish her off before the police get here! Set burning coals in the place of her sin!

ADELA [*clutching her belly*]. No! No!

BERNARDA. Kill her! Kill her!

CURTAIN

ACT 3

Four white walls, lightly tinged with blue, of the interior courtyard in BERNARDA's *house. It is night. The décor must be of the utmost simplicity. The doorways, illumined by light from inside the rooms, cast a delicate glow over the stage. In the centre, a table with an oil-lamp where* BERNARDA *and her* DAUGHTERS *are eating.* PONCIA *is serving them.* PRUDENCIA *is sitting apart.*

The curtain rises on a heavy silence broken only by the noise of plates and cutlery.

PRUDENCIA. I'll be going now. It's been a long visit.

[*She gets up*

BERNARDA. Don't go yet, Prudencia. We never see each other.

PRUDENCIA. Have they rung the last bell for the rosary?

PONCIA. Not yet. [PRUDENCIA *sits down*

BERNARDA. So how is your husband these days?

PRUDENCIA. Just the same.

BERNARDA. We never see him either.

PRUDENCIA. You know what he's like. Since he quarrelled with his brothers over the inheritance he hasn't used the front door. He gets a ladder and climbs over the wall of the yard.

BERNARDA. There's a real man for you! What news of your daughter?

PRUDENCIA. He's still not forgiven her.

BERNARDA. Quite right too.

PRUDENCIA. I don't know what to say about it. It makes me very unhappy.

BERNARDA. A daughter who is disobedient stops being a daughter and becomes an enemy.

PRUDENCIA. I just let things take their course. My only consolation is going to church to get away from it all, but now that my sight is failing I'll have to stop coming: the children tease me so much. [*A loud thud is heard as if the wall were being struck*] What's that?

BERNARDA. The breeding stallion; he's shut in and kicking the wall. [*Shouting*] Shackle him and let him out into the yard. [*In a low voice*] He must be hot.

PRUDENCIA. Are you going to put the new mares to him?

BERNARDA. First thing in the morning.

PRUDENCIA. You've built up your stock really well.

BERNARDA. Thanks to a lot of expense and unpleasantness.

PONCIA [*interjecting*]. But she does have the best herd for miles around. Pity the prices are so low.

BERNARDA. Would you like some cheese and honey?

PRUDENCIA. I've no appetite.   [*Another thud is heard*

PONCIA. For God's sake!

PRUDENCIA. That went right through me!

BERNARDA [*getting up, furious*]. Do I have to say everything twice? Let him out, so he can roll around on the piles of straw! [*Pause, then as if talking to the farmhands*] Shut the mares in the stable then, but let him loose before he kicks the walls down. [*She returns to the table and sits down again*] Ay, what a life!

PRUDENCIA. Having to fight like a man.

BERNARDA. That's right.   [ADELA *rises from the table*
Where are you off to?

ADELA. To get a drink of water.

BERNARDA [*shouting*]. Bring a jug of cool water. [*To* ADELA] You can sit down again.   [ADELA *sits down*

PRUDENCIA. So when is Angustias going to get married?

BERNARDA. They're coming to ask for her within the next few days.

PRUDENCIA. You must be pleased!

ANGUSTIAS. Oh, yes.

AMELIA [*to* MAGDALENA]. Now you've spilled the salt!

MAGDALENA. Well, your luck can't get any worse.

AMELIA. It's always a bad omen.

BERNARDA. That's enough!

PRUDENCIA [to ANGUSTIAS]. Has he given you the ring yet?

ANGUSTIAS. See.   [She holds it out

PRUDENCIA. It's lovely. Three pearls. In my day pearls were for tears.

ANGUSTIAS. But it's different now.

ADELA. I don't think so. What things stand for doesn't change. Engagement rings should be diamonds.

PRUDENCIA. It's more usual.

BERNARDA. Pearls or no pearls, things are what you make them.

MARTIRIO. Or as God disposes.

PRUDENCIA. I hear the furniture's lovely.

BERNARDA. Sixteen thousand *reales* it cost me.

PONCIA [interjecting]. The best piece is the wardrobe with a mirror.

PRUDENCIA. I've never seen one of those.

BERNARDA. A chest was all we had.

PRUDENCIA. What matters is that everything should work out.

ADELA. And that you can never be sure of.

BERNARDA. There's no reason why it shouldn't.

[Far-off bells are heard

PRUDENCIA. The last bell. [To ANGUSTIAS] I'll come another time so you can show me the clothes.

ANGUSTIAS. Whenever you like.

PRUDENCIA. Good-night and God bless.

BERNARDA. Goodbye, Prudencia.

THE FIVE DAUGHTERS [together]. God be with you!

[Pause. Exit PRUDENCIA

BERNARDA. Well that's supper over.   [They all get up

ADELA. I'll just walk as far as the gate to stretch my legs and get some air.

> [MAGDALENA *sits on a low chair and leans her head on the wall*

AMELIA. I'll go with you.

MARTIRIO. So will I.

ADELA [*with repressed hatred*]. I'm not going to get lost.

AMELIA. It's good to have company at night.

> [*They exit.* BERNARDA *sits, and* ANGUSTIAS *is clearing the table*

BERNARDA. Haven't I told you it's got to stop, this not speaking to your sister Martirio? What happened with the picture was just a joke, and you must put it out of your mind.

ANGUSTIAS. She has no love for me, you know that.

BERNARDA. Our private thoughts are our own business. I don't pry into other people's feelings, but I want proper appearances and family harmony. Do you understand that?

ANGUSTIAS. Yes.

BERNARDA. Then that's settled.

MAGDALENA [*almost asleep*]. Anyhow, you'll soon be away from here.   [*Falls asleep*

ANGUSTIAS. Not soon enough for me.

BERNARDA. What time did you finish talking last night?

ANGUSTIAS. At half past twelve.

BERNARDA. What does Pepe talk about?

ANGUSTIAS. I always feel he's not really there. He talks to me as if he were thinking of something else. If I ask him what's the matter, he says: 'Men have problems you wouldn't understand.'

BERNARDA. You shouldn't question him. Especially after you're married. Speak when he speaks, and look at him when he looks at you. Then you'll have no unpleasantness.

ANGUSTIAS. I think there are a lot of things he doesn't tell me, mother.

BERNARDA. Don't try to find out what they are; don't question him, and, it goes without saying, never let him see you cry.

ANGUSTIAS. I ought to be happy and I'm not.

BERNARDA. It's all the same.

ANGUSTIAS. I often look hard at Pepe through the bars of the window, and he becomes all blurred, as if a passing flock of sheep had covered him in a cloud of dust.

BERNARDA. That's what comes of having a weak constitution.

ANGUSTIAS. I hope you're right.

BERNARDA. Is he coming tonight?

ANGUSTIAS. No. He's gone to town with his mother.

BERNARDA. We'll have an early night, then. Magdalena!

ANGUSTIAS. She's asleep.

Enter ADELA, MARTIRIO, *and* AMELIA.

AMELIA. It's so dark tonight!

ADELA. You can't see your hand in front of your face.

MARTIRIO. A good night for robbers or anyone who doesn't want to be seen.

ADELA. The stallion was in the middle of the yard, all white! Looking twice as big, and looming in the dark.

AMELIA. That's right. It was quite frightening. He looked like a ghost!

ADELA. There are stars in the sky as big as your fist!

MARTIRIO. This one stared up at them so hard she almost cracked her neck.

ADELA. Don't they mean anything to you, then?

MARTIRIO. I've no interest in anything over the rooftop. What goes on inside the house gives me enough to think about.

ADELA. That's typical of you.

BERNARDA. She has her ways and you have yours.

ANGUSTIAS. Goodnight.

ADELA. Are you going to bed already?

ANGUSTIAS. Yes, Pepe isn't coming tonight.   [*She exits*

ADELA. Mother, when there's a shooting star or a flash of lightning, why do they say:

> Blessed St Barbara be nigh,
> whose name is written in the sky
> with holy water up on high?*

BERNARDA. In the old days they knew many things we've forgotten.

AMELIA. I close my eyes so I won't see them.

ADELA. I don't. I love it when things go rushing by blazing with light after lying quiet as a mouse for years on end.

MARTIRIO. But those things going on up there have nothing to do with us.

BERNARDA. It's best not to think about them.

ADELA. What a beautiful night! I'd like to stay up really late and enjoy the cool breeze from the fields.

BERNARDA. But it's time to go to bed. Magdalena!

AMELIA. She's gone right off.

BERNARDA. Magdalena!

MAGDALENA [*irritated*]. Leave me alone!

BERNARDA. Go to bed!

MAGDALENA [*getting up peevishly*]. Why can't you leave me in peace, all of you?   [*She goes off, grumbling*

AMELIA. Goodnight!   [*She exits*

BERNARDA. You two can go as well.

MARTIRIO. Why isn't Angustias's young man coming tonight?

BERNARDA. He's away.

MARTIRIO [*looking at* ADELA]. Ah!

ADELA. See you in the morning.   [*She exits*

> [MARTIRIO *takes a drink of water and exits slowly, looking towards the door that leads to the yard*

Enter PONCIA.

PONCIA. You're still here?

BERNARDA. Enjoying the peace and quiet, and not seeing much sign of the 'something very serious' that's going on here, according to you.

PONCIA. Bernarda, don't let's talk about that.

BERNARDA. There's not a squeak to be heard in this house. My vigilance has everything under control.

PONCIA. There's nothing to be seen or heard. That's true. Your daughters live and have their being as if they were stacked away in cupboards. But neither you nor anyone else can keep watch inside people's hearts.

BERNARDA. My daughters are breathing peacefully enough.

PONCIA. That's your business, you're their mother. I've got enough to do looking after your house.

BERNARDA. So now you're determined not to say anything.

PONCIA. I'm keeping to my place, and that's all there is to it.

BERNARDA. The truth is you've got nothing to say. If this house had grass in it, you'd make it your business to bring in all the sheep of the neighbourhood to browse.

PONCIA. I keep quiet about more than you think.

BERNARDA. Does your son still see Pepe at four in the morning? Do they go on reciting the same wicked tales about this house?

PONCIA. Nobody says anything.

BERNARDA. That's because they can't. Because there's no meat to chew on. Thanks to my watchful eye!

PONCIA. Bernarda, I don't want to speak, because I'm afraid of what you'll do. But don't feel so secure.

BERNARDA. I feel absolutely secure.

PONCIA. Lightning can strike without warning! A sudden rush of blood can stop your heart beating!

BERNARDA. Nothing will happen here. I'm on my guard against the kind of thing you're imagining.

PONCIA. So much the better for you.

BERNARDA. I should think so!

MAID [*entering*]. I've done the dishes. Is there anything else, Bernarda?

BERNARDA [*getting up*]. No. I'm going to bed.

MAID. What time shall I wake you?

BERNARDA. Don't. I'm going to have a good long sleep tonight.

[*Exit* BERNARDA

PONCIA. When you can't stop the tide, it's easier to turn your back on it and see nothing.

MAID. She's so proud, she puts a blindfold on herself.

PONCIA. There's nothing I can do. I tried to put a stop to it, but now I'm too scared. You see how quiet it is? Well, I tell you there are storms brewing in every room. The day they break we'll be swept away, all of us. I've said my say, that's it.

MAID. Bernarda thinks she's a match for everybody. She doesn't know the power a man has over a house full of women.

PONCIA. It's not all Pepe el Romano's fault. Of course, he was after Adela last year and she was mad about him, but she ought to keep her place now, and not lead him on. A man's a man after all.

MAID. Some people think there's many a night he's been talking to Adela.

PONCIA. He has. [*In a confidential tone*] And other things.

MAID. I dread to think what's going to happen here.

PONCIA. I wish I could go across the sea away from this battle-ground of a house.

MAID. Bernarda's speeding up the wedding, so perhaps it'll be all right.

PONCIA. Things have gone too far now. Adela's determined not to be stopped, and the others keep watch day and night.

MAID. Martirio too?

PONCIA. She's the worst. She's a sink of poison. She knows she won't get Romano, so she'd wreck the whole world if she could.

MAID. What a wicked lot they are!

PONCIA. They're women without a man, that's all. When that happens, not even the ties of blood mean anything any more. Shhh!   [*She listens*

MAID. What is it?

PONCIA [*getting up*]. The dogs are barking.

MAID. Someone must have gone past the gate.

    ADELA *enters wearing a white petticoat and a bodice.*

PONCIA. Aren't you in bed yet?

ADELA. I want a drink of water.

                            [*Drinks from a glass on the table*

PONCIA. I thought you were asleep.

ADELA. I woke up feeling thirsty. Aren't you two going to bed?

MAID. We're just going.   [*Exit* ADELA

PONCIA. Come on.

MAID. We've certainly earned our rest. Bernarda doesn't let me sit down all day.

PONCIA. Take the light.

MAID. The dogs have gone mad.

PONCIA. They're going to keep us awake.

             [*They exit. The stage is left in half darkness*

    Enter MARÍA JOSEFA *with a lamb in her arms.*

MARÍA JOSEFA.

Little lamb, my little baby,
to the sea-side off we go.
The ant will watch us from his doorway,
I'll give you suck and feed you bread.

We'll leave leopard-faced Bernarda
and Magdalena the hyena—
little lamb,
baa-baa, baa-baa—
for the palms that deck the stable in the town of Bethlehem.

                                [*She laughs*

You and I don't want to sleep.
The door will open by itself,
and we'll live snugly on the beach
in a little coral hut.

We'll leave leopard-faced Bernarda
and Magdalena the hyena—
little lamb,
baa-baa, baa-baa—
for the palms that deck the stable in the town of Bethlehem.

[She goes off singing

Enter ADELA. *She looks around furtively, and disappears
through the door leading out to the yard.* MARTIRIO *enters
by another door, and stands in an anguished state of
watchfulness in the centre of the stage. She too is in
her petticoats. She has put a little black shawl round her
shoulders.* MARÍA JOSEFA *enters and crosses in front of her.*

MARTIRIO. Grandma, where are you going?

MARÍA JOSEFA. Will you open the door for me? Who are you?

MARTIRIO. How did you get out here?

MARÍA JOSEFA. I escaped. Who are you?

MARTIRIO. Go to bed.

MARÍA JOSEFA. You're Martirio. I can see you now. Martirio:
martyr-face. When are you going to have a baby? I've had this
one.

MARTIRIO. Where did you get that lamb?

MARÍA JOSEFA. I know it's a lamb. But why can't a lamb be a
baby? Better to have a lamb than not have anything. Bernarda's
a leopard-face! Magdalena's a hyena.

MARTIRIO. Don't raise your voice.

MARÍA JOSEFA. It's true. Everything is very dark. Just because I
have white hair you think I can't have babies, but I can:
babies, and babies, and babies. This little one will have white
hair and she will have another little one, and that one will
have another, and all of us with snow-white hair will be like
the waves: first one, then another, and another. Then we'll all

sit down and we'll all have white hair and we shall be foam.
Why is there no foam here? Here there's nothing but black
cloaks for mourning.

MARTIRIO. Shhh, quiet now.

MARÍA JOSEFA. When my neighbour had a baby, I used to take
her chocolate, and then she'd bring it for me, and so it was
again, and again, and again. You will have white hair, but the
neighbours will never come to you. I must go away from here,
but I'm afraid the dogs will bite me. Will you come with me
away from this countryside? I don't like the country. I like
houses, but houses with their doors open, and neighbours in
bed with their little ones and the men outside sitting on their
chairs; Pepe el Romano is a giant. You all love him. But he's
going to eat you all up because you're grains of wheat. No,
not grains of wheat. You're frogs without tongues!

MARTIRIO [forcefully]. Come along, off you go to bed.

[She pushes her

MARÍA JOSEFA. All right, but you will let me out again, won't
you?

MARTIRIO. Of course I will.

MARÍA JOSEFA [weeping].
            Little lamb, my little baby,
            to the sea-side off we go.
            The ant will watch us from his doorway,
            I'll give you suck and feed you bread.
        [Exit MARÍA JOSEFA. MARTIRIO closes the door behind
        her, and moves towards the door leading to the
        yard. Then she hesitates, but takes a further two steps

MARTIRIO [softly]. Adela. [Pause. She moves right up to the
door. Loudly] Adela!

    ADELA appears. Her hair is somewhat dishevelled.

ADELA. Why are you looking for me?

MARTIRIO. Keep away from that man.

ADELA. Who are you to tell me what to do?

MARTIRIO. That's no place for a respectable woman.

ADELA. And haven't you just longed to be there!

MARTIRIO [*loudly*]. The time has come for me to speak out. This can't go on.

ADELA. This is only the beginning. I had the strength to take action. The spirit and the courage that you haven't got. Under this roof I saw death, and I went out to get what was mine, what belonged to me.

MARTIRIO. That brute came here for another woman. You came between them.

ADELA. He wanted her money, but his eyes were always on me.

MARTIRIO. I won't let you snatch him away. He's going to marry Angustias.

ADELA. You know even better than I do that he doesn't love her.

MARTIRIO. That's true.

ADELA. You know it's me he loves because you've seen him with me.

MARTIRIO [*desperately*]. Yes!

ADELA [*drawing close to her*]. He loves *me*, he loves *me*.

MARTIRIO. Stick a knife into me, if that's what you want, but don't say that to me again.

ADELA. That's why you want to stop me going with him. You don't care if he puts his arms round a woman he doesn't love. Neither do I. It's all right for him to spend a hundred years with Angustias. But, if he puts his arms round me, you can't bear it, because you love him too, you love him!

MARTIRIO [*dramatically*]. Yes, I do! Let me be honest and say it. I do! Let my breast burst with bitterness like a pomegranate. I love him!

ADELA [*impulsively, and hugging her*]. Martirio, oh Martirio, it's not my fault.

MARTIRIO. Don't touch me! Don't try to get round me. We're not the same blood any more; I'd like to look on you as my sister, but for me you're just another woman now.

[*She pushes her away*

ADELA. There's no way out of this. One of us must sink, the other swim. Pepe el Romano is mine. He takes me into the reed-beds by the river.

MARTIRIO. No!

ADELA. I can't stand the horrors of this house any more, not after feeling the taste of his mouth. I'll be whatever he wants me to be. The whole village will be against me, pointing their fiery fingers and burning me up, I'll be hounded by those that call themselves respectable, and in front of them all I'll put on the crown of thorns worn by every woman who's loved by a married man.

MARTIRIO. Be quiet!

ADELA. Yes, yes. [*Softly*] Let's go to bed, let's leave him to marry Angustias. I don't care any more. But I'll go and live in a little house by myself where he can come and see me when he wants to, whenever he feels like it.

MARTIRIO. That won't happen as long as I've a drop of blood left in my body.

ADELA. Oh, you won't stop me, you're feeble; I could bring a bucking stallion to his knees just with the strength in my little finger.

MARTIRIO. Don't raise that voice of yours, it makes me wild. My heart is filled with such a devilish strength, it's choking me and taking possession of me against my will.

ADELA. They tell us we should love our sisters. God must have abandoned me to dwell in darkness, because I look at you as if I'd never seen you before.

> [*A whistle is heard, and* ADELA *runs towards the door to the yard, but* MARTIRIO *bars her way*

MARTIRIO. Where are you going?

ADELA. Get away from the door.

MARTIRIO. Get past if you can.

ADELA. Get away!   [*They struggle*

MARTIRIO [*shouting*]. Mother, mother!

ADELA. Let me go!

BERNARDA *appears. She is in her petticoat with a black shawl.*

BERNARDA. Stop it, both of you! To be so helpless, oh! If only I had a thunderbolt in my hand!

MARTIRIO [*pointing to* ADELA]. She was with him! Look at her petticoat, with straw all over it!

BERNARDA. That is the bed of a harlot!

[*She moves furiously towards* ADELA

ADELA [*standing up to her*]. This place has sounded like a prison long enough. [*She snatches her mother's stick and breaks it in two*] That's what I do with the tyrant's rod. Don't take another step. Nobody but Pepe tells me what to do.

Enter MAGDALENA.

MAGDALENA. Adela!

Enter PONCIA *and* ANGUSTIAS.

ADELA. I am his woman. [*To* ANGUSTIAS] Get that into your head, and go out into the yard and tell him so. He will rule over everyone in this house. He's out there, breathing like a lion.

ANGUSTIAS. Oh, my God!

BERNARDA. The gun! Where's the gun?   [*She rushes off*

AMELIA *appears upstage; she looks on in terror with her head pressed against the wall.*

[MARTIRIO *exits*

ADELA. Nobody's going to stop me!   [*She makes to exit*

ANGUSTIAS [*restraining her*]. You're not leaving here with your triumphant little body, you thief! You've brought shame on our house!

MAGDALENA. Let her go where we'll never see her again!

[*A shot is heard*

BERNARDA [*entering*]. Go after him now, if you dare.

MARTIRIO [*entering*]. That's done for Pepe el Romano.

ADELA. Pepe! Oh, my God! Pepe!   [*She runs off*

PONCIA. Did you kill him, then?

MARTIRIO. No. He galloped off on his mare.

BERNARDA. All my fault. Women are no good with guns.

MAGDALENA. Why did you say that, then?

MARTIRIO. For her benefit. I'd like to drench her in blood.

PONCIA. You fiend!

MAGDALENA. She's in the grip of the devil!

BERNARDA. Still, it's better this way.   [*A thud is heard*

BERNARDA. Adela! Adela!

PONCIA [*at the door*]. Open the door!

BERNARDA. Open up! Don't think walls will hide your shame.

MAID [*entering*]. The neighbours are all out of bed!

BERNARDA [*in a low roar*]. Open the door or I break it down! [*Pause. There is not a sound*] Adela! [*She moves back from the door*] Bring me a hammer!

> [PONCIA *heaves open the door and goes in. She gives a shriek, and comes out*

BERNARDA. What is it?

PONCIA [*she puts her hands to her neck*]. God save us from ending like that!

> [*The sisters fall back. The* MAID *crosses herself.* BERNARDA *screams and steps forward*

PONCIA. Don't go in!

BERNARDA. No. I won't go in! Pepe: you're riding away alive now through the dark poplars, but one day your turn will come. Cut her down. My daughter died immaculate! Carry her to her room and dress her as if she were a virgin. Nobody is to say anything! She died a virgin. Tell them to toll the bells twice at sunrise.

MARTIRIO. Oh, she was happy! She knew what it was to have him!

BERNARDA. I want no weeping. We must look death in the face. Quiet! [*To one of the daughters*] Quiet, I said! [*To another daughter*] Keep your tears for when you're alone. We'll all drown ourselves in an ocean of mourning! She, the youngest daughter of Bernarda Alba, died a virgin. Do you hear me? Quiet, quiet, I said. Quiet!

CURTAIN

DOÑA ROSITA THE SPINSTER
or
THE LANGUAGE OF FLOWERS

A Poem of Granada at the
Turn of the Century,
divided into Various Gardens
with Scenes containing
Singing and Dancing

(1935)

CHARACTERS

Doña Rosita
The Uncle
The Aunt
The Housekeeper
The Nephew
First, Second, and Third Manola
First, Second, and Third Spinster
The Spinsters' Mother
First and Second Ayola
The Professor of Political Economy (Señor X)
Don Martín
The Youth
Two Workmen
Vendor's Voice

ACT 1

A room with an exit leading into a greenhouse.

UNCLE. Where are my seeds?

HOUSEKEEPER. They were there.

UNCLE. Well, they're not there now.

AUNT. Hellebore, fuchsias, the chrysanthemums, violet Louis-Passy, and snow-white altair with heliotrope tips.

UNCLE. You must look after the flowers.

HOUSEKEEPER. If it's me you mean. . .

AUNT. Be quiet. Don't answer back.

UNCLE. I mean everyone. Yesterday I found the dahlia seeds trampled all over the floor. [*He goes into the greenhouse*] You don't have a proper appreciation of my greenhouse: since 1807, when the first musk-rose was grown by the Countess of Wandes, nobody in Granada has managed to grow one but me, not even the botanist at the University. You must have more respect for my plants.

HOUSEKEEPER. Are you saying I don't respect them?

AUNT. Ssh! You're both as bad as each other.

HOUSEKEEPER. That's as may be, señora. But it's not me that says all that flower-watering flooding the place is going to make toads pop out of the sofa.

AUNT. You like the scent of the flowers all right.

HOUSEKEEPER. No, señora, I don't. To me they smell of the death of a child or nuns taking the veil or an altar in church. Sad things. Give me an orange or a ripe quince and I can do without the roses of this world. But in this place—roses on the right, basil on the left, anemones, salvias, petunias, and the latest fad, chrysanthemums, all ruffled like gypsy-girls' hair. If only this garden grew pears, or cherries, or date-plums!

AUNT. So that you could gobble them up!

HOUSEKEEPER. That's what mouths are for—as they used to say in my village:

> Mouths are made for eating,
> legs are made to dance,
> and women have a wee thing—

[*She breaks off, goes up to the* AUNT, *and whispers the rest in her ear*

AUNT. Good Heavens!   [*She crosses herself*

HOUSEKEEPER. That's country rudeness for you.

[*She crosses herself*

ROSITA [*entering swiftly, dressed in rose pink, in the 1900 style with leg-of-mutton sleeves and braid trimming*].* My hat! Where's my hat? The bells of St Luis* have rung thirty times already!

HOUSEKEEPER. I left it on the table.

ROSITA. Well, it's not there.   [*They search

[*The* HOUSEKEEPER *exits*

AUNT. Have you looked in the wardrobe?   [*The* AUNT *exits*

HOUSEKEEPER [*entering*]. I can't find it.

ROSITA. Surely somebody must know where my hat is!

HOUSEKEEPER. Wear the blue one with the daisies.

ROSITA. You must be mad.

HOUSEKEEPER. Not as mad as you.

AUNT [*returning*]. Here it is. Off you go!

[ROSITA *snatches it and runs out*

HOUSEKEEPER. She wants everything at the double. She'd like today to be the day after tomorrow. Off she goes and leaves us all standing. When she was a little girl every day I had to tell her the story of when she'd be an old woman: 'Now Rosita is eighty years old. . .'—always the same. When have you seen her sitting down with some tatting or chenille work or drawing the threads to trim a cap for herself?

AUNT. Never.

HOUSEKEEPER. She never stops: 'in and out and round about and in my lady's chamber. . .'

AUNT. If you knew what that meant, you wouldn't say it!

HOUSEKEEPER. Well, it doesn't shock you, I know that!

AUNT. It's true I've always let her have her own way; I mean, who could hurt a poor creature with no father or mother?

HOUSEKEEPER. No daddy, no mummy, no puppy to bark for her, but she has got an uncle and auntie worth their weight in gold. [She embraces the AUNT

UNCLE [within]. This really is too much!

AUNT. Holy Mary!

UNCLE. It's one thing to have the seeds trampled on, it's quite another to have the little leaves torn off the rose bush I love most of all. Much more than the musk-rose or the hispid or the pompon or the damask or even Queen Isabella's eglantine. [To the AUNT] Come in here and you'll see.

AUNT. Is it ruined?

UNCLE. No, nothing much happened to it, but it might have.

HOUSEKEEPER. Oh, for Heaven's sake!

UNCLE. Who knocked over the flowerpot, I wonder?

HOUSEKEEPER. Don't you look at me.

UNCLE. Did I do it, then?

HOUSEKEEPER. So there are no cats, and no dogs, and no gusts of wind blowing through the window?

AUNT. Go and sweep up the mess in the greenhouse.

HOUSEKEEPER. I see I'm not allowed to speak in this house.
[She exits

UNCLE [entering]. It's a rose you've never seen: a surprise I had ready for you. Because, incredible though they all are—the *rosa declinata* with its drooping buds, the *inermis* that has no thorns (isn't that amazing, not a single thorn?), the *myrtifolia* from Belgium and the *sulfurata* that glows in the dark—this one is the rarest of all. Botanists call it *rosa mutabilis*; that means 'mutable', 'which changes'. . . Here in this book there's a description and a picture of it, look! [*He opens the book*] It's red in the morning, turns white in the evening, and at night it loses its petals.

In the morning, when it opens,
it's red, as red as blood;
the dew will not dare touch it
for fear of being burnt.
At midday fully opened
like coral it is hard.
The sun peers through the window
to see how bright it shines.
When the birds light on the branches
and break into their song,
and evening sinks into
the violets of the sea,
it whitens with the whiteness
of salt upon the cheek.
And when night plays upon
the moon's soft metal horn,
the stars step slowly forward
and the breezes drop away,
then on the edge of darkness
its petals start to fall.

AUNT. Is it in bloom yet?

UNCLE. There's one flower just opening.

AUNT. And it lasts only one day?

UNCLE. One day, but I'm going to spend the whole day beside it to watch it turning white.

ROSITA [*entering*]. My sunshade.

UNCLE. Her sunshade.

AUNT [*shouting off*]. Her sunshade!

HOUSEKEEPER [*appearing*]. Here's the sunshade!
   [ROSITA *takes the sunshade and kisses her* AUNT *and* UNCLE

ROSITA. What do you think?

UNCLE. Charming.

AUNT. Delightful.

ROSITA [*opening the sunshade*]. And now?

HOUSEKEEPER. For God's sake, shut the sunshade, it mustn't be opened in the house! It's bad luck!

> By Bartholomew's wheel,*
> by Joseph's staff,
> by the holy laurel bough,
> begone, begone thou enemy:
> fly from Jerusalem now!

[They all laugh. The UNCLE *exits*

ROSITA [*shutting the sunshade*]. There!

HOUSEKEEPER. Never do that again... Shi—Shame on you!

ROSITA. Eh??

AUNT. What were you going to say?

HOUSEKEEPER. Well, I didn't say it!

ROSITA [*exits, laughing*]. Bye now!

AUNT. Who's going with you?

ROSITA [*popping back*]. I'm going with the Manolas.

HOUSEKEEPER. And her young man.

AUNT. I think he has things to do.

HOUSEKEEPER. I don't know which I like best, the young man or her.   [*The* AUNT *sits down to make lace with bobbins* A pair of cousins pretty enough to be modelled in icing sugar, and, if they should die, which God forbid, they should be embalmed and put in a glass case all mirrors and snow. Which one do you like best?   [*She starts dusting*

AUNT. They're my nephew and niece: I love them both.

HOUSEKEEPER. One for Saturday and one for Sunday; all the same...

AUNT. Of course, Rosita grew up with me...

HOUSEKEEPER. Exactly. I don't believe in blood-ties. As far as I'm concerned, that's what counts. The same blood may flow down there in the veins, but you can't see it. A second cousin you see every day means more than a brother who's over the hills and far away. Why? I'll tell you why.

AUNT. Get on with your cleaning, woman.

HOUSEKEEPER. All right. I know I'm not allowed to open my mouth in this place. That's what I get after bringing up a pretty little girl. I abandon my own children in a hovel·shivering with hunger. . .

AUNT. With cold, you mean.

HOUSEKEEPER. Shivering with everything you can think of, only to be told: 'Shut up!' And because I'm only a servant I just have to shut up, which is what I do, I can't speak my mind and say. . .

AUNT. And say what?

HOUSEKEEPER. Do stop clicking those bobbins, my head's going to burst with all that click, click, clicking.

AUNT [*laughing*]. Go and see who's at the door.
[*The stage is silent except for the clicking of the bobbins*

VOICE OFF. Caaa-mo-miiile! Best mountain caa–mo—mile!

AUNT [*talking to herself*]. We should buy some more camomile. There are times when it's useful. Another day when he comes by. . . thirty-seven, thirty-eight. . .

VENDOR'S VOICE [*very distant*]. Best mountain caa–mo—mile!

AUNT [*placing a pin*]. Forty.

NEPHEW [*entering*]. Aunt.

AUNT [*without looking at him*]. Hello. Sit down if you like. Rosita's already gone.

NEPHEW. Who did she go with?

AUNT. The Manolas. [*Pause. Looking at the* NEPHEW] You're upset.

NEPHEW. Yes.

AUNT [*uneasily*]. I think I know why. I hope I'm wrong.

NEPHEW. You're not. Read this.

AUNT [*reads*]. Of course, it was bound to happen. That's why I was against your getting involved with Rosita. I knew that sooner or later you'd have to go to your parents. And they're not exactly next door. Forty days it takes to get to Tucumán.* If I were a man and still young I'd punch your face. . .

NEPHEW. I can't help being in love with my cousin. Do you think I want to go away? It's because I want to stay that I've come here now.

AUNT. Stay? Stay? Your duty is to go. There are all those acres to be farmed out there, and your father is old. I've no choice but to make sure you get on that ship. But you'll be leaving a great bitterness in my life. And I can't bear to think what you'll do to your cousin. You're going to drive an arrow tipped with sorrow through her heart. Now she will have to learn that linen is not just for embroidering flowers on but for wiping tears away.

NEPHEW. What do you think I should do?

AUNT. Go, of course. Remember, your father is my brother. Here you just idle your time strolling among the flowers; there you will be a farmer.

NEPHEW. But I'd like to. . .

AUNT. Get married? Are you crazy? Not until you've got some prospects. And you'd like to take Rosita with you, eh? Over my dead body and your uncle's.

NEPHEW. It's just talk. I know only too well that I can't. But I want Rosita to wait for me. Because I'll soon be back.

AUNT. If you don't fall for some girl in Tucumán. I should have bitten my tongue off before letting you get engaged; now my little girl will be left alone in these four walls while you roam freely over the sea, up those rivers, through groves of grape-fruit; and my little girl still here, every day the same, and you over there: horse and shotgun at the ready to bring down the pretty pheasants.

NEPHEW. You've no call to speak to me like that. I gave my word and I'll keep it. It's through keeping his word that my father is in South America, and you know very well. . .

AUNT [softly]. Quiet.

NEPHEW. I'll be quiet, but don't mistake respect for lack of self-respect.

AUNT [with Andalusian irony]. Oh, please forgive me!
I forgot that you are a man now.

HOUSEKEEPER [*enters weeping*]. If he were a man, he wouldn't go.

AUNT [*sharply*]. That's enough!

> [*The* HOUSEKEEPER *weeps with great sobs*

NEPHEW. I'll come back in a few minutes. Please break it to her.

AUNT. Don't you worry. It's always the old who have to deal with painful situations.   [*The* NEPHEW *exits*

HOUSEKEEPER. Oh! How sad! Oh, my poor little girl! Oh! How sad! That's how men are these days! I wouldn't abandon such a treasure if I had to beg in the streets. Once more this house will be a house of tears. Oh! Señora! [*Her mood changes*] I hope he gets devoured by a sea serpent!

AUNT. That is for God to decide!

HOUSEKEEPER.   By sesame seed,
By the three holy questions,
By cinnamon flower,
May his nights be troubled,
May his seedings be barren.
By St Nicholas' well
May his salt turn to poison.

> [*She takes a pitcher of water and makes a cross on the ground*

AUNT. Stop that cursing. Go about your work.

> [*The* HOUSEKEEPER *exits. Bursts of laughter are heard. The* AUNT *exits*

FIRST MANOLA [*entering and shutting her sunshade*]. Ah!

SECOND MANOLA [*likewise*]. Ah, how cool it is!

THIRD MANOLA [*likewise*]. Ah!

ROSITA [*likewise*].
For whom are you sighing,
my three lovely manolas?

FIRST MANOLA.
For no one.

SECOND MANOLA.
          For the wind.

THIRD MANOLA.

> For a young man who is courting me.

ROSITA.

> Whose hands will gather
> the sighs that you breathe?

FIRST MANOLA.

> The wall.

SECOND MANOLA.

> Someone's picture.

THIRD MANOLA.   The lace on my pillow.

ROSITA.

> I too want to sigh,
> Ah! my friends! Ah! my manolas!

FIRST MANOLA.

> Who will gather your sighs?

ROSITA.   Two eyes
> that lighten the darkness,
> whose long lashes are vines
> where dawn lies sleeping,
> and even in their blackness glow
> like poppies in the dusk.

FIRST MANOLA.

> Bind a ribbon round that sigh!

SECOND MANOLA.

> Ah!

THIRD MANOLA.

> Lucky you!

FIRST MANOLA.   So lucky!

ROSITA.

> Don't deceive me, for I know
> certain rumours about you.

FIRST MANOLA.

> Rumours are wild mustard.

SECOND MANOLA.

> And the chorus of the waves.

ROSITA.
> I'll tell you, shall I...

FIRST MANOLA.   Yes, begin.

THIRD MANOLA.
> Rumours are garlands.

ROSITA.
> Elvira Street, Granada,
> where the Manolas* live,
> who go to the Alhambra
> all three, or four, alone.
> One of them's dressed in green,
> and one in mauve; the third?
> She wears a tartan bodice
> with ribbons to her train.
> The two in front are herons,
> the one behind, a dove;
> they spread their wings of muslin,
> mysterious in the grove.
> Ah! dark is the Alhambra!
> Where will the Manolas go
> while the fountain and the rose
> are pining in the gloom?
> What lovers will they meet there?
> Beneath what myrtle rest?
> What hands will steal the perfume
> from their two rounded blooms?
> No one goes with them, no one,
> two herons and one dove;
> But lovers in the world there are
> who hide among the leaves;
> the bells of the Cathedral
> are carried by the breeze.
> The Genil lulls its oxen,
> the Darro its butterflies;*
> the night comes over-burdened
> with deeply shadowed hills.
> Among the lacy flounces
> one shows her dainty shoes;

the eldest has wide-open eyes,
the youngest's are half-closed.
Who can they be, those three,
high-breasted and long-trained?
Why wave their handkerchiefs?
So late where are they going?
Elvira Street, Granada,
where the Manolas live,
who go to the Alhambra
all three, or four, alone.

FIRST MANOLA.
Throughout Granada let the ripples
of the rumour spread.

SECOND MANOLA.
And have we sweethearts?

ROSITA.   None of you.

SECOND MANOLA.
Now shall I tell the truth?

ROSITA.   Yes, tell.

THIRD MANOLA.
Our bridal shifts are trimmed
with lace of frost.

ROSITA.
But why. . .

FIRST MANOLA. We like to walk the night.

ROSITA.
But where. . .

SECOND MANOLA. Through streets where shadows fall.

FIRST MANOLA.
We climb to the Alhambra
all three, or four, alone.

THIRD MANOLA.
Ah!

SECOND MANOLA.
Hush!

THIRD MANOLA.
Why should we?

SECOND MANOLA.   Ah!

FIRST MANOLA.
Ah, nobody must hear!

ROSITA.
Alhambra, mournful jasmine,
where the moon sinks down to rest.

The HOUSEKEEPER *enters.*

HOUSEKEEPER [*very sad*]. Child, your aunt wants you.

ROSITA. Have you been crying?

HOUSEKEEPER [*controlling herself*]. No, it's just that there's something that. . .

ROSITA. Don't frighten me. What's happened?
[ROSITA *exits swiftly, looking at the* HOUSEKEEPER. *When she's gone, the* HOUSEKEEPER *breaks into silent weeping*

FIRST MANOLA [*loudly*]. What's the matter?

SECOND MANOLA. Tell us.

HOUSEKEEPER. Be quiet.

THIRD MANOLA [*softly*]. Bad news?
[*The* HOUSEKEEPER *leads them to the door and looks after* ROSITA

HOUSEKEEPER. She's telling her now!
[*Pause, while they all listen*

FIRST MANOLA. Rosita is crying, let's go in.

HOUSEKEEPER. Come with me and I'll tell you. Leave her alone now. You can go out by the garden gate.   [*They exit*

The stage remains empty. A very distant piano plays a Czerny étude. Pause. The NEPHEW *enters and when he reaches the middle of the room he stops because* ROSITA *comes in. They stand facing each other. The* NEPHEW *steps forward. He puts his arm round her waist. She leans her head on his shoulder.*

ROSITA. Why did your faithless eyes
melt into mine?
Why did your hands weave flowers
into my hair?
The grieving of the nightingale
you leave to my young heart,
For by your shape and presence now
I breathe and steer my course:
Forsaking me you break
the strings of my lute.

NEPHEW [*he leads her to a love-seat and sits*].
Ah, no, my precious cousin!
Be like the snowbound nightingale
and let your mouth be closed
against imagined cold;
No frost drives me away from you,
for, though I go across the sea,
I'll have to borrow from the waves
cool blooms of tranquil spray
to curb my raging fire
when it would burn me.

ROSITA. Half-slumbering one night
on my jasmine balcony,
I saw two cherubs flying down
to join a love-sick rose;
I saw her then turn scarlet,
though white had been her hue.
But, as she was a fragile flower,
her petals, being set aflame,
went scattering bruised and frayed
with love's first kiss.
So I, my innocent cousin,
within my myrtle grove
gave all my yearning to the wind,
and to the fountain my virginity.
A trusting, tender gazelle,
I raised my eyes, saw you,
and in my heart I felt

the trembling of needles
that are tearing wounds in me
as red as gillyflowers.

NEPHEW.

I will come back, my cousin,
to take you away with me
in a ship all gleaming bright with gold
and sails of happiness;
light and dark, night and day,
I'll think only of loving you.

ROSITA. But the poison that love pours out
on the soul that is left alone
will weave the distance of land and sea
into a shroud for me.

NEPHEW.

When my stallion slowly
crops grass that's wet with dew,
when the river-mist clouds over
the clammy wall of wind;
when the stormy blaze of summer
splashes crimson on the plain,
and when hoar-frost leaves on me
the sparkling of the stars,
I tell you now, because I love you,
I shall die for you.

ROSITA. I long to see you coming home
one evening through Granada,
and all the light shot through with salt
from yearning for the sea;
the yellow lemon-grove
and the bloodless jasmine-tree
all tangled up with stones
will slow your path to me;
and whirls of twisting spikenards
will drive my rooftop wild.
Will you come back?

NEPHEW.   I will. I will come back.

ROSITA. What shining dove will be
    the herald of your coming?

NEPHEW.

    My true faith is your dove.

ROSITA. Then mind I shall embroider
    the sheets that we will share.

NEPHEW.

    By the diamond tears of Christ
    and the red bloom in his side
    I swear I will come back to be with you.

ROSITA. Farewell, my cousin.

NEPHEW.

    Cousin, fare you well.
    *[They embrace on the love-seat. The distant piano is
    heard. The* NEPHEW *exits.* ROSITA *is left weeping.
    The* UNCLE *appears and crosses towards the green-
    house. On seeing her* UNCLE, ROSITA *picks up the
    rose-book, which is within reach of her hand*

UNCLE. What were you doing?

ROSITA. Nothing.

UNCLE. Were you reading?

ROSITA. Yes.   *[The* UNCLE *exits. She reads aloud*

ROSITA. In the morning, when it opens,
    it's red, as red as blood;
    the dew will not dare touch it
    for fear of being burnt.
    At midday fully opened
    like coral it is hard.
    The sun peers through the window
    to see how bright it shines.
    When the birds light on the branches
    and break into their song,
    and evening sinks into
    the violets of the sea,
    it whitens with the whiteness
    of salt upon the cheek.

And when night plays upon
the moon's soft metal horn,
the stars step slowly forward
and the breezes drop away,
then on the edge of darkness
its petals start to fall.

CURTAIN

ACT 2

The drawing-room in DOÑA ROSITA's *house. The garden can be seen in the background.*

SEÑOR X. So I will always be a man of this century.

UNCLE. The century that's just begun will be an age of materialism.

SEÑOR X. But much more advanced than the last one. My friend Señor Longoria, of Madrid, has just bought a motor car which goes whizzing along at the fantastic speed of thirty kilometres an hour; and the Shah of Persia, who is without doubt a most delightful fellow, has acquired a Panhard-Levassor with a twenty-four horsepower engine.

UNCLE. And I say: where do they think they're going in such a hurry? You saw what happened in the Paris–Madrid rally: they had to call it off because all the drivers had killed themselves before they got to Bordeaux.

SEÑOR X. Count Zbronsky, who died in the accident, and Marcel Renault, or Renol as it may be and frequently is pronounced, who also died in the accident, are martyrs to science: when the religion of positivism* is proclaimed, they will be beatified. I knew Renol quite well. Poor Marcel!

UNCLE. You'll never convince me.   *[He sits*

SEÑOR X [*his foot on a chair, playing with his cane*]. I most assuredly shall; although a professor of Political Economy ought not to get involved in disputes with a rose-grower. Still, in this day and age, believe me, there's no place for quietist attitudes or obscurantist ideas. Today the pace is set by men like Jean-Baptiste Say, or Sé as it may be and frequently is pronounced, or Count Leo Tolstwa, or in common parlance, Tolstoy, whose writing is as elegant in form as it is profound in content. My habitat is the relevantly constituted polity;* I hold no brief for *natura naturata*.

UNCLE. We each of us live from day to day as best we can or as best we know how.

SEÑOR X. Oh, the planet Earth is mediocre, we know that; still, one ought to do one's bit for civilization. If Santos Dumont, instead of studying comparative meteorology, had gone in for rose-growing, the dirigible balloon would still be in Brahma's bosom.*

UNCLE [*offended*]. Botany is a science too.

SEÑOR X [*contemptuously*]. Yes; but an applied one: for studying the juices of the fragrant Anthemis or rhubarb or the giant Pulsatila or the narcotic secretions of the Datura Stramonium.

UNCLE [*innocently*]. Are you interested in those plants?

SEÑOR X. My experience of them is insufficiently extensive. I am interested in general culture, which is an entirely different matter. *Voilà.* [*Pause*] Is. . . er. . . Rosita at home?

UNCLE. Rosita? [*Pause. Loudly*] Rosita!

VOICE [*within*]. She's not here.

UNCLE. She's not here.

SEÑOR X. I am sorry.

UNCLE. So am I. As it's her saint's day,* she must have gone to church to say her forty credos.

SEÑOR X. Will you give her this *pendentif** from me. It's a mother-of-pearl Eiffel Tower with two doves beneath, bearing in their beaks the wheel of industry.

UNCLE. She will be most grateful.

SEÑOR X. I almost brought her a little silver cannon through the mouth of which could be seen the Virgin of Lourdes, or Lordes; or a belt-buckle shaped like a snake and four dragonflies; but I chose this as being in better taste.

UNCLE. Thank you.

SEÑOR X. I'm enchanted by your auspicious welcome.

UNCLE. Thank you.

SEÑOR X. Convey my devoted homage to your wife.

UNCLE. Thank you so much.

SEÑOR X. Convey my devoted homage to your charming niece, to whom I offer heartfelt felicitations on the feast day of her saint.

UNCLE. Thank you very much.

SEÑOR X. Your most devoted servant, my dear sir!

UNCLE. Thank you very much indeed.

SEÑOR X. May I say again. . .

UNCLE. Thank you, thank you, thank you.

SEÑOR X. I bid you farewell.   [*He goes*

UNCLE [*shouting after him*]. Thank you, thank you, thank you.

HOUSEKEEPER [*enters, laughing*]. I don't know where you find
    the patience. What with that gentleman and the other one,
    Don Confucio Montes de Oca, baptized in Lodge No. 43,*
    one day there'll be an explosion in this house.

UNCLE. I've told you I don't like you eavesdropping on my
    conversations.

HOUSEKEEPER. There's ingratitude for you. I was behind the door,
    it's true, señor, but I wasn't there to listen, only to put a
    broom upside-down so that the gentleman would go.

AUNT [*entering*]. Has he gone?

UNCLE. Yes.   [*He exits*

HOUSEKEEPER. Is he another one courting Rosita?

AUNT. What do you mean, courting? You don't know Rosita!

HOUSEKEEPER. No, but I know these fellows who come courting.

AUNT. My niece is engaged.

HOUSEKEEPER. Don't make me say it! Don't make me say it!
    Don't make me say it! Don't make me say it!

AUNT. Keep quiet then.

HOUSEKEEPER. Does it seem right to you for a man to go away
    for fifteen years and desert a pearl among women? She ought
    to get married. My arms ache from storing away so many
    table-cloths of Marseilles lace and sets of bedlinen with gui-
    pure trimming and table-runners and gauze bedspreads with
    embossed flowers. She ought to be using them now, wearing
    them out, but she just doesn't realize how time is passing.
    When her hair has turned white she'll still be sewing shiny
    satin ribbons on the frills of her honeymoon nightdress.

AUNT. Why do you always have to get involved in matters that are none of your business?

HOUSEKEEPER [*surprised*]. I don't *get* involved, I *am* involved.

AUNT. Well I have no doubt that she's happy.

HOUSEKEEPER. She only thinks she is. Yesterday she had me waiting around with her all day at the entrance to the circus because she would have it that one of the puppeteers looked like her cousin.

AUNT. And did he?

HOUSEKEEPER. He was as handsome as a young priest saying his first mass, but your nephew would give a lot to have that slender waist, that mother-of-pearl throat and that trim moustache. He wasn't a bit like him. There aren't any good-looking men in your family.

AUNT. Thanks for the compliment.

HOUSEKEEPER. They're all squat and a bit round-shouldered.

AUNT. Really!

HOUSEKEEPER. It's the honest truth, señora. What happened was that Rosita took a fancy to the puppeteer just as I did and just as you would have done. But she always has to bring her cousin into it. Sometimes I feel like throwing a shoe at her head. If she goes on gazing up at the skies she'll end up with eyes like a cow's.

AUNT. That's it! Not another word! Clowns have licence to speak but not to bark.

HOUSEKEEPER. You can't say I don't love her.

AUNT. Sometimes I wonder if you do.

HOUSEKEEPER. I'd give her the bread from my mouth and the blood from my veins if she wanted them.

AUNT [*fiercely*]. Honey-tongued hypocrite! Words, words, words!

HOUSEKEEPER [*fiercely*]. And deeds! I've proved what I feel for her by what I've done. I love her more than you do.

AUNT. That's a lie.

HOUSEKEEPER [*fiercely*]. It's the truth!

AUNT. Don't you raise your voice to me.

HOUSEKEEPER [*shouting*]. Why do you think the good God gave me a tongue?

AUNT. Be quiet, you uncouth woman!

HOUSEKEEPER. Forty years I've been with you.

AUNT [*near tears*]. Well, you're dismissed!

HOUSEKEEPER [*shouting*]. Thank God I shan't have to look at you any more!

AUNT [*weeping*]. Out of the house this instant!

HOUSEKEEPER [*breaking into tears*]. Out of the house!
[*She goes to the door, and as she is leaving drops something. The two women are in tears. Pause*

AUNT [*drying her eyes. Gently*]. What's that you dropped?

HOUSEKEEPER [*still weeping*]. It's a thermometer-stand—eighteenth-century style—French. . .

AUNT. Really?

HOUSEKEEPER. Yes, señora.   [*They are both weeping*

AUNT. May I see?

HOUSEKEEPER. It's for Rosita's saint's day.
[*She goes to the* AUNT

AUNT [*sniffing*]. It's exquisite.

HOUSEKEEPER [*tearfully*]. It's got a velvet base, and in the middle there's a fountain made of real shells; over the fountain there's an arbour made of wire with green roses; the water in the basin is made of blue sequins and the water shooting up is the thermometer itself. The pools around are painted in oil, and above them there's a nightingale drinking, embroidered in gold thread. I wanted it to wind up and sing, but that wasn't possible.

AUNT. That wasn't possible.

HOUSEKEEPER. But there's no need for it to sing: we have real ones in the garden.

AUNT. That's true. [*Pause*] Why have you been so extravagant?

HOUSEKEEPER [*weeping*]. Everything I have I give to Rosita.

AUNT. Because you love her more than anyone else does.

HOUSEKEEPER. Except you.

AUNT. No. You've given her your blood.

HOUSEKEEPER. You've sacrificed your life for her.

AUNT. But I gave out of duty; you gave freely, from the heart.

HOUSEKEEPER [*louder*]. Don't say that!

AUNT. You've shown that you love her more than anyone else does.

HOUSEKEEPER. I've only done what anybody would have done in my situation. I'm a servant. You pay me and I serve you.

AUNT. We've always looked on you as one of the family.

HOUSEKEEPER. I'm a poor servant; I give what I have, and that's all.

AUNT. You're really trying to tell me that's all?

HOUSEKEEPER. Well, am I anything more?

AUNT [*irritated*]. How can you say that? I'm leaving the room so as not to hear you.

HOUSEKEEPER [*irritated*]. And so am I.

[*They walk briskly out by different exits. The* AUNT, *as she goes, runs into the* UNCLE

UNCLE. You two have lived together so long, you peck each other on sight.

AUNT. It's because she always wants to have the last word.

UNCLE. Don't tell me, I know it all by heart. . . All the same, you'd be lost without her. Yesterday I heard you giving her all the details of our current account at the bank. You just can't keep your proper distance. That doesn't seem to me the kind of conversation one ought to have with a servant.

AUNT. She is not a servant.

UNCLE [*softly*]. All right, all right; I'm not going to argue with you.

AUNT. You mean it's impossible to speak to me?

UNCLE. It's possible, but I prefer to hold my tongue.

AUNT. And smoulder with silent resentment.

UNCLE. What would be the good of my saying anything at this stage? Rather than have an argument I'd make my own bed, clean my suits with a bar of soap, and buy new rugs for my room.

AUNT. It's not fair for you to put on this air of a superior being who's not properly looked after, when this entire house is geared to your tastes and your convenience.

UNCLE [softly]. Quite the contrary, my dear.

AUNT [seriously]. Completely and utterly. Instead of making lace I prune plants. What do you do for me?

UNCLE. Forgive me. There comes a time when people who've lived together for many years take offence and get worked up over the slightest thing in order to stir some life and passion into what is irretrievably dead. When we were twenty we didn't have this sort of conversation.

AUNT. No. When we were twenty the windows used to shatter. . .

UNCLE. And the cold was a toy for us to play with.

ROSITA appears. She is dressed in rose pink. The fashion has changed from leg-of-mutton sleeves to that of 1900. Her skirt is bell-shaped. She crosses swiftly with a pair of scissors in her hand and stops centre stage.

ROSITA. Has the postman been?

UNCLE. Has he been?

AUNT. I don't know. [Shouting] Has the postman been? [Pause] No, not yet.

ROSITA. He always comes at this time.

UNCLE. He should have been here some time ago.

AUNT. But he's often delayed.

ROSITA. The other day I found him playing hopscotch with three boys and a great pile of letters lying on the ground.

AUNT. He'll soon be here.

ROSITA. Let me know when he comes.

[*She makes to exit quickly*

UNCLE. Where are you going with those scissors?

ROSITA. I'm going to cut some roses.

UNCLE [*unbelieving*]. What? Who gave you permission?

AUNT. I did. It's her saint's day.

ROSITA. I want to put some in the jardinières and in the vase in the hall.

UNCLE. Every time you cut a rose it's like cutting off one of my fingers. That doesn't matter, I know. [*Looking at his wife*] All right, I don't want to argue. I know they don't last long. [*The* HOUSEKEEPER *enters*] That's what it says in the *Waltz of the Roses*, which is one of my favourite modern songs, but I can't help getting upset when I see them in vases.   [*Exits*

ROSITA [*to the* HOUSEKEEPER]. Has the postman been?

HOUSEKEEPER. All roses are good for is to make rooms look pretty.

ROSITA [*irritated*]. I asked you if the postman had been.

HOUSEKEEPER [*irritated*]. Do I keep the letters to myself when they come?

AUNT. Go and cut the flowers.

ROSITA. In this house there's a streak of bitterness for everything.

HOUSEKEEPER. That's right. We find arsenic in all the holes and corners.   [*She exits*

AUNT. Are you happy?

ROSITA. I don't know.

AUNT. What do you mean?

ROSITA. When I don't see people I'm happy, but as I can't avoid seeing them. . .

AUNT. I should think not! I don't like the kind of life you lead. Your fiancé doesn't expect you to be a recluse. In his letters he's always telling me you should go out.

ROSITA. But when I go out I can't help being aware of how time is passing, and I don't want to have my dreams destroyed. They've built yet another new house in the little square. I don't want to know that time is passing.

AUNT. But it is! So often I've advised you to write to your cousin and get married here to someone else. You've got spirit. I know there are men old and young who've fallen for you.

ROSITA. Aunt, you don't understand! My roots go deep down, down into my feeling for him. If I didn't have to see people, I'd believe it was only a week since he went away. I'm waiting for him now exactly as I was on the first day. And anyway what is a year, or two years, or five? [*A bell rings*] The post.

AUNT. I wonder what he's sent you.

HOUSEKEEPER [*entering*]. The old maids are here—the three frights.

AUNT. Holy Mary!

ROSITA. Show them in.

HOUSEKEEPER. The mother and the three girls. Dressed to kill and stale breadcrumbs to eat. A good walloping on their— that's what I'd give them!   [*She exits*

Enter the three vulgarly overdressed girls and their MOTHER. *The three* SPINSTERS *are wearing enormous hats with gaudy feathers, outlandish outfits, elbow-length gloves with bracelets over them and fans dangling from long chains. The* MOTHER *is wearing a faded black dress and a hat made of old purple ribbons.*

MOTHER. Congratulations!   [*They kiss*

ROSITA. Thank you.   [*She kisses the* SPINSTERS
Faith! Charity! Clemency!*

FIRST SPINSTER. Congratulations!

SECOND SPINSTER. Congratulations!

THIRD SPINSTER. Congratulations!

AUNT [*to the* MOTHER]. And how are those poor feet?

MOTHER. Getting worse. If it weren't for the girls I'd never go out of the house.   [*They sit*

AUNT. Don't you rub them with lavender?

FIRST SPINSTER. Every night.

SECOND SPINSTER. And the mallow poultice.

AUNT. No rheumatism can survive that.   [*Pause*

MOTHER. And how is your husband?

AUNT. He's well, thank you.   [*Pause*

MOTHER. Still busy with his roses.

AUNT. Still busy with his roses.

THIRD SPINSTER. Flowers are so beautiful!

SECOND SPINSTER. We have a St Francis rose bush in a pot.

ROSITA. But St Francis roses have no smell.

FIRST SPINSTER. Very little.

MOTHER. What I like best is philadelphus*—so like orange blossom.

THIRD SPINSTER. Violets are very pretty too.   [*Pause*

MOTHER. Well, girls, did you bring the card?

THIRD SPINSTER. Yes. It's a little girl dressed in rose pink and, you see, she's a barometer as well. The ones with the hooded friar are too common now. The little girl's skirt is made of very thin paper and it opens or closes according to how damp it is.

ROSITA [*reading*].

> The nightingales one morning
>   were singing in their nest,
> and in their song were saying:
>   Rosita is the best.

You really shouldn't have bothered.

AUNT. It's very tasteful.

MOTHER. It's not taste I'm short of; what I'm short of is money!

FIRST SPINSTER. Mama!

SECOND SPINSTER. Mama!

THIRD SPINSTER. Mama!

MOTHER. No, girls, here I can speak freely. Nobody can hear us. [*To the* AUNT] But you know very well: since my poor husband passed away I've been working miracles to manage on our little pension. I can still hear these girls' father, generous and gentlemanly as he was, saying to me: 'Enriqueta, spend, spend, I'm earning seventy duros* now'; but those days are gone for ever. Even so, we haven't gone downhill socially. And what agony I've suffered, señora, so that these girls could go on wearing hats! The tears I've shed, the misery I've suffered just to see them with a new ribbon or a bunch of ringlets. Many a sleepless night those feathers and those wires have cost me.

THIRD SPINSTER. Mama!

MOTHER. It's the plain truth, my dear child. We daren't overspend by a single centimo. Often I have to put it to them: 'Which would you prefer, my darlings, eggs for lunch or seats in the Alameda* to watch the promenade?' And they answer all together: 'Seats!'

THIRD SPINSTER. Mama, don't go on about it any more. The whole of Granada knows.

MOTHER. Well, naturally: what would you expect them to say? And so off we go, with only a few potatoes and a bunch of grapes to eat, but decked out with the latest Mongolian capes, or painted parasols, or poplinette blouses and all the accessories. Because what else can we do? But it's wearing me out! And my eyes fill with tears when I see them hobnobbing with girls who have everything.

SECOND SPINSTER. Don't you go to the Alameda now, Rosita?

ROSITA. No.

THIRD SPINSTER. We always join up there with the Ponce de León girls, or the Herrasti girls, or the daughters of the Baroness of Santa Matilda of the Apostolic Blessing. The cream of Granada.

MOTHER. Naturally. They were all together at the Porta Coeli Convent.*

[*Pause*

AUNT [*rising*]. You must have a little something.

[*They all rise*

MOTHER. Nobody can hold a candle to you when it comes to candied pine nuts and glory cake.*

FIRST SPINSTER [*to* ROSITA]. Have you had any news?

ROSITA. The last letter promised me some real news soon. We'll see what this one brings.

THIRD SPINSTER. Have you finished the set with the Valencian lace?

ROSITA. Finished it! I've done another one since then, of nainsook with moiré butterflies.

SECOND SPINSTER. The day you get married you'll have the best trousseau that ever was seen.

ROSITA. Oh, there can't be too much! They say men get bored if they see a woman always in the same clothes.

HOUSEKEEPER [*entering*]. The Ayolas are here, the photographer's girls.

AUNT. What you mean is: The Señoritas de Ayola have called.

HOUSEKEEPER. I beg leave to announce the la-di-da daughters of the toffee-nosed Ayola, photographer to His Majesty the King and winner of the Gold Medal in the Madrid Exhibition.

[*She exits*

AUNT. One has to put up with her, but there are times when she plays havoc with my nerves. Servants are impossible.

[*The* SPINSTERS *are looking at samples of material with* ROSITA

MOTHER. They're all so insolent. I have a girl who comes to clean the apartment in the afternoon; she used to be paid what they've always had: one peseta a month and the leftovers. Which is quite enough in times like these; but the other day she upped and told us she wanted five pesetas. Well, I can't afford that!

AUNT. I don't know where it's all going to end.

Enter the AYOLA GIRLS, *who gaily greet* ROSITA. *They are expensively dressed in the wildly exaggerated fashion of the period.*

ROSITA. Don't you know one another?

FIRST AYOLA. Only by sight.

ROSITA. The Señoritas de Ayola: the Señora and the Señoritas de Escarpina.

SECOND AYOLA. We've seen them sitting in their seats in the Alameda.   [*They try to conceal their mirth*

ROSITA. Do sit down.   [*The* SPINSTERS *sit*

AUNT [*to the* AYOLAS]. Will you take a little something?

SECOND AYOLA. No thank you: we've just eaten. Do you know, I had four eggs with tomato chutney and I could hardly get up from my chair.

FIRST AYOLA. She's such a scream!   [*They laugh*
[*Pause. The* AYOLAS *break into a fit of giggling which infects* ROSITA; *she tries to restrain them. The* SPINSTERS *and their* MOTHER *are quite serious. Pause*

AUNT. Silly things!

MOTHER. Youth!

AUNT. Ah, happy days!

ROSITA [*walking round the room as if setting things to rights*]. Do please be quiet.   [*They calm down*

AUNT [*to* THIRD SPINSTER]. How's your piano?

THIRD SPINSTER. I don't practise much these days. I have so much needlework to do.

ROSITA. It's a long time since I heard you play.

MOTHER. If it weren't for me, she'd have let her fingers seize up. But I'm always at her, nag, nag, nag.

SECOND SPINSTER. Since poor papa died she hasn't the heart for it. He did so love hearing her play!

THIRD SPINSTER. I remember sometimes he was moved to tears.

FIRST SPINSTER. When she played Popper's *Tarantella*.*

SECOND SPINSTER. And *The Maiden's Prayer.**

MOTHER. Such a big heart he had, that man!

> [*The* AYOLAS, *who have been restraining their mirth,*
> *break out into great bursts of laughter.* ROSITA,
> *with her back to the* SPINSTERS, *also laughs, but*
> *controls herself*

AUNT. What children you are!

FIRST AYOLA. We're laughing because, just before we came in
here. . .

SECOND AYOLA. She tripped and nearly went head over heels. . .

FIRST AYOLA. And I. . .

> [*They collapse into laughter. The* SPINSTERS *force a*
> *slight laugh tinged with a weary sadness*

MOTHER. We'd best be going.

AUNT. Certainly not.

ROSITA [*to all*]. Let's celebrate your not falling down! [*To the*
HOUSEKEEPER] Bring us the St Catherine's Bones.*

THIRD SPINSTER. Oh, delicious marzipan!

MOTHER. Last year we were given a whole half-kilo.

> *The* HOUSEKEEPER *enters with the pastries.*

HOUSEKEEPER. A special treat for special people. [*To* ROSITA]
The postman's coming down the avenue.

ROSITA. Wait for him at the door.   [*The* HOUSEKEEPER *exits*

FIRST AYOLA. I don't want anything to eat. I'd rather have a
pastis.*

SECOND AYOLA. I'd like some grape juice.

ROSITA [*to* FIRST AYOLA]. You like your tipple, don't you!

FIRST AYOLA. When I was six I used to come here and Rosita's
fiancé got me used to drinking pastis. Don't you remember,
Rosita?

ROSITA [*serious*]. No!

SECOND AYOLA. Rosita and her fiancé used to teach me my
ABC. . . How long ago was that?

AUNT. Fifteen years.

FIRST AYOLA. I almost, almost can't remember your fiancé's face.

SECOND AYOLA. Didn't he have a scar on his lip?

ROSITA. A scar? Aunt, did he have a scar?

AUNT. Don't you remember, dear? It was the only thing that marred his looks a little.

ROSITA. But it wasn't a scar; it was a burn, a little red mark. Scars are deeper.

FIRST AYOLA. I do wish Rosita would get married!

ROSITA. Oh, my goodness!

SECOND AYOLA. No, really. I do too.

ROSITA. Why?

FIRST AYOLA. So as to have a wedding to go to. I'm going to get married as soon as I can.

AUNT. Really!

FIRST AYOLA. I'll marry anybody rather than be left on the shelf.

SECOND AYOLA. That's what I say.

AUNT [to the MOTHER]. What do you think?

FIRST AYOLA. Oh, yes! That's why I'm friends with Rosita, because I know she's got a young man! Women who don't have a young man are dried up and depressed, they're all. . . [Seeing the SPINSTERS] Well, not all; some of them. . . Anyway, they're all frantic with frustration!

AUNT. Hey! That's quite enough.

MOTHER. Let her be.

FIRST SPINSTER. Many women don't get married because they don't want to.

SECOND AYOLA. I don't believe that.

FIRST SPINSTER [meaningfully]. I happen to know that it's true.

SECOND AYOLA. A woman who didn't want to get married would stop using face-powder and padding out her bosom, and wouldn't spend all her time peering out of the window at all the passers-by.

SECOND SPINSTER. She might like fresh air!

ROSITA. What an absolutely ridiculous conversation.

[*They force themselves to laugh*

AUNT. Well now, why don't we have some music?

MOTHER. Go on, dear!

THIRD SPINSTER [*getting up*]. But what shall I play?

SECOND AYOLA. Play *Viva Frascuelo*!

SECOND SPINSTER. The barcarolle from *The Frigate Numancia*.

ROSITA. Why not *What the Flowers say*?

MOTHER. Oh, yes, *What the Flowers say*! [*To the* AUNT] Have you heard her? She recites and plays at the same time. It's charming!

THIRD SPINSTER. Or I can recite 'The swallows dark will soon return, to nest upon your balcony.'

FIRST AYOLA. That's very sad.

FIRST SPINSTER. Sad things are nice too.

AUNT. Come along! Come along!

THIRD SPINSTER [*at the piano*].
 Mother, walk me through the fields
 in the light of early morning
 to see the flowers opening
 as the boughs are slowly swaying.
 A thousand flowers say a thousand things
 to a thousand lovelorn girls,
 and the babbling spring tells everything
 that the nightingale conceals.

ROSITA. Already open was the rose
 in the light of early morning;
 so red it was with tender blood,
 the dew would not come near it;
 so hot it was upon the stem,
 the gentle breeze was burning;
 How tall it is! And how it glows!
 Already it was open!

THIRD SPINSTER.

> 'My eyes are set on you alone,'
> the heliotrope confesses.
> 'I'll never love you while I live,'
> the basil-flower professes.
> 'I'm shy,' complains the violet.
> 'I'm cold,' the white rose tells us.
> The jasmine says, 'I will be true;'
> And 'passionate,' the carnation.

SECOND SPINSTER.

> The hyacinth's for bitterness;
> For pain the passion-flower.

FIRST SPINSTER.

> The mustard-flower speaks disdain,
> and lilies stand for hope.

AUNT.   Says the gardenia: 'I'm your friend.'
> The passion-flower means trust.
> The honeysuckle cradles you;
> the immortelle brings death.

MOTHER.

> Immortelle that stands for death,
> flower of the folded hands;
> with what content you feel the air
> shed tears upon your wreath!

ROSITA.   Already open was the rose,
> but evening was approaching;
> now a suspicion of sad snow
> weighed down its slender branches;
> and as the darkness came again
> and the nightingale was singing,
> it pined away, its flowers grew pale
> like a girl who'd died of sorrow;
> and when the mighty metal horn
> of night was heard resounding,
> and when the winds lay intertwined
> and sleeping in the mountains,
> it let its petals fall, and sighed
> for the crystal light of morning.

THIRD SPINSTER.

> The flowers of grief are culled and set
> into your long dark hair;
> and some will bring you the pain of wounds,
> some water, others fire.

FIRST SPINSTER.

> Flowers have tongues with which they speak
> for girls who are in love.

ROSITA.

> The willow-herb spells jealousy;
> the dahlia scornful pride;
> the spikenard breathes deep sighs of love;
> laughter, the fleur-de-lis.
> A yellow flower speaks of hate;
> a scarlet one of rage;
> white flowers mean a wedding feast;
> and blue foretell a shroud.

THIRD SPINSTER.

> Mother, walk me through the fields
> in the light of early morning
> to see the flowers opening
> as the boughs are slowly swaying.
>
> [*A final scale on the piano, and the music stops*

AUNT. Ah! How charming!

MOTHER. They can also recite the language of the fan, the language of gloves, the language of postage-stamps, and the language of the hours. It gives me the shivers when they come to:

> Far and wide the clock strikes twelve
> with harsh and fearful sound:
> bethink you, sinner, the hour of your death
> will shortly you confound.

FIRST AYOLA [*her mouth full of pastry*]. How ghastly!

MOTHER. And when they say:

> At the hour of one we may be born,
> la, ra, lilli la ra,
> and when at that time we see the dawn,

la, ra, lilli la ra,
we open our eyes one early morn
on a field of flowers and waving corn,
la, ra, lilli la ra la ray.

SECOND AYOLA [*to her sister*]. I think she's getting squiffy. [*To the* MOTHER] Would you like another drink?

MOTHER. With the greatest pleasure and the utmost willingness, as we used to say in my day.

[ROSITA *has been looking out for the postman*

HOUSEKEEPER [*entering*]. The letter!   [*General excitement*

AUNT. He couldn't have timed it better.

THIRD SPINSTER. He must have worked it out so that it would arrive today.

MOTHER. It's perfect!

SECOND AYOLA. Open it!

FIRST AYOLA. Perhaps you should read it in private, in case he's said naughty things.

MOTHER. Good gracious!   [ROSITA *goes out with the letter*

FIRST AYOLA. A love letter is not a prayer book.

THIRD SPINSTER. It's a prayer book of love.

SECOND AYOLA. Oh, such delicacy!   [*The* AYOLAS *laugh*

FIRST AYOLA. She's obviously never received one.

MOTHER [*firmly*]. So much the better for her.

FIRST AYOLA. Much good may it do her.

AUNT [*to the* HOUSEKEEPER, *who is going out to join* ROSITA]. Where are you going?

HOUSEKEEPER. Aren't I allowed to move?

AUNT. You leave her alone.

ROSITA [*entering*]. Aunt! Aunt!

AUNT. What is it, my dear?

ROSITA [*in a state*]. Oh, aunt!

FIRST AYOLA. What?

THIRD SPINSTER. Tell us!

SECOND AYOLA. What?

HOUSEKEEPER. Say!

AUNT. Out with it!

MOTHER. A glass of water!

SECOND AYOLA. Do tell!

FIRST AYOLA. Quickly!   [*Flurry*

ROSITA [*in a choking voice*]. He's getting married. [*General alarm*]
    He's going to marry me, because he can't bear to wait any
    longer, but. . .

SECOND AYOLA [*hugging her*]. Hooray! How wonderful!

FIRST AYOLA. I want to hug you!

AUNT. Let her finish.

ROSITA [*calmer*]. But, as he can't come here at the moment, the
    marriage will be by proxy, and he will come later.

FIRST SPINSTER. Congratulations!

MOTHER [*almost weeping*]. May God grant you all the happi-
    ness you deserve.   [*Embraces her*

HOUSEKEEPER. So: and what's this proxy business? What does it
    mean?

ROSITA. Nothing. It's just that somebody stands in for the groom
    at the ceremony.

HOUSEKEEPER. And?

ROSITA. Then I'm married!

HOUSEKEEPER. And what happens at night?

ROSITA. Heavens!

FIRST AYOLA. Good question. What happens at night?

AUNT. Really, girls!

HOUSEKEEPER. Let him come himself and marry you. 'Proxy!'
    I've never heard of such nonsense. The bed and its covers all
    shivering with cold and the bride's nightdress still buried in
    the trunk. Señora, don't you let any proxies into this house.

[*They all laugh*] Señora, I don't want anything to do with proxies.

ROSITA. But he'll soon be here himself. This is further proof of how much he loves me!

HOUSEKEEPER. All right. Let him come and take you by the arm and stir the sugar in your coffee and taste it first to see if it's too hot!   [*Laughter. She exits*

The UNCLE *appears with a rose.*

ROSITA. Uncle!

UNCLE. I heard everything, and almost without realizing I cut the only mutable rose I had in the greenhouse. It was still red:

>   At midday fully opened,
>   like coral it is hard.

ROSITA.   The sun peers through the window
>   to see how bright it shines.

UNCLE. If I'd waited two hours more before cutting it, I'd be giving you a completely white flower.

ROSITA.   White as a dove,
>   as the laugh of the sea;
>   white as the white
>   of a salt-white cheek.

UNCLE. But now it still has the warm fire of its youth.

AUNT [*to the* UNCLE]. Have a little drink with me, come on. It's just the day for it.

>   [*Flurry. The* THIRD SPINSTER *sits at the piano and
>   plays a polka.* ROSITA *is looking at the rose. The
>   FIRST and SECOND SPINSTERS dance with the
>   AYOLAS and sing*

FIRST AND SECOND SPINSTERS.
>   I saw you standing there,
>   a woman on the shore,
>   your sweet and dreamlike air
>   has made me yearn the more.

And that rare sweetness born
of my fatal fantasy
you saw beneath the moon
sink deep into the sea.

[*The* AUNT *and* UNCLE *dance.* ROSITA *moves to the couple formed by the* SECOND SPINSTER *and* AYOLA. *She dances with the* SPINSTER. *The* AYOLA *claps her hands on seeing the old couple dancing. The* HOUSEKEEPER *enters and joins in the clapping*

CURTAIN

ACT 3

A small sitting-room with green-shuttered french windows leading into the garden. The stage is silent. A clock strikes 6 p.m. The HOUSEKEEPER *crosses the stage with a box and a suitcase. Ten years have passed. The* AUNT *appears and sits on a low chair, centre stage. Silence. The clock again strikes 6. Pause.*

HOUSEKEEPER [*entering*]. Six o'clock twice.

AUNT. Where's the little one?

HOUSEKEEPER. Up top, in the tower. Where have you been?

AUNT. Clearing the last flowerpots out of the greenhouse.

HOUSEKEEPER. I didn't catch sight of you all morning.

AUNT. Since my husband died, the house is so empty it seems twice as big; we have to go searching for one another. Some nights when I cough in my room I hear an echo as if I were in a church.

HOUSEKEEPER. It's true the house is much too big now.

AUNT. If he were only with us still, with all that clarity of mind he had, all that cleverness. . . [*almost weeping*]

HOUSEKEEPER [*singing*]. La la la-la-la la. . . No, señora, no crying, I won't have it. It's six years since he died, and I'm not going to have you the way you were on the first day. We've shed quite enough tears for him. On we go, señora, best foot forward. Let the sun shine in to the darkest corners. Let him wait for us many years yet, still busy with his roses.

AUNT [*rising*]. I'm so old now. And our downfall is a great burden to bear.

HOUSEKEEPER. We shall survive. I'm old too, you know!

AUNT. Oh, if only I were your age!

HOUSEKEEPER. There's not much between us, but I've had to work hard, so I'm well oiled, whereas your legs have seized up from so much sitting around.

AUNT. Do you think I haven't worked?

HOUSEKEEPER. Oh, yes, with the tips of your fingers, with sewing, pruning, making jam, but I've had to work with my back, with my knees, and my nails.

AUNT. So running a house is not work?

HOUSEKEEPER. Scrubbing its floors is a lot harder.

AUNT. I'm not going to argue.

HOUSEKEEPER. Why not? It helps to pass the time. Go on. Contradict me. We've lost the use of our tongues. In the old days we used to shout at each other: If you don't do this, if you don't do that! Where's the egg custard? If you don't get on with the ironing. . .!

AUNT. There's no fight left in me. All I want is soup one day, a bit of bread the next, my glass of water, my rosary in my bag, and I could just wait for death with dignity. . . But when I think of poor Rosita!

HOUSEKEEPER. Ah, that's what rankles!

AUNT [*vehemently*]. When I think of the wrong that's been done her, the terrible deception that was kept up, and the lying heart of that man who is no part of my family and is not worthy to be part of my family, I wish I were twenty still so I could get on a ship and go to Tucumán and take a horsewhip. . .

HOUSEKEEPER [*interrupting her*]. And cut off his head with a sword and smash it between two stones and cut off his hand that signed false oaths and wrote love letters full of filthy lies.

AUNT. That's right: what has cost blood he should pay for with blood, though it were all my blood, and then. . .

HOUSEKEEPER. Scatter his ashes over the sea.

AUNT. Bring him to life again and back to Rosita so that I could breathe easy knowing my family's honour had been restored.

HOUSEKEEPER. Now you'll admit that I was right.

AUNT. You were.

HOUSEKEEPER. Over there he met the rich girl he went looking for, and he married her. But he should have come clean straight away. I mean, who's going to want this woman now? She's over the hill! Señora, couldn't we send him a poisoned letter, so that when he opened it he'd fall down dead?

AUNT. Such notions! Eight years he's been married, and the scoundrel didn't write and tell me the truth until last month. I could tell by his letters there was something fishy: the power of attorney that never came, a kind of shiftiness about it all—he didn't have the nerve to confess, then at last he came out with it. After his father's death, of course! And now this poor creature. . .

HOUSEKEEPER. Sssh!

AUNT. And bring in the two big jars.

ROSITA *appears. She's wearing pale rose pink in the fashion of 1910. Her hair is in ringlets. She has aged very much.*

HOUSEKEEPER. There you are, pet!

ROSITA. What are you doing?

HOUSEKEEPER. Having a moan. Where are you going?

ROSITA. To the greenhouse. Have they taken the flowerpots?

AUNT. There are still a few left.

[ROSITA *exits. The two women wipe away their tears*

HOUSEKEEPER. And that's it? You sit there and I sit here? Just waiting to give up the ghost? Is there no law? Has no one got the guts to make mincemeat of him. . .?

AUNT. Hush! Don't go on.

HOUSEKEEPER. It's just not in my nature to suffer these things without my heart racing around in my breast like a dog on the run. When I buried my husband I was really sorry, but deep down I felt a great joy—no, not joy exactly—but my heart beat all the faster to know that I wasn't the one being buried. When I buried my little girl—you understand me?—when I buried my little girl, it was as if my insides were being trampled on, but, after all, the dead are dead and gone. They die, we shed tears, the door closes, and we get on with our lives! But this business with my little Rosita is worse than anything. It's loving someone you can't put your hands on, weeping and not knowing who for; sighing for someone you know isn't worth your sighs. It's an open wound that never stops trickling blood, and nobody, absolutely nobody can ever bring you the swabs you need, the bandages or the blessed lump of ice.

AUNT. What do you want me to do?

HOUSEKEEPER. Just let the river carry us along.

AUNT. When we get old we don't count any more.

HOUSEKEEPER. As long as I have a pair of arms you won't lack for anything.

AUNT [*pause; very softly, as if ashamed*]. I'm sorry to tell you this, but I can't afford to pay you any longer. You'll have to leave us.

HOUSEKEEPER. Wheeee! What a draught there is blowing through the window! Wheee! Or am I going deaf? Then... why do I suddenly feel like singing? Like the children coming out of school! [*Children's voices are heard*] Can you hear them, señora? My señora, my señora more than ever now.

[*Hugging her*

AUNT. Listen to me.

HOUSEKEEPER. I'm going to cook now. I'm going to do you baked mackerel with fennel.

AUNT. Listen!

HOUSEKEEPER. And an ice pudding!* I'm going to make you an ice pudding with hundreds and thousands all over it!

AUNT. But I tell you, woman...

HOUSEKEEPER [*loudly*]. Well I never! Here's Don Martín! Don Martín, do come in! Come in! Keep the señora company for a while.   [*She exits swiftly*

DON MARTÍN *enters. He's an old man with red hair. He uses a crutch to support a lame leg. A noble breed of man, with great dignity and an air of irredeemable sadness.*

AUNT. How good to see you!

DON MARTÍN. So when is the final uprooting?

AUNT. Today.

DON MARTÍN. You're really going then!

AUNT. The new house is not the same. But it has good views and a little patio with two fig trees where we can grow flowers.

DON MARTÍN. Just right for you.   [*They sit*

AUNT. And how are you?

DON MARTÍN. I carry on as usual. I've just given my Rhetoric class. Absolute torture! It was a delightful topic: 'The Concept and Definition of Harmony', but it was of no interest to the children. And what children they are! They can see I'm disabled, so they treat me with a little respect: a drawing-pin on my chair maybe, or a paper doll stuck on my back, but they do the most horrible things to my colleagues. They're the sons of wealthy fathers and, since they're paying, they can't be punished. That's what the Headmaster is always telling us. Yesterday they would have it that Señor Canito, the new Geography master, wore a corset, just because he's a little pigeon-chested; and when they found him alone in the playground the big bullies and the boarders all got together, stripped him to the waist, tied him to one of the pillars of the portico, and threw a pitcher of water over him from the balcony.

AUNT. Poor man!

DON MARTÍN. Every day I go to school in fear and trembling of what they might do to me, although, as I say, they do have some respect for my misfortune. A little while ago there was an almighty row because Señor Consuegra, who's a brilliant teacher of Latin, found cat's mess on his mark book.

AUNT. Aren't they the very devil!

DON MARTÍN. They pay, so we put up with them. And, I tell you, the parents only laugh at their outrageous behaviour because we're mere assistant teachers and so we won't be the ones to examine their children. So they look on us as people without feelings, white-collar workers, just, but on the bottom rung of the ladder.

AUNT. Oh dear, Don Martín! What a world we live in!

DON MARTÍN. What a world! I always dreamed of being a poet. I won a prize for poetry once, and I wrote a play, but I've never managed to get it put on.

AUNT. You mean *Jephtha's Daughter*?

DON MARTÍN. That's right.

AUNT. But we've read it, Rosita and I. You lent it to us. We've read it four or five times.

DON MARTÍN [*eagerly*]. And what. . .?

AUNT. I liked it very much. I've often told you so. Especially when she's about to die and remembers her mother and calls out to her.

DON MARTÍN. It's powerful stuff, isn't it? Really dramatic. A play sound in form and concept. But I've never managed to get it put on. [*He begins to recite*]

> O mother without parallel! Look down
> on her who swooning lies in mortal throe;
> receive unto yourself these sparkling treasures
> and the expiring groan that ends my woe.

Can you say that's not well done? And doesn't the last line sound rather splendid with its balance and sense of finality?

> And the expiring groan that ends my woe.

AUNT. Thrilling! Quite thrilling!

DON MARTÍN. And when Glucinius goes to challenge Isaiah and lifts up the hangings of his tent. . .

HOUSEKEEPER [*interrupting him*]. This way.

> *Two* WORKMEN *enter dressed in overalls.*

FIRST WORKMAN. Good evening.

AUNT AND DON MARTÍN [*together*]. Good evening.

HOUSEKEEPER. That's the one!

> [*She indicates a large divan at the back of the room. The men take it out slowly as if it were a coffin. The* HOUSEKEEPER *follows them. Silence. Two strokes of a church bell are heard while the* WORKMEN *are going out with the divan*

DON MARTÍN. Is that the novena of St Gertrude the Great?

AUNT. Yes, at St Anthony's.

DON MARTÍN. It's very hard to be a poet.

[*The* WORKMEN *go out*

After that I wanted to be a pharmacist. That's a quiet life.

AUNT. My brother, God rest his soul, was a pharmacist.

DON MARTÍN. But that wasn't for me. I had to help my mother, so I became a schoolmaster. That's why I envied your husband so much. He was what he wanted to be.

AUNT. And it cost him everything he had.

DON MARTÍN. Yes, but I'm in a worse case.

AUNT. Still, you go on writing.

DON MARTÍN. I don't know why I write, because I don't delude myself, but it's still the only thing I like doing. Did you read my short story yesterday in the second number of the *Granada Outlook*?

AUNT. 'Matilda's Birthday'? Yes, we read it; it's a little gem.

DON MARTÍN. Do you really think so? I was trying to rejuvenate myself in that by producing something more up-to-date: I even mention an aeroplane! The fact is that one has to keep up with the times. Obviously what *I* like best are my sonnets.

AUNT. To the nine muses of Parnassus!

DON MARTÍN. The ten, the ten! Don't you remember I made Rosita the tenth muse?

HOUSEKEEPER [*entering*]. Señora, will you help me fold this sheet? [*They set about folding the sheet between them*] Don Martín with his ginger hair! Why haven't you married, you good Christian man? You wouldn't be so alone in this life.

DON MARTÍN. Nobody's ever wanted me.

HOUSEKEEPER. No one has good taste any more, that's why. When you speak so beautifully!

AUNT. You'll make him fall in love with you if you're not careful!

DON MARTÍN. I'm not complaining!

HOUSEKEEPER. When he's teaching in the downstairs classroom at the school, I go to the coalyard where I can hear him. 'What is meant by an idea?' 'It's the representation in the mind of a thing or an object.' Isn't that right?

DON MARTÍN. Listen to her! Listen to her!

HOUSEKEEPER. Yesterday he was shouting: 'No, no: this is a case of hyperbaton', and then he talked about 'the epinicion'*—I only wish I understood, but, since I don't, it makes me laugh, and the coalman, who's always reading a book called *The Ruins of Palmyra*, he glares at me with eyes like two crazy cats. Oh yes, I laugh like a proper dunce; but Don Martín is really clever, I do see that.

DON MARTÍN. There's no appreciation of Rhetoric and Poetry these days; nor even of a university education.

[*The* HOUSEKEEPER *exits swiftly with the folded sheet*

AUNT. What can we do about it? We don't have much time left on this stage.

DON MARTÍN. And what we have we must devote to kindness and self-sacrifice.   [*Voices are heard*

AUNT. What's happening?

HOUSEKEEPER [*reappearing*]. Don Martín, will you go to the school; the children have banged a nail through the water pipes and all the classrooms are flooded.

DON MARTÍN. I'm on my way. I dreamt of Parnassus and I end up a builder and plumber. As long as they don't push me or I slip. . . [*The* HOUSEKEEPER *helps him up. Voices are heard*

HOUSEKEEPER. He's coming! Keep calm!
Let's hope the water rises till not a single child is left alive!

DON MARTÍN [*leaving*]. God's will be done!

AUNT. Poor man! What a sad lot he has to endure!

HOUSEKEEPER. What must it be like! He irons his own collars and darns his own socks, and, when he was ill and I took him some egg custard, the sheets on his bed were black as coal, and as for the walls and the wash-basin—ugh!

AUNT. And other people have so much.

HOUSEKEEPER. That's why I shall always say: Damn the rich, damn them all! Let them burn down to their last finger-nail!

AUNT. Let them be.

HOUSEKEEPER. I'm quite sure they're all going head first to hell. Where do you think Don Rafael Salé will be now, that exploiter of the poor they buried two days ago, God forgive him, with all those priests and nuns and weeping and wailing? In hell, that's where he'll be. And he'll be saying, 'I've got twenty million pesetas, don't grab me with your tongs! I'll give you forty thousand duros if you take these burning coals away from my feet!' But the demons will bash him this way and bash him that way and kick him all over and smash his face till his blood turns to charcoal.

AUNT. All we Christians know that the rich can't enter the kingdom of Heaven, but if you talk like that you're liable to end up going head first to hell yourself.

HOUSEKEEPER. Me, go to hell? I'll give Old Nick's cauldron such an almighty shove, the boiling water will splash over to the very ends of the earth. No, señora, oh no. I'll fight my way into Heaven. [*Sweetly*] And I'll take you with me. We shall sit in armchairs of sky-blue silk that rock all by themselves, fanning ourselves with fans of scarlet satin. And in between us there'll be Rosita, swinging to and fro on a swing made of jasmine and sprigs of rosemary; and behind will be your husband all covered with roses, just as he left this room in his coffin; with the same smile, the same forehead white as crystal; and you will be rocking like this, and I like this, and Rosita like this, and from behind the good Lord will be throwing roses over us as if the three of us were in the Holy Week procession framed in mother-of-pearl and all decked out with candles and frills.

AUNT. And our tear-stained handkerchiefs we'll have left down here below.

HOUSEKEEPER. That's right, let them all get on with it. For us it will be a party in Paradise!

AUNT. Because we shan't have a single tear anywhere in our hearts.

FIRST WORKMAN [*at the door*]. What next, ladies?

HOUSEKEEPER. Come with me. [*From the door, leaving*] On we go!

AUNT. God bless you!   [*Sits slowly*

ROSITA *appears with a bundle of letters in her hand. Silence.*

AUNT. Have they taken the bureau?

ROSITA. Just now. A child came for a screwdriver for your cousin Esperanza.

AUNT. They'll be getting the beds ready for tonight. We ought to have gone on ahead so as to have everything arranged to our liking. My cousin will have put the furniture just anywhere.

ROSITA. But I'd rather leave here when it's dark in the street. I'd put out the street lamp if I could. The neighbours are sure to be peering out to see us go. With the removal men here there's been a crowd of youngsters round the door all day, as if there were a dead body in the house.

AUNT. If I'd known, I'd never have allowed your uncle to mortgage the house with all the furniture and everything. What we're taking are just the barest necessities, chairs to sit on and beds to sleep in.

ROSITA. To die in.

AUNT. A pretty pickle he left us in! Tomorrow the new owners will be here. I wish your uncle could see us now. The old fool. When it came to business, he simply wasn't up to it. Potty about his blessed roses! A man with no idea about money! Every day he plunged me deeper into debt. 'Señor So-and-so is here', and he'd say, 'Show him in'; and Señor So-and-so would come in with empty pockets and go out bulging with banknotes and always the same plea: 'Don't say anything to my wife.' What a waster! No will-power! And there was no disaster he wouldn't try to put right, no child he wouldn't try to save, because... because he had the kindest heart that a man ever had... and the purest Christian soul; no, no, you silly old woman, be quiet! Hold your babbling tongue and accept God's will! We've lost everything! So be it, I'll say no more. But when I look at you...

ROSITA. Don't worry about me, aunt. I know he arranged the mortgage to pay for my furniture and my trousseau, and that's what grieves me.

AUNT. He was right to do it. You deserved it all, and everything that was bought does you credit and will look beautiful the day you use it.

ROSITA. The day I use it?

AUNT. Of course! Your wedding day.

ROSITA. Don't force me to speak.

AUNT. That's the trouble with well-brought-up women in these parts: not speaking! We don't speak—and we need to speak. [*Calling to the* HOUSEKEEPER *off-stage*] Has the postman been?

ROSITA. What do you intend to do?

AUNT. I intend to live, so as to set you an example.

ROSITA [*hugging her*]. Don't say any more.

AUNT. There comes a time when I have to speak. Break out from your four walls, my pet. Don't resign yourself to being unhappy.

ROSITA [*on her knees before her*]. For many years I've grown used to living outside myself, thinking of things that were far away, and now that those things don't exist any more, I still go on spinning round and round in an icy space, seeking a way out that I shall never be able to find. I knew perfectly well what had happened, I knew he'd got married; a kindly soul had been thoughtful enough to tell me that, but I went on receiving his letters with a heartbroken sense of hope that surprised even me. If nobody had said anything; if you hadn't known, if nobody had known but me, his letters and his lies would have gone on feeding my dream just as they did in the first year after he went away. But everyone knew, and I found myself pointed at in a way that made it ludicrous for me to go on behaving as though I were engaged, and grotesque to be carrying the kind of fan used by single women. Each year that passed was like an intimate piece of clothing torn from my body. One day a friend gets married, then another, and another, and the next day she has a baby and the baby grows older and comes to show me his exam marks, and new houses are put up and new songs written, and I'm still the same, still quivering with forlorn hope, still exactly the same; I'm just as I was before, cutting the same carnations, looking up at the same clouds; then one day I go down to walk in the Alameda and I realize that I don't know anybody; the girls and boys leave me behind because I get tired, and one boy says: 'There's the old maid,' and another, a good-looking boy with curly hair, says, 'No one's going to fall for her now.' And I hear him and I can't even scream, but on I go, my mouth brimming with poison, and longing, longing to run away, to kick off my shoes, to sink into my little corner, and never, never move out of it again.

AUNT. Rosita! My poor pet!

ROSITA. Now I'm old. Yesterday I heard the housekeeper say I could still get married. There's no question of it. Don't think of it. I've lost the hope of marrying the man I loved with every drop of my blood, the man I loved—and whom I love still. Everything is over—the dream is shattered; and yet every day I go to bed and every day I get up with the most terrible feeling there can be: the feeling that in me all hope is dead. I want to run away, to stop seeing, to become tranquil, empty—doesn't a poor woman have the right to breathe freely?—but still that hope hounds me, haunts me, gnaws at me; like a wolf in its death-throes gritting its fangs for the last time.

AUNT. Why didn't you listen to me? Why didn't you marry someone else?

ROSITA. My hands were tied. And besides, did any man ever come to this house with a sincere and burning desire to win my affection? Never.

AUNT. You paid no attention to them. You were wrapped up in that sugar-tongued scoundrel.

ROSITA. I've always acted responsibly.

AUNT. You've clung to your obsession with no regard for reality or thought for your future.

ROSITA. I am as I am. And I can't change myself. All I have left now is my dignity. What I feel inside I keep to myself.

AUNT. That's just what I don't want you to do.

HOUSEKEEPER [*suddenly appearing*]. And nor do I! Why don't you speak, let it all come out, we'll all three of us have a good cry, we'll all share the sorrow between us.

ROSITA. What should I say to you? There are things which can't be said because there are no words to say them; and, if there were, no one would understand what they meant. You understand me if I ask for bread and water or even a kiss, but you could never understand or take away that shadowy hand which freezes or burns my heart—I'm not sure which—whenever I find myself alone.

HOUSEKEEPER. Now you're beginning to say something.

AUNT. There's consolation for everything.

ROSITA. My story would be the one that never ended. I know my eyes will always be young, and I know too that my back will become more bent with every day that passes. It's nothing new; what has happened to me has happened to thousands of women. [*Pause*] But why am I saying all this? [*To the* HOUSEKEEPER] You, go and see to things; in a few minutes we're going to leave this house, and this garden; and you, aunt, don't worry about me. [*Pause. To the* HOUSEKEEPER] Go on! I can't stand you looking at me like that. I won't be stared at with the eyes of a faithful dog.

[*The* HOUSEKEEPER *goes*

Pitying looks; they upset me, they make me furious.

AUNT. My dear, what do you want me to do?

ROSITA. Just accept that I'm a lost cause. [*Pause. She walks up and down*] I know you're thinking of your unmarried sister—the old maid, like me. She became bitter, she hated children, she hated any girl who wore a new dress—but I won't be like that. [*Pause*] I'm sorry.

AUNT. Don't be silly.

At the rear of the room appears an eighteen-year-old YOUTH.

ROSITA. Come in.

YOUTH. Are you moving, then?

ROSITA. In a few minutes. When it gets dark.

AUNT. Who is it?

ROSITA. He's María's son.

AUNT. What María?

ROSITA. The eldest of the three Manolas.

AUNT. Ah!

> Who go to the Alhambra
> all three, or four, alone.

Forgive my poor memory, my boy.

YOUTH. You haven't seen me very often.

AUNT. That's true, but I was very fond of your mother. She was such fun! She died about the same time as my husband.

ROSITA. Before.

YOUTH. Eight years ago.

ROSITA. He has her face.

YOUTH [*cheerfully*]. Mine's not quite so pretty. It was bashed into shape with a hammer.

AUNT. And the same sense of humour; the same character!

YOUTH. It's true, I do look like her. At carnival time once I put on one of my mother's dresses, one she'd had donkey's years ago, green it was. . .

ROSITA [*in a melancholy tone*]. With black bows and flounces of nile-green silk.

YOUTH. Yes.

ROSITA. And a huge velvet bow at the waist.

YOUTH. That's the one.

ROSITA. Which fell on either side of the bustle.

YOUTH. That's right! What a ridiculous fashion!   [*He smiles*

ROSITA [*sadly*]. It was a pretty fashion.

YOUTH. Oh, come on! Anyway, there I was coming down the stairs laughing my head off dressed up in that ancient outfit and filling the hall with the smell of mothballs, when suddenly my aunt got all upset and started crying because she said it was just like seeing my mother again. Then of course I got upset as well, so I left the dress and the carnival mask on my bed.

ROSITA. Memories have more life in them than anything else. In the end they make it impossible for us to go on living. That's why I can understand those little old women you see wandering drunk about the streets trying to blot out the world, or sitting on the benches in the Alameda singing to themselves.

AUNT. And how is your married aunt?

YOUTH. She writes from Barcelona. Less and less often though.

ROSITA. Has she any children?

YOUTH. Four.   [Pause

HOUSEKEEPER [entering]. Give me the keys to the store-cupboard. [The AUNT hands them over. Referring to the YOUTH] This young man was out with his sweetheart yesterday. I saw them in the Plaza Nueva. She wanted to walk one way, and he wouldn't let her.   [She laughs

AUNT. Come now, leave the boy alone!

YOUTH [embarrassed]. We were only playing.

HOUSEKEEPER [leaving]. There's no need to blush!

ROSITA. That's quite enough!

YOUTH. What a wonderful garden you've got!

ROSITA. Used to have!

AUNT. Come on, we'll go and cut some flowers.

YOUTH. Good luck, Doña Rosita!

ROSITA. God bless you, my boy. [The YOUTH and the AUNT go out. Evening is falling] Doña Rosita!* Doña Rosita!

> In the morning, when it opens
> it's red, as red as blood;
> the evening sees it whiten,
> as white as foam or salt.
> And when the night is coming
> its petals start to fall.   [Pause

HOUSEKEEPER [*enters wearing a shawl*]. Time to be off.

ROSITA. Yes, I'm going to slip my coat on.

HOUSEKEEPER. I've taken down the coat-rack: you'll find it hanging from the window-catch.   [*Exit* ROSITA

Enter the THIRD SPINSTER *in dark clothes with a mourning veil over her head and a ribbon round her neck in the fashion of 1912. They speak quietly.*

THIRD SPINSTER. Still here?

HOUSEKEEPER. In a few minutes we shall be gone.

THIRD SPINSTER. I've just been giving a piano lesson near by, so I came to see if you needed anything.

HOUSEKEEPER. That's very kind of you.

THIRD SPINSTER. What a dreadful thing!

HOUSEKEEPER. Yes, yes, but don't you get me all emotional; don't you pull the plaster off the wound, because I'm the one who has to keep everyone going in this funeral-without-a-corpse that you're watching.

THIRD SPINSTER. I'd like to see them.

HOUSEKEEPER. Much better not. Call on them in the new house!

THIRD SPINSTER. Yes, that would be better. But, if they need anything, you know that I'll do whatever I can.

HOUSEKEEPER. This bad time won't last for ever.

[*The wind is heard*

THIRD SPINSTER. There's a wind rising!

HOUSEKEEPER. Yes. It looks as if it's going to rain.

[*The* THIRD SPINSTER *leaves*

AUNT [*entering*]. With this wind there won't be a single rose left alive. The cypresses by the arbour are almost touching the walls of my room. It's as if someone were trying to make the garden look ugly so that we shouldn't feel sorry to leave it.

HOUSEKEEPER. It was never all that beautiful. Let's get your coat on. And this scarf as well. There you are, well wrapped up. [*She fusses over her*] Now when we get there I've got a meal all ready. Egg custard for pudding. Your favourite. A golden egg custard, just like a marigold. [*The* HOUSEKEEPER *speaks in a voice choked by deep emotion.*]   [*A bang is heard*

AUNT. It's the door of the greenhouse. Why don't you close it?

HOUSEKEEPER. It won't close. It's swollen with the damp.

AUNT. It will be banging all night.

HOUSEKEEPER. Well, we shan't hear it. . .!
                    [*The stage glows in the soft half-light of dusk*

AUNT. I shall. I shall hear it.

  ROSITA *appears. She is pale, dressed in white, with a coat reaching down to the hemline of her dress.*

HOUSEKEEPER [*bravely*]. Off we go!

ROSITA [*in a faint voice*]. It's started to rain. That means no one will be out watching us go.

AUNT. So much the better.

ROSITA [*she sways a little, clings to a chair, and falls between the* HOUSEKEEPER *and the* AUNT, *whose support prevents her from total collapse*].
              And when the night is coming
              its petals start to fall.
              [*They exit, leaving the stage empty. The door is heard banging. Suddenly one of the french windows at the rear of the stage opens and the white curtains flutter in the wind*

              CURTAIN

EXPLANATORY NOTES

BLOOD WEDDING

The play is based on an incident reported in the Madrid daily, *ABC*, on 25 July 1928. In Níjar, in the province of Almería, a guest on his way to a wedding found a young man dead by the roadside. It was eventually discovered that the dead man was a previous lover of the bride who had absconded with her the night before the wedding, and that he had been killed by the groom's outraged brother. Lorca's brother Francisco remembers him closely following the reports of the crime. See I. Gibson, *Federico García Lorca: A Life* (London: Faber & Faber, 1989).

2 *Moon*: the moon appears regularly in Lorca's works and is often a harbinger of death. See, for example, 'Arc of Moons', 'Song of the Rider', and 'Ballad of the Moon, Moon', in *Federico García Lorca: Selected Poems*, trans. Merryn Williams (Newcastle upon Tyne: Bloodaxe Books, 1992).

Death: the use of a female figure to represent this character is not surprising since the noun is feminine in Spanish, 'la muerte', and the Spanish counterpart of Old Father Time is the feminine 'la Parca'.

3 *palm-leaf put on his chest*: in Roman times, gladiators who were victorious in the arena were given a branch of the palm tree.

7 *arms cut off by the machine*: an early, mechanical threshing-machine, made of wood, would be capable of taking off a man's arms.

9–11 *Hushaby . . . cry*: with its images of blood and suffering, this lullaby might seem a little gruesome for sending a baby to sleep, but Lorca pointed out that Spain 'made use of its texts of most melancholy expression to tinge the first sleep of its children' and that in his country 'all regions accentuate their poetic character and background of sadness in this type of song' ('Las nanas infantiles', *OC* iii).

23 *orange blossom*: a symbol of innocence and chastity.

27 *Oh, let the bride awaken . . . bay*: it was a custom in rural Andalusia, where weddings began early to avoid the summer heat, for the bride to be wakened with a song on her wedding day. Lorca's poetry here evokes that tradition.

36 *Get the trays of wheat ready*: the wheat represents a wish for prosperity for the couple.

37 *Let's go and take out your pins*: traditionally, the first person to receive a pin from the dress of the newly married bride would be the next to get married. (The dress would be one handed down through the family and would be adjusted with pins to fit for the few hours it was worn.)

42 *the Wheel*: a dance in which the participants form a circle around one person or a couple, in this case the bride and groom, and dance around them singing.

49 *coffers*: in the Spanish, *cofre*, the chest where the best linen, used for laying out family corpses, would be kept.

55 *my wedding sheets displayed*: this refers to the custom of the bride displaying her bloodstained bed sheets the morning after the wedding night to prove that she had been a virgin.

63 *rosebay*: another name for oleander, a plant poisonous to humans and animals. This may be contrasted with the *palm-leaf* of p. 3.

YERMA

68 *Yerma*: the name means 'barren' and is usually applied to the land.

69 *climbing on to the roof*: the roofs of houses in rural Andalusia were, and still are, often flat, tiled, and easily accessible.

81 *in October we're going to the Saint*: as a child Lorca watched the annual pilgrimage to Moclín in Andalusia, where there was a picture of Christ gifted to the village in 1492 by King Ferdinand and Queen Isabella and to which the power of curing infertility was attributed. Because of the orgiastic nature of the celebrations, it is suggested that any ensuing pregnancies were more a result of human than of divine intervention. See Gibson, *Federico García Lorca: A Life*.

84 *I shall be watering all night*: because of the shortage of water in Andalusia, as in other parts of Spain, specific times were allotted for each farmer to irrigate his land from a common source. These times were strictly adhered to.

103 *St Anne*: mother of Mary, patron saint of motherhood.

THE HOUSE OF BERNARDA ALBA

124 *Requiem aeternam . . . luceat eis*: 'Lord grant them eternal rest. And illuminate them with perpetual light.' These words are taken from the funeral mass.

125 *May the corn of your marriage-harvest never fail you*: a reference to the wheat which was given to a couple on their marriage and which represented a wish for their prosperity. See also note for p. 36 of *Blood Wedding*.

146 *rattles*: in the Spanish 'carrañacas', these musical instruments were, and still are, often used in carnival celebrations. They consist of small metal plates which make a noise when scraped with sticks.

148 *St Bartholomew*: one of the twelve Apostles, often depicted in Christian iconography as a handsome, naked male.

162 *Blessed . . . high*: a falling star or a flash of lightning was thought to presage bad luck, and any person witnessing these events would recite the lines quoted to ensure that he or she would not be the victim of that bad luck. This is why Amelia says a few lines later that she closes her eyes rather than look at them.

DOÑA ROSITA THE SPINSTER

176 There are some inconsistencies in Lorca's stage directions. When Rosita enters in Act 1 she is wearing a dress 'in the 1900 style, with leg-of-mutton sleeves'. This style of dress was fashionable, at least in England, around 1893–5. It is clear from the opening dialogue in Act 2 that it is this Act which takes place in 1900, and, indeed, Lorca's stage direction for Rosita's entrance here states that the fashion has now 'changed from leg-of-mutton sleeves to that of 1900'. The Housekeeper's remark in this Act, that the cousin 'has been gone fifteen years', places Act 1 in 1885. At the beginning of Act 3 Lorca states that 'ten years have passed', and this is consistent with his stage direction that she is 'wearing pale rose pink in the fashion of 1910'. However, when the Third Spinster enters later in this Act she is dressed in 'the fashion of 1912'.

In his statements to the press while working on the play, Lorca was inconsistent about the dates in which the actions of the three Acts were set. In 1934 and 1935 he placed them in 1890, 1900, and 1910. In his first formal talk about the play, he stated that it began in 1885 and ended in 1900. At the première he intimated the years 1885, 1900, and 1911. See Luis Martínez Cuitiño's introduction to *Doña Rosita la soltera o El lenguaje de las flores* (Madrid, Colección Austral, 1993), 17–18. The text of the play, however, clearly places the action in 1885, 1900, and 1910.

St Luis: a church in the Albaicín area of Granada.

179 *Bartholomew's wheel*: St Bartholomew, one of the twelve Apostles, was flayed to death, and is usually depicted naked or with a flaying knife. There seems to be no obvious reason for his being associated with a wheel.

180 *Tucumán*: a province of north-western Argentina.

184 *Manolas*: according to his brother, Lorca took great delight in making these characters in a song from Granada, a 'granadina', characters in his play. See Francisco García Lorca's introduction to *Lorca: Three Tragedies* (New York, New Directions Publishing Company, 1955), 12.

Genil . . . butterflies: the Genil and Darro are two rivers which meet in Granada.

191 *positivism*: this movement did, at one time, put itself forward as an appropriate religion for the modern age.

the relevantly constituted polity: in the Spanish 'la Polis viviente', used here to mean 'contemporary, of our times'. Señor X is proclaiming his allegiance to the current of advanced Liberalism of those times.

192 *in Brahma's bosom*: Brahma is the supreme god of Hindu mythology, of whom the whole universe is no more than a manifestation. Hence, something which remains an unrealized possibility can be said to be 'in Brahma's bosom'. The reference to oriental myth would have been fashionable at the time of the action—or, typically, a little before.

saint's day: Spaniards who take their name from a particular saint celebrate that saint's feast day, just as they would a birthday.

pendentif: a pendant necklace.

193 *Don Confucio Montes de Oca, baptized in Lodge No. 43*: bearing the surname of one of nineteenth-century Spain's best known military conspirators, and an impossibly secular first name, this Masonic gentleman caricatures yet more of the elements of Granadine bourgeois 'advanced' culture.

199 *Faith! Charity! Clemency!*: in the Spanish, the name of the first sister is 'Amor', literally 'Love' which would be unlikely as a Christian name in English.

200 *philadelphus*: commonly known as 'mock orange' and often used as a substitute for orange blossom in wedding flowers.

201 *70 duros*: 350 pesetas.

the Alameda: a tree-lined avenue in Granada where it was fashionable to take an evening stroll or hire a seat to watch occasional entertainments.

202 *Porta Coeli Convent*: in the Spanish, 'el Colegio de la Puerta del Cielo', but the Latin equivalent is more commonly used in English-speaking countries.

glory cake: in the Spanish 'pastel de gloria', an Andalusian pastry cake.

203 *Popper's Tarantella*: the tarantella is a very fast, whirling dance. David Popper (1843–1913) was a composer of cello music.

204 *The Maiden's Prayer*: a piece of music by the Polish composer Thekle Bederzewska which is, according to the *Concise Oxford Dictionary of Music* of 1952, 'a tasteless piano composition which has been (and perhaps still is) one of the best sellers the music trade has ever known'.

St Catherine's Bones: long marzipan sweets with a chocolate or other sweet filling. They were usually made by nuns, so in this case they probably came from St Catherine's Convent.

pastis: another name for anisette.

216 *ice pudding*: in the Spanish 'un monte nevado', a dessert made with meringue which resembles a snowy mountain.

220 '*the epinicion*': a term used in Greek poetics, meaning 'a victory ode'.

227 *Doña Rosita!*: 'Doña' is a title which comes with age. It has just been brought home to Rosita that she is no longer considered a 'Señorita'.

ANTON CHEKHOV

Early Stories
Five Plays
The Princess and Other Stories
The Russian Master and Other Stories
The Steppe and Other Stories
Twelve Plays
Ward Number Six and Other Stories

FYODOR DOSTOEVSKY

Crime and Punishment
Devils
A Gentle Creature and Other Stories
The Idiot
The Karamazov Brothers
Memoirs from the House of the Dead
Notes from the Underground and
    The Gambler

NIKOLAI GOGOL

Dead Souls
Plays and Petersburg Tales

ALEXANDER PUSHKIN

Eugene Onegin
The Queen of Spades and Other Stories

LEO TOLSTOY

Anna Karenina
The Kreutzer Sonata and Other Stories
The Raid and Other Stories
Resurrection
War and Peace

IVAN TURGENEV

Fathers and Sons
First Love and Other Stories
A Month in the Country

Bhagavad Gita

The Bible Authorized King James Version
With Apocrypha

Dhammapada

Dharmasūtras

The Koran

The Pañcatantra

**The Sauptikaparvan (from the
Mahabharata)**

**The Tale of Sinuhe and Other Ancient
Egyptian Poems**

Upaniṣads

ANSELM OF CANTERBURY **The Major Works**

THOMAS AQUINAS **Selected Philosophical Writings**

AUGUSTINE **The Confessions**
On Christian Teaching

BEDE **The Ecclesiastical History**

HEMACANDRA **The Lives of the Jain Elders**

KĀLIDĀSA **The Recognition of Śakuntalā**

MANJHAN **Madhumalati**

ŚĀNTIDEVA **The Bodhicaryàvatàra**

The Oxford World's Classics Website

www.worldsclassics.co.uk

- Information about new titles
- Explore the full range of Oxford World's Classics
- Links to other literary sites and the main OUP webpage
- Imaginative competitions, with bookish prizes
- Peruse the Oxford World's Classics Magazine
- Articles by editors
- Extracts from Introductions
- A forum for discussion and feedback on the series
- Special information for teachers and lecturers

www.worldsclassics.co.uk

American Literature

British and Irish Literature

Children's Literature

Classics and Ancient Literature

Colonial Literature

Eastern Literature

European Literature

History

Medieval Literature

Oxford English Drama

Poetry

Philosophy

Politics

Religion

The Oxford Shakespeare

A complete list of Oxford Paperbacks, including Oxford World's Classics, Oxford Shakespeare, Oxford Drama, and Oxford Paperback Reference, is available in the UK from the Academic Division Publicity Department, Oxford University Press, Great Clarendon Street, Oxford OX2 6DP.

In the USA, complete lists are available from the Paperbacks Marketing Manager, Oxford University Press, 198 Madison Avenue, New York, NY 10016.

Oxford Paperbacks are available from all good bookshops. In case of difficulty, customers in the UK can order direct from Oxford University Press Bookshop, Freepost, 116 High Street, Oxford OX1 4BR, enclosing full payment. Please add 10 per cent of published price for postage and packing.